European War and Diplomacy, 1337–1815

European War and Diplomacy, 1337–1815

◆

A Bibliography

William Young

iUniverse, Inc.

New York Lincoln Shanghai

European War and Diplomacy, 1337–1815
A Bibliography

iUniverse, Inc.

For information address:
iUniverse, Inc.
2021 Pine Lake Road, Suite 100
Lincoln, NE 68512
www.iuniverse.com

ISBN: 0-595-29874-5

Printed in the United States of America

For
my children,

Mark Edward Young,
William Anthony Young, Jr.
Geoffrey Arthur Young
and
Heather Ashley Young

Contents

ACKNOWLEDGMENTS

The genesis of this bibliography is rooted in my avid collection of books and journal articles during the last twenty years. I started collecting books about the topics considered in this work while I was in the Air Force stationed in the United Kingdom. My wife, Patricia, and sons, Mark and William, spent numerous hours assisting me (as well as waiting for me) while I scoured through book stores in Cambridge, Oxford, London, Norwich, Canterbury, Colchester, Bristol, Hay-on-Wye, Shrewsbury, Ipswich, and numerous other cities and small villages in England and Wales. My next military assignment resulted in book hunting in the Kingdom of the Netherlands in such cities as Utrecht, Amsterdam, and The Hague.

The opportunity to search for books about war and diplomacy during the early modern era in used and rare book stores was severely hampered with my military assignment to Grand Forks Air Force Base, North Dakota, in late 1990. However, this posting provided the opportunity to study at the University of North Dakota. Graduate work included the opportunity to conduct research on diplomatic relations and warfare during the late seventeenth and early eighteenth centuries, resulting in my study *War and Diplomacy in the Age of Louis XIV: A Historical Study and Annotated Bibliography* (2000). This study, as well as the present one, was assisted by the avid support of the Chester Fritz Library Inter-Library Loan staff. The advent of on-line computer research and on-line book search dealers during the 1990s was a tremendous help in the research and purchasing of numerous studies listed in the present volume. Nevertheless, the patience and support of my wife and children were the greatest contribution to my academic endeavor.

William Young
Grand Forks, North Dakota
September 2003

PREFACE

For most of the twentieth century diplomatic history, or international history, was not held in high esteem by American historians. It was considered old fashion. These same historians did not even consider military history worthy of academic pursuit. This seems strange when the twentieth century witnessed the rise of a global system of interdependence as well as numerous military confrontations including two world wars.

In spite of historical research focusing on social, economic, and other worthy subjects, a limited number of historians continued to produce studies concerning diplomacy and warfare. Only a small share of these historians devoted their efforts toward early modern Europe. However, Anglo-American historians have rekindled an interest in the history of international relations and warfare during the last decades of the century. This bibliography contains a listing of monographs, journal articles, and other sources regarding war and diplomacy from 1337 to 1815 which were published in the English language during the twentieth and early twenty-first centuries.

The bibliography is set up in parts. It contains fifteen parts. Part I contains a listing of general studies concerning international history from 1337 to 1815. This is followed by parts devoted to the practice of diplomacy, military and naval affairs, the Military Revolution, trade and finance, international relations theory, as well as historiographies and bibliographies. The final seven parts, the heart of the bibliography, contains listings of studies concerning European diplomacy and warfare during the fourteenth and fifteenth centuries, the Age of the Habsburg-Valois Wars, the era of Philip II of Spain, the Thirty Years' War, the Age of Louis XIV, the eighteenth century, and the Age of the French Revolution and Napoleonic Wars.

The bibliography will be useful for history teachers, researchers, and students interested in the history of international relations and warfare during the early modern European period.

PART I
INTERNATIONAL HISTORY,
1337–1815

GENERAL STUDIES—EUROPEAN HISTORY

Andrews, Stuart. *Eighteenth Century Europe: The 1680s to 1815*. London: Longmans, Green and Company, 1965.

Black, Jeremy. *Eighteenth Century Europe, 1700–1789*. New York: St. Martin's Press, 1990.

_____. "Warfare, Crisis, and Absolutism." In *Early Modern Europe: An Oxford History*. Edited by Euan Cameron. Oxford: Oxford University Press, 1999.

Bonney, Richard. *The European Dynastic States, 1494–1660*. Oxford: Oxford University Press, 1991.

Bush, M.L. *Renaissance, Reformation and the Outer World, 1450–1660*. Second edition. London: Blandford Press, 1971.

Cameron, Euan, editor. In *Early Modern Europe: An Oxford History*. Oxford: Oxford University Press, 1999.

Carter, Charles H. *The Western European Powers, 1500–1700*. Ithaca: Cornell University Press, 1971.

Christiansen, Eric. *The Northern Crusades: The Baltic and the Catholic Frontier, 1100–1525*. London: Macmillan, 1980.

Deakin, Quentin. *Expansion, War and Rebellion: Europe, 1598–1661*. Cambridge: Cambridge University Press, 2000.

Dickens, A.G., editor. *The Courts of Europe: Politics, Patronage and Royalty, 1400–1800.* London: Thames and Hudson, 1977.

Dunn, Richard S. *The Age of Religious Wars, 1559–1715.* Second edition. New York: W.W. Norton and Company, 1979.

Glete, Jan. *War and the State in Early Modern Europe: Spain, the Dutch Republic and Sweden as Fiscal-Military States, 1500–1660.* London: Routledge, 2002.

Gunn, Steven. "War, Religion, and the State." In *Early Modern Europe: An Oxford History.* Edited by Euan Cameron. Oxford: Oxford University Press, 1999.

Holmes, George. *Europe: Hierarchy and Revolt, 1320–1450.* Brighton: Harvester Press, 1975.

Harris, R.W. *Absolutism and Enlightenment, 1660–1789.* Second edition. Poole: Blandford, 1967.

Hay, Denys. *Europe in the Fourteenth and Fifteenth Centuries.* London: Longmans, Green and Company, 1966.

Jensen, De Lamar. *Reformation Europe: Age of Reform and Revolution.* Second edition. Lexington: D.C. Heath and Company, 1992.

_____. *Renaissance Europe: Age of Recovery and Reconciliation.* Second edition. Lexington: D.C. Heath and Company, 1992.

Jones, Martin. *Clash of Empires: Europe 1498–1560.* Cambridge: Cambridge University Press, 2000.

Kirby, David. *Northern Europe in the Early Modern Period: The Baltic World, 1492–1772.* London: Longman, 1990.

Kirchner, Walther. *The Rise of the Baltic Question.* Westport: Greenwood Press, 1970.

Koenigsberger, Helmut G. *The Habsburgs and Europe, 1516–1660.* Ithaca: Cornell University Press, 1971.

_____ and George L. Mosse. *Europe in the Sixteenth Century*. London: Longmans, Green and Company, 1968.

Krieger, Leonard. *Kings and Philosophers, 1689–1789*. New York: W.W. Norton and Company, 1970.

Langley, Lester D. *The Americas in the Age of Revolution, 1750–1850*. New Haven: Yale University Press, 1996.

Lee, Stephen. *Aspects of European History, 1494–1789*. London: Methuen, 1978.

Lockyer, Roger. *Habsburg and Bourbon Europe, 1470–1720*. London: Longman, 1974.

Mackenney, Richard. *Sixteenth Century Europe: Expansion and Conflict*. New York: St. Martin's Press, 1993.

Maland, David. *Europe in the Seventeenth Century*. New York: St. Martin's Press, 1966.

_____. *Europe in the Sixteenth Century*. London: Macmillan, 1973.

Mulgan, Catherine. *The Renaissance Monarchies, 1469–1558*. Cambridge: Cambridge University Press, 1998.

Munck, Thomas. *Seventeenth Century Europe: State, Conflict and the Social Order in Europe, 1598–1700*. London: Macmillan, 1990.

Ogg, David. *Europe in the Seventeenth Century*. Revised eighth edition. London: Adam and Charles Black, 1965.

Pennington, D.H. *Seventeenth Century Europe*. London: Longman, 1970.

Rice, Eugene F., Jr. *The Foundations of Early Modern Europe, 1460–1559*. London: Weidenfeld and Nicolson, 1970.

Subtelny, Orest. *Domination of Eastern Europe: Native Nobilities and Foreign Absolutism, 1500–1715*. Gloucester: Alan Sutton, 1986.

Symcox, Geoffrey, editor. *War, Diplomacy and Imperialism, 1618–1763*. London: Macmillan, 1973.

Tracy, James D. *Europe's Reformations, 1450–1650*. New York: Rowman and Littlefield, 1999.

Treasure, Geoffrey. *The Making of Modern Europe, 1648–1780*. London: Methuen, 1985.

Williams, E.N. *The Ancien Regime in Europe: Government and Society in the Major States, 1648–1789*. London: Bodley Head, 1970.

GENERAL STUDIES—INTERNATIONAL RELATIONS

Anderson, Matthew S. *The Eastern Question 1774–1923*. London: Macmillan, 1966.

_____. *The Origins of the Modern European State System, 1494–1618*. London: Longman, 1999.

Black, Jeremy. *European International Relations, 1648–1815*. New York: Palgrave, 2002.

_____, editor. *The Origins of War in Early Modern Europe*. Edinburgh: John Donald, 1987.

_____. *The Rise of the European Powers, 1679–1793*. London: Edward Arnold, 1990.

Duchhardt, Heinz. "International Relations, the Law of Nations, and the Germanies: Structures and Changes in the Second Half of the Seventeenth Century." In *State and Society in Early Modern Austria*. Edited by Charles W. Ingrao. West Lafayette: Purdue University Press, 1994.

Frost, Robert I. *The Northern Wars: War, State, and Society in Northeastern Europe, 1558–1721*. London: Longman, 2000.

Gierowski, Józef Andrzej. "The International Position of Poland in the Seventeenth and Eighteenth Centuries." In *A Republic of Nobles: Studies in Polish History to 1864*. Edited by J.K. Fedorowicz. Cambridge: Cambridge University Press, 1982.

Hill, David Jayne. *A History of Diplomacy in the International Development of Europe.* London: Longman, Green and Company. 1906.

Lewitter, L.R. "Poland, the Ukraine and Russia in the Seventeenth Century." *Slavonic and East Europe Review* 27 (1948–49): 157–171, 414–28.

Lisk, Jill. *The Struggle for Supremacy in the Baltic, 1600–1725.* London: Hodder and Stoughton, 1967.

Lukowski, Jerzy. *The Partitions of Poland, 1772, 1793, 1795.* London: Addison, Wesley, Longman, 1999.

McKay, Derek and H.M. Scott. *The Rise of the Great Powers, 1648–1815.* London: Longman, 1983.

McNeill, William H. *Europe's Steppe Frontier, 1500–1800.* Chicago: University of Chicago Press, 1964.

Mowat, Robert B. *A History of European Diplomacy, 1451–1789.* London: Edward Arnold, 1928.

Oakley, Stewart P. *War and Peace in the Baltic, 1560–1790.* London: Routledge, 1992.

_____. "War in the Baltic, 1550–1790." In *The Origins of War in Early Modern Europe.* Edited by J. Black. Edinburgh: John Donald, 1987.

Petrie, Charles. *Earlier Diplomatic History, 1492–1713.* London: Hollis and Carter, 1949.

Roider, Karl. "Origins of Wars in the Balkans, 1660–1792." In *The Origins of Wars in Early Modern Europe.* Edited by J. Black. Edinburgh: John Donald, 1987.

Schroeder, Paul W. *The Transformation of European Politics, 1763–1848.* Oxford: Oxford University Press, 1994.

Setton, Kenneth M. *Venice, Austria, and the Turks in the Seventeenth Century.* Philadelphia: American Philosophical Society, 1991.

Shennan, J.H. *International Relations in Europe, 1689–1789*. London: Routledge, 1995.

Stiles, Andrina. *Russia, Poland and the Ottoman Empire, 1725–1800*. London: Hodder and Stoughton, 1991.

Wolf, John B. *Toward a European Balance of Power, 1620–1715*. Chicago: Rand McNally, 1970.

GENERAL STUDIES—GREAT BRITAIN

Aylmer, G.E. *The Struggle for the Constitution, 1603–1689*. Fourth edition. London: Blandford Press, 1975.

Anderson, Matthew S. *Britain's Discovery of Russia, 1553–1815*. London: Macmillan, 1958.

Black, Jeremy. *A System of Ambition?: British Foreign Policy, 1660–1793*. London: Longman, 1991.

_____. "Britain and the Continent, 1688–1815: Convergence or Divergence?" *British Journal for Eighteenth-Century Studies* 15 (1992): 145–49.

_____. *Convergence or Divergence?: Britain and the Continent*. New York: St. Martin's Press, 1994.

_____, editor. *Knights Errant and True Englishmen: British Foreign Policy, 1600–1800*. Edinburgh: John Donald, 1989.

Corbett, Julian S. *England in the Mediterranean: A Study of the Rise and Influence of British Power within the Straits, 1603–1713*. London: Longmans, Green and Company, 1904; reprint, Westport: Greenwood Press, 1987.

Coward, Barry. *The Stuart Age: A History of England, 1603–1714*. London: Longman, 1980.

Crowson, P.S. *Tudor Foreign Policy*. London: Adam and Charles Black, 1973.

Doran, Susan. *England and Europe, 1485–1603*. Second edition. London: Longman, 1996.

_____. *England and Europe in the Sixteenth Century.* New York: St. Martin's Press, 1999.

Guy, John. *Tudor England.* Oxford: Oxford University Press, 1988.

Harris, R.W. *England in the Eighteenth Century, 1689–1793: A Balanced Constitution and New Horizons.* London: Blandford Press, 1963.

Howat, G.M.D. *Stuart and Cromwellian Foreign Policy.* London: Adam and Charles Black, 1974.

Jarrett, Derek. *Britain, 1688–1815.* London: Longmans, Green and Company, 1965.

Jones, James R. *Britain and Europe in the Seventeenth Century.* London: Edward Arnold, 1966.

_____. *Britain and the World, 1649–1815.* Brighton: Harvester Press, 1980.

Kenyon, John. *Stuart England.* London: Allen Lane, 1978.

Kishlansky, Mark. *A Monarchy Transformed: Britain, 1603–1714.* London: Allen Lane, 1996.

Langford, Paul. *The Eighteenth Century, 1688–1815.* London: Adam and Charles Black, 1976.

Lockyer, Roger. *Tudor and Stuart Britain, 1471–1714.* London: Longman, 1964.

Maltby, William S. "The Origins of a Global Strategy: England from 1558 to 1713." In *The Making of Strategy: Rulers, States, and War.* Edited by Williamson Murray, MacGregor Knox, and Alvin Bernstein. Cambridge: Cambridge University Press, 1994.

Marshall, Dorothy. *Eighteenth Century England.* London: Longman, 1962.

Palmer, William. *The Problem of Ireland in Tudor Foreign Policy, 1485–1603.* Woodbridge: Boydell, 1994.

Petrie, Charles. "Ireland in Spanish and French Strategy, 1558–1815." *The Irish Sword* 6 (1964): 154–65.

Pickering, Andrew. *Lancastrians to Tudors: England, 1450–1509*. Cambridge: Cambridge University Press, 2000.

Quinn, David and A.N. Ryan. *England's Sea Empire, 1550–1642*. London: George Allen and Unwin, 1983.

Reitan, Earl A. *Politics, War, and Empire: The Rise of Britain to a World Power, 1588–1792*. Arlington Heights: Harlan Davidson, 1994.

Savelle, M. *The Origins of American Diplomacy: The International History of Anglo-America, 1492–1763*. New York: Macmillan, 1967.

Wernham, R.B. *Before the Armada: The Growth of English Foreign Policy, 1485–1588*. London: Jonathan Cape, 1966.

Williamson, James A. *The Tudor Age*. Third edition. London: Longman, 1964.

GENERAL STUDIES—FRANCE

Baumgartner, Frederic J. *France in the Sixteenth Century*. New York: St. Martin's Press, 1995.

Black, Jeremy. *From Louis XIV to Napoleon: The Fate of a Great Power*. London: University College London Press, 1999.

Briggs, Robin. *Early Modern France, 1560–1715*. Oxford: Oxford University Press, 1977.

Brown, W.E. *The First Bourbon Century*. London: University of London Press, 1968.

Collins, James B. *The State in Early Modern France*. Cambridge: Cambridge University Press, 1995.

Knecht, Robert J. *The Rise and Fall of Renaissance France*. London: Harper-Collins, 1996.

Potter, David. *A History of France, 1460–1560: The Emergence of a Nation State.* London: Macmillan, 1995.

Treasure, Geoffrey. *Seventeenth Century France.* London: Rivingtons, 1966.

GENERAL STUDIES—AUSTRIA AND GERMAN EMPIRE

Bérenger, Jean. *A History of the Habsburg Empire, 1273–1700.* London: Longman, 1994.

Chudoba, Bohdan. *Spain and the Empire, 1519–1643.* Chicago: University of Chicago Press, 1952; reprint, New York: Octagon, 1969.

Clasen, Claus-Peter. *The Palatinate in European History, 1559–1660.* Oxford: Basil Blackwell, 1963.

Evans, R.J.W. *The Making of the Habsburg Monarchy, 1550–1700: An Interpretation.* Oxford: Oxford University Press, 1979.

Fay, Sidney B. *The Rise of Brandenburg-Prussia to 1786.* New York: Holt, Rinehart and Winston, 1964.

Gagliardo, John. *Germany under the Old Regime, 1600–1790.* London: Longman, 1991.

Hochedlinger, Michael. *Austria's Wars of Emergence, 1683–1797.* London: Longman, 2003.

Holborn, Hajo. *A History of Modern Germany.* 3 volumes. New York: Alfred Knopf, 1964–67.

Hughes, Michael. *Early Modern Germany, 1477–1806.* Philadelphia: University of Pennsylvania Press, 1992.

Ingrao, Charles W. editor. *State and Society in Early Modern Austria.* West Lafayette: Purdue University Press, 1994.

_____. *The Habsburg Monarchy, 1618–1815*. Cambridge: Cambridge University Press, 1994.

Koch, H.W. *A History of Prussia*. London: Longman, 1978.

Köpeczi, Béla. "The Hungarian Wars of Independence of the Seventeenth and Eighteenth Centuries in their European Context." In *From Hunyadi to Rákóczi: Wars and Society in Late Medieval and Early Modern Hungary*. Edited by J. Bak and B. Király. New York: Brooklyn College Press, 1982.

Oppenheim, Walter. *Habsburgs and Hohenzollerns, 1713–1786*. London: Hodder and Stoughton, 1993.

Press, Volker. "Austria and the Rise of Brandenburg-Prussia." In *State and Society in Early Modern Austria*. Edited by Charles W. Ingrao. West Lafayette: Purdue University Press, 1994.

Shennan, Margaret. *The Rise of Brandenburg-Prussia*. London: Routledge, 1995.

Tapié, Victor-L. *The Rise and Fall of the Habsburg Monarchy*. London: Pall Mall, 1971.

Vierhaus, Rudolf. *Germany in the Age of Absolutism*. Cambridge: Cambridge University Press, 1988.

Wilson, Peter H. *War, State and Society in Württemberg, 1677–1793*. Cambridge: Cambridge University Press, 1995.

GENERAL STUDIES—SPAIN AND PORTUGAL

Boxer, C.R. *The Portuguese Seaborne Empire, 1415–1825*. London: Hutchinson, 1969.

Chudoba, Bohdan. *Spain and the Empire, 1519–1643*. Chicago: University of Chicago Press, 1952; reprint, New York: Octagon, 1969.

Darby, Graham. *Spain in the Seventeenth Century*. London: Longman, 1994.

Elliott, John H. "A Question of Reputation?: Spanish Foreign Policy in the Seventeenth Century." *The Journal of Modern History* 55 (September 1983): 475–83.

_____. *Imperial Spain, 1469–1714*. London: Edward Arnold, 1963.

_____. *Spain and Its World, 1500–1700: Selected Essays*. New Haven: Yale University Press, 1989.

Israel, Jonathan I. *Conflicts of Empires: Spain, the Low Countries and the Struggle for World Supremacy, 1585–1713*. London: Hambledon Press, 1997.

Kamen, Henry. *Spain, 1469–1714: A Society of Conflict*. London: Longman, 1983.

Kilsby, Jill. *Spain: Rise and Decline, 1474–1643*. London: Hodder and Stoughton, 1989.

Lovett, A.W. *Early Habsburg Spain, 1517–1598*. Oxford: Oxford University Press, 1986.

Lynch, John. *Bourbon Spain, 1700–1808*. Oxford: Basil Blackwell, 1989.

_____. *Spain under the Habsburgs*. 2 volumes. Oxford: Blackwell, 1981.

Parry, J.H. *The Spanish Seaborne Empire*. London: Hutchinson, 1966.

Stradling, Robert A. *Europe and the Decline of Spain: A Study of The Spanish System, 1580–1720*. London: George Allen and Unwin, 1981.

_____. "Seventeenth-Century Spain: Decline or Survival?." *European Studies Review* 9 (1979): 157–94; reprinted in *Spain's Struggle for Europe, 1598–1668*. London: Hambledon Press, 1994.

_____. *Spain's Struggle for Europe, 1598–1668*. London: Hambledon Press, 1994.

GENERAL STUDIES—DUTCH NETHERLANDS

Boxer, C.R. *The Dutch Seaborne Empire, 160–1800*. London: Hutchinson, 1965.

Carter, Alice Clare. *Neutrality or Commitment: The Evolution of Dutch Foreign Policy, 1667–1795*. London: Edward Arnold, 1975.

Geyl, Pieter. *The Netherlands in the Seventeenth Century*. 2 volumes. London: Ernest Benn, 1961.

Haley, Kenneth. *The Dutch in the Seventeenth Century*. London: Thames and Hudson, 1972.

Israel, Jonathan I. *The Dutch Republic: Its Rise, Greatness, and Fall, 1477–1806*. Oxford: Oxford University Press, 1994.

Price, J.L. "A State Dedicated to War?: The Dutch Republic in the Seventeenth Century." In *The Medieval Military Revolution: State Society and Military Change in Medieval and Early Modern Europe*. Edited by Andrew Ayton. London: I.B. Tauris Publishers, 1995.

_____. *The Dutch Republic in the Seventeenth Century*. London: Macmillan, 1998.

Rowen, Herbert H. *The Princes of Orange: The Stadholders in the Dutch Republic*. Cambridge: Cambridge University Press, 1988.

Smit, J.W. "The Netherlands and Europe in the Seventeenth and Eighteenth Centuries." In *Britain and the Netherlands in Europe and Asia: Papers Delivered to the Third Anglo-Dutch Historical Conference*. Edited by J.S. Bromley and E.H. Kossman. London: Macmillan, 1968.

Wilson, Charles. *The Dutch Republic and the Civilisation of the Seventeenth Century*. New York: McGraw-Hill, 1968.

GENERAL STUDIES—ITALY

Carpanetto, Dino and Giuseppe Ricuperati. *Italy in the Age of Reason, 1685–1789*. London: Longman, 1987.

Cochrane, Eric. *Italy, 1530–1630.* London: Longman, 1988.

Hale, John R. *Florence and the Medici: The Pattern of Control.* London: Thames and Hudson, 1977.

Hay, Denys and John Law. *Italy in the Age of the Renaissance, 1380–1530.* London: Longman, 1989.

Parrott, David A. and Robert Oresko. "The Sovereignty of Monferrato and the Citadel of Casale as European Problems in the Early Modern Period." In *Stefano Guazzo e Casale tra Cinque e Seiento.* Edited by Daniela Ferrari and A. Quondam. Rome: Bulzoni, 1997.

Sella, Domenico. *Italy in the Seventeenth Century.* London: Longman, 1997.

GENERAL STUDIES—RUSSIA

Crummey, R. *The Formation of Muscovy, 1304–1613.* London and New York: Longman, 1987.

Dukes, Paul. *The Making of Russian Absolutism, 1613–1801.* London: Longman, 1982.

——————, editor. *Russia and Europe.* London: Collins and Brown, 1991.

Esper, Thomas. "Russia and the Baltic, 1494–1558." *Slavic Review* 25 (1966): 458–74.

Fuller, William C., Jr. *Strategy and Power in Russia, 1600–1914.* New York: Free Press, 1992.

Hellie, Richard. "Warfare, Changing Military Technology, and the Evolution of Muscovite Society." In *Tools of War: Instruments, Ideas, and Institutions of Warfare, 1445–1871.* Edited by John A.Lynn. Urbana: University of Illinois Press, 1990.

Hoetzsch, Otto. *The Evolution of Russia.* London: Thames and Hudson, 1966.

LeDonne, John P. *The Russian Empire and the World, 1700–1917: The Geopolitics of Expansion and Containment*. New York: Oxford University Press, 1997.

Martin, Janet. *Medieval Russia, 980–1584*. Cambridge: Cambridge University Press, 1995.

Rady, Martyn. *The Tsar's Russia, Poland and the Ukraine, 1462–1725*. London: Hodder and Stoughton, 1990.

Vernadsky, George. *The Tsardom of Moscow, 1547–1682*. New Haven: Yale University Press, 1969.

Wittram, Reinhard. *Russia and Europe*. London: Thames and Hudson, 1973.

GENERAL STUDIES—SWEDEN AND DENMARK

Böhme, K.-R. "Building a Baltic Empire: Aspects of Swedish Expansion, 1560–1660." In *In Quest of Trade and Security: The Baltic in Power Politics, 1500–1990*. Edited by G. Rystad, K.-R. Böhme, and W. Carlgren. Lund: University of Lund Press, 1994.

Lundkvist, Sven. "The European Powers and Sweden in the Reign of Gustav Vasa." In *Politics and Society in Reformation Europe: Essays for Sir Geoffrey Elton on his Sixty-Fifth Birthday*. Edited by E.I. Kouri and Tom Scott. London: Macmillan, 1987.

Oakley, Stewart P. *The Story of Sweden*. New York: Frederick A. Praeger, 1966.

Roberts, Michael. *Essays in Swedish History*. Minneapolis: University of Minnesota Press, 1967.

_____. *Gustavus Adolphus: A History of Sweden, 1611–1632*. 2 volumes. London: Longmans, Green and Company, 1953–58.

_____, editor. *Sweden as a Great Power, 1611–1697: Goverment, Society, and Foreign Policy*. London: Edward Arnold, 1968.

_____, editor. *Sweden's Age of Greatness, 1632–1718*. London: Macmillan 1973.

_____. *The Age of Liberty: Sweden 1719–1772.* Cambridge: Cambridge University Press, 1986.

_____. *The Early Vasas: A History of Sweden, 1523–1611.* Cambridge: Cambridge University Press, 1968.

_____. *The Swedish Imperial Experience, 1560–1718.* Cambridge: Cambridge University Press, 1979.

Scott, F.D. *Sweden, the Nation's History.* Minneapolis: University of Minnesota Press, 1977.

Stiles, Andrina. *Sweden and the Baltic, 1523–1721.* London: Hodder and Stoughton, 1992.

GENERAL STUDIES—POLAND

Davies, Norman. *God's Playground: A History of Poland.* 2 volumes. Oxford: Oxford University Press, 1981.

Rady, Martyn. *The Tsar's Russia, Poland and the Ukraine, 1462–1725.* London: Hodder and Stoughton, 1990.

Reddaway, W.F. and others. *The Cambridge History of Poland.* 2 volumes. Cambridge: Cambridge University Press, 1950.

GENERAL STUDIES—OTTOMAN EMPIRE

Coles, Paul. *The Ottoman Impact on Europe.* London: Thames and Hudson, 1968.

DeVries, Kelly. "The Lack of Western European Military Response to the Ottoman Invasions of Eastern Europe from Nicopolis (1396) to Mohács (1526)." *The Journal of Military History* 63 (July 1999): 539–60.

Friedman, Ellen G. "North African Piracy on the Coasts of Spain in the Seventeenth Century: A New Perspective on the Expulsion of the Moriscos." *The International History Review* 1 (January 1979): 1–16.

Guilmartin, John F., Jr. "Ideology and Conflict: The Wars of the Ottoman Empire, 1453–1606." *Journal of Interdisciplinary History* 18 (1988): 721–47; reprinted in *The Origin and Prevention of Wars*. Edited by R.I. Rotberg and T.K. Rabb. Cambridge and New York: Cambridge University Press, 1989.

Housley, Norman. *The Later Crusades, 1274–1580: From Lyons to Alcazar.* Oxford: Oxford University Press, 1992.

Lewis, Bernard. *Cultures in Conflict: Christians, Muslims and Jews in the Age of Discovery.* Oxford: Oxford University Press, 1995.

_____. *The Muslim Discovery of Europe.* New York: W.W. Norton and Company, 1982.

Sugar, Peter F. *Southeastern Europe under Ottoman Rule, 1354–1804.* Seattle: University of Washington Press, 1977.

Tenenti, A. *Piracy and the Decline of Venice, 1580–1615.* Berkeley: University of California Press, 1967.

Turnbull, Stephen. *The Ottoman Empire 1326–1699.* Botley: Osprey, 2003.

Valensi, Lucette. *The Birth of a Despot: Venice and the Sublime Porte.* Ithaca: Cornell University Press, 1995.

Vaughan, Dorothy M. *Europe and the Turk: A Pattern of Alliances, 1350–1700.* Liverpool: Liverpool University Press, 1954; reprint, New York: AMS Press, 1976.

GENERAL STUDIES—AGE OF DISCOVERY

Elliott, John H. *The Old World and the New, 1492–1650.* Cambridge: Cambridge University Press, 1972.

Hassig, Ross. *Mexico and the Spanish Conquest.* London: Longman, 1994.

O'Sullivan, Dan. *The Age of Discovery, 1400–1550.* London: Longman, 1984.

Parry, J.H. *The Age of Reconnaissance: Discovery, Exploration and Settlement, 1450–1650.* London: Weidenfeld and Nicolson, 1964.

Robinson, Charles M., III. *The Spanish Invasion of Mexico 1519–1521.* Botley: Osprey, 2003.

PART II
DIPLOMATS AND
DIPLOMACY,
1337–1815

Adair, Edward R. *The Exterritoriality of Ambassadors in the Sixteenth and Seventeenth Centuries*. London: Longmans, 1929.

Aksan, Virginia. *An Ottoman Statesman in War and Peace: Ahmed Resmi Enfedi, 1700–1783*. Leiden: E.J. Brill, 1995.

Allen, E. John B. *Post and Courier Service in the Diplomacy of Early Modern Europe*. The Hague: Martinus Nijhoff, 1972.

Altbauer, Dan. "The Diplomats of Peter the Great." *Jahrbücher für Geschichte Osteuropas* 28 (1980): 1–16.

_____. "The Diplomats of Peter the Great, 1689–1725." Ph.D. thesis, Harvard University, 1976.

Anderson, Matthew S. *The Rise of Modern Diplomacy, 1450–1919*. London and New York: Longman, 1993.

Baack, Lawrence J. "State Service in the Eighteenth Century: The Bernstorffs in Hanover and Denmark." *The International History Review* 1 (July 1979): 323–48.

Black, Jeremy. *British Diplomats and Diplomacy, 1688–1800*. Exeter: University of Exeter Press, 2001.

Bohlen, Avis. "Changes in Russian Diplomacy under Peter the Great." *Cahiers du monde russe et sovietique* 7 (1966): 341–58.

Carter, Charles H. "Wicquefort on the Ambassador and His Functions." In *Studies in History and Politics* 2 (1981–82): 37–59.

Chance, James F. and L.G. Wickham Legg. *British Diplomatic Instructions, 1689–1789*. 7 volumes. London: Royal Historical Society, 1922–34.

Clark, Ruth. *Sir William Trumbull in Paris, 1685–1686*. Cambridge: Cambridge University Press, 1938.

Contini, Alessandra. "Aspects of Medicean Diplomacy in the Sixteenth Century." In *Politics and Diplomacy in Early Modern Italy: The Structure of Diplomatic Practice, 1450–1800*. Edited by Daniela Frigo. Cambridge: Cambridge University Press, 2000.

Croskey, Robert M. *Muscovite Diplomatic Practice in the Reign of Ivan III*. New York: Garland, 1987.

Dover, Paul M. "Letters, Notes and Whispers: Diplomacy, Ambassadors and Information in the Italian Renaissance Princely State." Ph.D. diss., Yale University, 2002.

Frey, Linda S. and Marsha L. Frey. *The History of Diplomatic History*. Columbus: Ohio State University Press, 1999.

_____. "The Reign of the Charlatan is Over: The French Revolutionary Attack on Diplomatic Practice." *The Journal of Modern History* 65 (December 1993): 706–45.

Frigo, Daniela. "'Small States' and Diplomacy: Mantua and Modena." In *Politics and Diplomacy in Early Modern Italy: The Structure of Diplomatic Practice, 1450–1800*. Edited by Daniela Frigo. Cambridge: Cambridge University Press, 2000.

Gilbert, Felix. "The 'New' Diplomacy of the Eighteenth Century." *World Politics* 5 (October 1951): 1–38.

Hamilton, Keith and Richard Langhorne. *The Practice of Diplomacy: Its Evolution, Theory and Administration*. London: Routledge, 1995.

Hartley, Janet M. *Charles Whitworth: Diplomat in the Age of Peter the Great*. Aldershot: Ashgate, 2002.

Hatton, Ragnhild M. "Gratifications and Foreign Policy: Anglo-French Rivalry in Sweden during the Nine Years' War." In *William III and Louis XIV: Essays 1680–1720 by and for Mark A. Thomson*. Edited by R.M. Hatton and J.S. Bromley. Liverpool: Liverpool University Press, 1968.

Henneke, Christian E. "The Art of Diplomacy under the Early Stuarts, 1603–1642." Ph.D. diss., University of Virginia, 1999.

Horn, David Bayne. *British Diplomatic Representatives, 1689–1789*. London: Royal Historical Society, 1932.

_____. *Scottish Diplomats, 1689–1789*. London: Historical Assocation, 1944.

_____. *The British Diplomatic Service, 1689–1789*. Oxford: Clarendon Press, 1961.

_____. "The Diplomatic Experience of Secretaries of State, 1660–1852." *History* 41 (1956): 88–99.

_____. "The Machinery for the Conduct of British Foreign Policy in the Eighteenth Century." *Journal of the Society of Archivists* 3 (1965–69): 229–40.

_____. "Rank and Emolument in the British Diplomatic Service, 1689–1789." *Transactions of the Royal Historical Society*, Fifth series, 9 (1959): 19–50.

Israel, Jonathan I. "The Diplomatic Career of Jeronimo Nunes da Costa: An Episode in Dutch-Portuguese Relations of the Seventeenth Century." *Bijdragen en Mededelingen betreffende de geschiedenis der Nederlanden* 98 (1983): 67–90.

Jusserand, J.J. *A French Ambassador at the Court of Charles the Second*. New York: G.P. Putnam's and Sons, 1892.

Keens-Soper, H.M.A. *Abraham de Wicquefort and Diplomatic Theory*. Leicester: Centre for the Study of Diplomacy, University of Leicester, 1996.

_____. "The French Political Academy: A School for Ambassadors." *European Studies Review* 2 (1972): 329–55; reprinted in *François de Callières:*

The Art of Diplomacy. Edited by H.M.A. Keens-Soper and K.W. Schweizer. New York: Holmes and Meier, 1983.

_____. "François de Callières and Diplomatic Theory." *Historical Journal* 16 (1973): 485–508.

_____ and Karl W. Schweizer, editors. *François de Callières: The Art of Diplomacy.* New York: Holmes and Meier, 1983.

Klaits, Joseph. "Men of Letters and Political Reform in France at the End of the Reign of Louis XIV: The Founding of the *Académie Politique.*" *The Journal of Modern History* 43 (December 1971): 577–97.

Lachs, Phyllis S. *The Diplomatic Corps under Charles II and James II.* New Brunswick: Rutgers University Press, 1965.

Lane, Margery. "The Diplomatic Service under William III." *Transactions of the Royal Historical Society,* Fourth Series 10 (1927): 87–110.

Langhorne, Richard. "The Development of International Conferences, 1648–1830." *Studies in History and Politics* 2 (1981–82): 61–91.

Levin, Michael Jacob. "A Spanish Eye on Italy: Spanish Ambassadors in the Sixteenth Century." Ph.D. diss., Yale University, 1997.

Loomie, Albert J. "The *Conducteur des Ambassadeurs* of Seventeenth Century France and Spain." *Revue Belge de Philologie et d'Historie* 53 (1975): 333–56.

Lundell, Richard E. "The Mask of Dissimulation: Eustace Chapuys and Early Modern Diplomatic Technique, 1536–1545." Ph.D diss., University of Illinois at Urbana-Champaign, 2001.

Maiorini, Maria Grazia. "Neapolitan Diplomacy in the Eighteenth Century: Policy and the Diplomatic Apparatus." In *Politics and Diplomacy in Early Modern Italy: The Structure of Diplomatic Practice, 1450–1800.* Edited by Daniela Frigo. Cambridge: Cambridge University Press, 2000.

Mattingly, Garrett. *Renaissance Diplomacy.* London: Jonathan Cape, 1955.

Middleton, C.R. *The Administration of British Foreign Policy, 1782–1846*. Durham: Duke University Press, 1977.

Murray, John J. "The Görtz-Gyllenborg Arrests: A Problem in Diplomatic Immunity." *The Journal of Modern History* 28 (December 1956): 325–37.

Naff, Thomas. "Reform and the Conduct of Ottoman Diplomacy, 1789–1807." *Journal of the American Oriental Society* 83 (1963): 295–315.

Neale, John E. "The Diplomatic Envoy." In *The Age of Catherine de Medici and Essays in Elizabethan History*. London: Jonathan Cape, 1963.

Nicolson, Harold. *The Evolution of Diplomatic Method*. London: Constable and Company, 1954.

Oakley, Stewart P. "The Interception of Posts in Celle, 1694–1700." In *William III and Louis XIV: Essays 1680–1720 by and for Mark A. Thomson*. Edited by R.M. Hatton and J.S. Bromley. Liverpool: Liverpool University Press, 1968.

O'Brien, Dennis H. "Louis XIV's Diplomatic Corps, 1648–1671." Ph.D. diss., University of Illinois at Chicago Circle, 1973.

_____. "Mazarin's Diplomatic Corps, 1648–1661." *North Dakota Quarterly* (Winter 1977): 31–42.

Platt, F. Jeffrey. "The Elizabethan 'Foreign Office'." *The Historian* 56 (Summer 1994): 725–40.

Przezdziecki, Count Renaud. *Diplomatic Ventures and Adventures: Some Experiences of British Envoys at the Court of Poland*. London: The Polish Research Centre, 1953.

Queller, Donald E. *The Office of Ambassador in the Middle Ages*. Princeton: Princeton University Press, 1967.

Riccardi, Lucca. "An Outline of Vatican Diplomacy in the Early Modern Age." In *Politics and Diplomacy in Early Modern Italy: The Structure of Diplomatic Practice, 1450–1800*. Edited by Daniela Frigo. Cambridge: Cambridge University Press, 2000.

Rice, Geoffrey W. "British Consuls and Diplomats in the Mid-Eighteenth Century: An Italian Example." *The English Historical Review* 92 (1977): 834–46.

Roelofsen, C.G. "The Negociations about Nijmegen's Juridical Status during the Peace Congress." In *The Peace of Nijmegen, 1676–1678/79*. Edited by J.A.H. Bots. Amsterdam: APA-Holland University Press, 1980.

Roider, Karl A., Jr. "The Oriental Academy in the *Thereisenzeit*." In *The Habsburg Dominions under Maria Theresa*. Edited by W.J. McGill. Washington, Pa.: Washington and Jefferson College, 1980.

Roosen, William J. "A New Way of Looking at Early Modern Diplomacy-Quantification." *Proceedings of the Annual Meeting of the Western Society for French History* 5 (1978): 1–13.

_____. "Early Modern Diplomatic Ceremonial: A Systems Approach." *The Journal of Modern History* 52 (September 1980): 452–76.

_____. "How Good were Louis XIV's Diplomats?" In *Studies in History and Politics* 4 (1985): 89–102.

_____. "Seventeenth Century Diplomacy: French or European?" *Proceedings of the Annual Meeting of the Western Society for French History* 2 (1975): 89–93.

_____. *The Age of Louis XIV: The Rise of Modern Diplomacy*. Cambridge, Mass.: Schenkman, 1976.

_____. "The Ambassador's Craft: A Study of the Functioning of French Ambassadors under Louis XIV." Ph.D. diss., University of Southern California, 1967.

_____. "The Functioning of Ambassadors under Louis XIV." *French Historical Studies* 6 (Spring 1970): 311–32.

_____. "The True Ambassador: Occupational and Personal Characteristics of French Ambassadors under Louis XIV." *European Studies Review* 3 (1973): 121–39.

Rule, John C. "Gathering Intelligence in the Age of Louis XIV." *The International History Review* 14 (November 1992): 732–52.

_____. "The *Commis* of the Department of Foreign Affairs under the Administration of Colbert of Croissy and Colbert de Torcy, 1680–1715." *Proceedings of the Annual Meeting of the Western Society for French History* 8 (1980): 69–80.

Russell, Joycelyne G. *Diplomats at Work: Three Renaissance Studies*. Stroud: Alan Sutton, 1992.

_____. "Language: A Barrier or a Gateway?" In *Diplomats at Work: Three Renaissance Studies*. Stroud: Alan Sutton, 1992.

Schweizer, Karl W. "Scotsmen and the British Diplomatic Service, 1714–1789." *Scottish Tradition* 7–8 (1977–78): 115–36.

Simpson, John. "Arresting a Diplomat, 1717." *History Today* 34 (January 1985): 32–37.

Snyder, Henry L. "The British Diplomatic Service during the Godolphin Ministry." In *Studies in Diplomatic History: Essays in Memory of David Bayne Horn*. Edited by R.M. Hatton and M.S. Anderson. London: Longman, 1970.

Storrs, Christopher. "Savoyard Diplomacy in the Eighteenth Century (1684–1798)." In *Politics and Diplomacy in Early Modern Italy: The Structure of Diplomatic Practice, 1450–1800*. Edited by Daniela Frigo. Cambridge: Cambridge University Press, 2000.

Stradling, Robert A. "A Spanish Statesman of Appeasement: Medina de las Torres and Spanish Policy, 1639–1670." *Historical Journal* 19 (1976): 1–31; reprinted in *Spain's Struggle for Europe, 1598–1668*. London: Hambledon Press, 1994.

Strasser, G. "Diplomatic Cryptology and Universal Languages in the Sixteenth and Seventeenth Centuries." In *Go Spy the Land: Military Intelligence in History*. Edited by Keith Neilson and B.J.C. McKercher. Westport: Praeger, 1992.

Thompson, James Westfall and Saul K. Padover. *Secret Diplomacy: Espionage and Cryptography, 1500–1815*. New York: Frederick Unger, 1937.

Thomson, Mark A. *The Secretaries of State, 1681–1782*. Oxford: Clarendon Press, 1932; reprint, London: Frank Cass and Company, 1968.

Walsh, Micheline Kerney. "Toby Bourke, Ambassador of James III at the Court of Philip V, 1705–1713." In *The Stuart Court in Exile and the Jacobites*. Edited by Eveline Cruickshanks and Edward Corp. London: Hambledon Press, 1995.

Whitcomb, Edward A. *Napoleon's Diplomatic Service*. Durham: Duke University Press, 1979.

_____. "The Duties and Functions of Napoleon's External Agents." *History* 57 (June 1972): 189–204.

Williams, Basil. "A Short Comparison between the Secretaries of State in France and in England during the Eighteenth Century." In *Studies in Anglo-French History during the Eighteenth, Nineteenth, and Twentieth Centuries*. Edited by Alfred Coville and Harold Temperly. Cambridge: Cambridge University Press, 1935.

_____. "The Foreign Office of the First Two Georges." *Blackwood's Magazine* 181 (Jan-Jun 1907): 92–105

Wilson, Lester N. "François de Callières (1645–1717): Diplomat and Man of Letters." Ph.D. thesis, University of Illinois, 1963.

Wolff, Lawrence. "A Duel for Ceremonial Precedence: The Papal Nuncio Versus the Russian Ambassador at Warsaw, 1775–1785." *The International History Review* 7 (May 1985): 235–44.

Wood, A.C. "The English Embassy at Constantinople, 1660–1762." *The English Historical Review* 40 (1925): 533–61.

Woodley, Jocelyn. "The Development of the French Diplomatic System under Richelieu, 1624–1642." M.Phil., Cambridge University, 1989.

Zannini, Andrea. "Economic and Social Aspects of the Crisis of Venetian Diplomacy in the Seventeenth and Eighteenth Centuries." In *Politics and Diplo-*

macy in Early Modern Italy: The Structure of Diplomatic Practice, 1450–1800. Edited by Daniela Frigo. Cambridge: Cambridge University Press, 2000.

Zeller, Gaston. "French Diplomacy and Foreign Policy in Their European Setting." In *The New Cambridge Modern History*, Volume V. Edited by F.L. Carsten. Cambridge: Cambridge University Press, 1961.

PART III
ARMIES AND NAVIES,
1337–1815

Åberg, Alf. "Scottish Soldiers in the Swedish Armies in the Sixteenth and Seventeenth Centuries." In *Scotland and Scandinavia 800–1800*. Edited by Grant G. Simpson. Edinburgh: John Donald, 1990.

_____. "The Swedish Army: From Lutzen to Narva." In *Sweden's Age of Greatness, 1632–1718*. Edited by M. Roberts. London: Macmillan, 1973.

Adair, E.R. "English Galleys in the Sixteenth Century." *The English Historical Review* 35 (1920): 497–512.

Ágoston, G. "Gunpowder for the Sultan's Army: New Sources on the Supply of Gunpowder to the Ottoman Army in the Hungarian Campaigns of the Sixteenth and Seventeenth Centuries." *Turcica* 25 (1993): 75–96.

_____. "Ottoman Artillery and European Military Technology in the Fifteenth and Seventeenth Centuries." *Acta Orientalia Academiae Scientiarum Hungaricae* 47 (1994): 15–48.

Aksan, Virginia. "Breaking the Spell of the Baron de Tott: Reframing the Question of Military Reform in the Ottoman Empire, 1760–1830." *The International History Review* 24 (June 2002): 253–77.

_____. "Feeding the Ottoman Troops on the Danube, 1768–1774." *War and Society* 13 (May 1995): 1–14.

_____. "Ottoman War and Warfare, 1453–1812." In *War in the Early Modern World, 1450–1815*. Edited by J. Black. Boulder: Westview Press, 1999.

_____. "The One-Eyed Fighting the Blind: Mobilization, Supply, and Command in the Russo-Turkish War of 1768–74." *The International History Review* 15 (1993): 221–38.

Albion, R.G. *Forests and Sea Power: The Timber Problem of the Royal Navy, 1652–1862*. Cambridge, Mass.: Harvard University Press, 1926.

Aldridge, David. "The Navy as Handmaid for Commerce and High Policy, 1680–1720." In *The British Navy and the Use of Naval Power in the Eighteenth Century*. Edited by J. Black and P. Woodfine. Atlantic Highlands: Humanities Press International, 1989.

Alef, Gustave. "Muscovite Military Reforms in the Second Half of the Fifteenth Century." *Forschungen zur Osteuropäischen Geschichte* 18 (1973): 73–108.

Allmand, Christopher. "War" In *The New Cambridge Medieval History*, Volume VII. Cambridge: Cambridge University Press, 1998.

Anderson, Matthew S. *War and Society in Europe of the Old Regime, 1618–1789*. New York: St. Martin's Press, 1988.

Anderson, R.C. *Naval Wars in the Baltic during the Sailing Ship Epoch, 1522–1850*. London: C. Gilbert Wood, 1910; reprinted, London: Francis Edwards, 1969.

_____. *Naval War in the Levant, 1559–1853*. Princeton: Princeton University Press, 1952.

Anglo, Sydney. *The Martial Arts of Renaissance Europe*. New Haven: Yale University Press, 2000.

Arnold, Thomas F. *Renaissance at War*. London: Cassell and Company, 2001.

Asher, E. *The Resistance to the Maritime Classes: The Survival of Feudalism in the France of Colbert*. Berkeley: University of California Press, 1960.

Bak, János and Béla K. Király, editors. *From Hunyadi to Rákóczi: War and Society in Late Medieval and Early Modern Hungary*. Brooklyn: Columbia University Press, 1982.

Balisch, Alexander. "Infantry Battlefield Tactics in the Seventeenth and Eighteenth Centuries on the European and Turkish Theatres of War: The Austrian Response to Different Conditions." *Studies in History and Politics* 3 (1983/84): 43–60.

Bamford, Paul W. *Fighting Ships and Prisons: The Mediterranean Galleys of France in the Age of Louis XIV.* Minneapolis: University of Minnesota Press, 1973.

_____. *Forests and French Sea Power, 1660–1789.* Toronto: University of Toronto Press, 1956.

Barford, H.J. *Niels Juel: A Danish Admiral of the Seventeenth Century.* Copenhagen: Marinehistorisk Selskab, 1977.

Barker, Thomas M. *Army, Aristocracy, Monarchy: Essays on War, Society, and Government in Austria, 1618–1780.* New York: Columbia University Press, 1982.

_____. *Double Eagle and Crescent: Vienna's Second Turkish Siege and Its Historical Setting.* Albany: State University of New York Press, 1967.

Barnett, Correlli. *Britain and Her Army, 1509–1970: A Military, Political and Social Survey.* London: Allen Lane, 1970.

Barthorp, Michael. *Marlborough's Army, 1702–1711.* London: Osprey, 1980.

Bartlett, Olive. *English Longbowmen 1330–1515.* Botley: Osprey, 1999.

Bartusis, Mark C. *The Late Byzantine Army: Arms and Society, 1204–1453.* Philadelphia: University of Pennsylvania Press, 1992.

Baugh, Daniel A. *British Naval Administration in the Age of Walpole.* Princeton: Princeton University Press, 1965.

_____. "Great Britain's 'Blue-Water' Policy, 1689–1815." *The International History Review* 10 (February 1988): 33–58.

Baumber, Michael. "Cromwell's Soldier-Admirals." *History Today* 39 (October 1989): 42–47.

_____. *General at Sea: Robert Blake and the Seventeenth Century Revolution in Naval Warfare.* London: John Murray, 1989.

Baxter, Douglas Clark. "*Premiers Commis* in the War Department in the Later Part of the Reign of Louis XIV." *Proceedings of the Annual Meeting of the Western Society for French History* 8 (1980): 81–89.

_____. *Servants of the Sword: French Intendants of the Army, 1630–1670.* Urbana: University of Illinois Press, 1976.

Black, Jeremy. *Britain as a Military Power, 1688–1815.* London: University College London Press, 1999.

_____, editor. *European Warfare, 1453–1815.* New York: St. Martin's Press, 1999.

_____. *European Warfare, 1494–1660.* London and New York: Routledge, 2002.

_____. *European Warfare, 1660–1815.* New Haven: Yale University Press, 1994.

_____. *The Cambridge Illustrated Atlas of Warfare: Renaissance to Revolution, 1492–1792.* Cambridge and New York: Cambridge University Press, 1996.

_____, editor. *The Origins of War in Early Modern Europe.* Edinburgh: John Donald, 1987.

_____. *War and the World: Military Power and the Fate of Continents, 1450–2000.* New Haven: Yale University Press, 1998.

_____, editor. *War in the Early Modern World, 1450–1815.* Boulder: Westview Press, 1999.

_____. *Warfare in the Eighteenth Century.* London: Cassell, 1999.

_____ and Philip Woodfine, editors. *The British Navy and the Use of Naval Power in the Eighteenth Century.* Leicester: Leicester University Press, 1988.

Blok, Petrus J. *The Life of Admiral de Ruyter*. London: Ernest Benn, 1933; reprint, Westport: Greenwood Press, 1975.

Blomfield, Reginald. *Sébastien Le Prestre de Vauban, 1633–1707*. London: Methuen, 1938; reprint, New York: Barnes and Noble, 1971.

Boyton, Linda. *The Elizabethan Militia, 1558–1638*. London: Routledge and Kegan Paul, 1976.

Bradbury, Jim. *The Medieval Archer*. London: Boydell and Brewer, 1985.

Brockington, William S. "Robert Monro: Professional Soldier, Military Historian and Scotsman." In *Scotland and the Thirty Years' War, 1618–1648*. Edited by Steve Murdoch. Leiden: Brill, 2001.

Bromley, John S. *Corsairs and Navies, 1660–1760*. London: Hambledon Press, 1987.

_____and A.N. Ryan. "Navies." In *The New Cambridge Modern History*, Volume VI. Edited by J.S. Bromley. Cambridge: Cambridge University Press, 1970.

Broucek, Peter. "The Border Defenses of Lower Austria, Styria, and Moravia against the Turks and Rákóczi's Insurgents." In *From Hunyadi to Rákóczi: War and Society in Late Medieval and Early Modern Hungary*. Edited by J. Bak and B. Király. New York: Brooklyn College Press, 1982.

Bruijn, J.R. "The Dutch Navy in its Political and Social Economic Setting of the Seventeenth Century." In *1688: The Seaborne Alliance and Diplomatic Revolution*. Edited by C. Wilson and D. Proctor. London: Roundwood Press, 1989.

_____. *The Dutch Navy of the Seventeenth and Eighteenth Centuries*. Columbia: University of South Carolina Press, 1993.

Brzezinski, Richard. *Polish Armies, 1569–1696*. 2 volumes. London: Osprey, 1987–91.

Capp, Bernard. *Cromwell's Navy: The Fleet and the English Revolution, 1648–1660*. Oxford and New York: Oxford University Press, 1989.

Chandler, David G. *Marlborough as Military Commander*. London: B.T. Batsford, 1973.

_____. "Regular and Irregular Warfare." *The International History Review* 11 (February 1989): 2–13.

_____, editor. *Robert Parker and Comte de Mérode-Westerloo: The Marlborough Wars*. Hamden: Archon, 1968.

_____. *The Art of Warfare in the Age of Marlborough*. London: B.T. Batsford, 1976.

_____. "The Art of War on Land." In *The New Cambridge Modern History*, Volume VI. Edited by J.S. Bromley. Cambridge: Cambridge University Press, 1970.

Chartrand, René. *Louis XIV's Army*. London: Osprey, 1988.

_____. *The French Soldier in Colonial America*. Bloomfield, Ont.: Museum Restoration Service, 1984.

Childs, John. "A Patriot for Whom? 'For God and Honour': Marshal Schomberg." *History Today* 38 (July 1988): 46–52.

_____. *Armies and Warfare in Europe, 1648–1789*. New York: Holmes and Meier, 1982.

_____. *The Army of Charles II*. London: Trinity Press, 1976.

_____. *The Army of James II and the Glorious Revolution*. Manchester: Manchester University Press, 1980.

_____. *The British Army of William III, 1689–1697*. Manchester: Manchester University Press, 1987.

_____. *The Nine Years War and the British Army, 1688–1697*. Manchester: Manchester University Press, 1991.

_____. "The Scottish Brigade in the Service of the Dutch Republic, 1689–1782." *Documentatieblad Werkgroep Achttiende Eeuw* 16 (1984): 59–75.

_____. *Warfare in the Seventeenth Century*. London: Cassel and Company, 2001.

Cipolla, Carlo M. *Guns and Sails in the Early Phase of European Expansion, 1400–1700*. London: Collins, 1965.

Clark, George N. *War and Society in the Seventeenth Century*. Cambridge: Cambridge University Press, 1958.

Contamine, Philippe. *War in the Middle Ages*. Oxford: Basil Blackwell, 1984.

Cooper, J.P. "Sea-Power." In *The New Cambridge Modern History*, Volume IV. Edited by J.P. Cooper. Cambridge: Cambridge University Press, 1970.

Corvisier. Andre. *Armies and Societies in Europe, 1494–1789*. Translated by Abigail Siddall. Bloomington: Indiana University Press, 1979.

Creveld, Martin van. *Supplying War: Logistics from Wallenstein to Patton*. Cambridge: Cambridge University Press, 1977.

Cruickshank, Charles. *Elizabeth's Army*. Second edition. Oxford and New York: Oxford University Press, 1966.

Dalton, Charles. *George the First's Army, 1714–1727*. 2 volumes. London: Eyre and Spottiswoode, 1910–12.

Dávid, Géza and Pál Fodor, editors. *Ottomans, Hungarians, and Habsburgs in Central Europe: The Military Confines in the Era of Ottoman Conquest*. Leiden: Brill, 2000.

Davies, J.D. *Gentlemen and Tarpaulins: The Officers and Men of the Restoration Navy*. Oxford: Clarendon Press, 1992.

Delbrück, Hans. *History of the Art of War*. 4 volumes. Westport: Greenwood Press, 1985.

DeVries, Kelly. "Gunpowder Weapons at the Siege of Constantinople, 1453." In *War and Society in the Eastern Mediterranean, 7th–15th Centuries*. Edited by Y. Lev. Leiden: E.J. Brill, 1997.

_____. *Infantry Warfare in the Early Fourteenth Century: Discipline, Tactics, and Technology*. Woodbridge: Boydell Press, 1996.

_____. *Medieval Military Technology*. Peterborough, Canada: Broadview Press, 1992.

_____. "The Impact of Gunpowder Weaponry on Siege Warfare in the Hundred Years' War." In *The Medieval City under Siege*. Edited by Ivy A. Corfis and Michael Wolfe. Woodbridge: Boydell Press, 1995.

_____. "The Use of Gunpowder Weaponry by and against Joan of Arc during the Hundred Years' War." *War and Society* 14 (1996): 1–16.

Duffy, Christopher. *Fire and Stone: The Science of Fortress Warfare, 1660–1860*. Newton Abbot: David and Charles, 1975.

_____. *Instrument of War: Volume I of the Austrian Armies in the Seven Years' War*. Rosemont, Ill.: Emperor's Press, 2000.

_____. *Russia's Military Way to the West: Origins and Nature of Russian Military Power, 1700–1800*. London: Routledge and Kegan Paul, 1981.

_____. *Siege Warfare: The Fortress in the Early Modern World, 1494–1660*. London: Routledge and Kegan Paul, 1979.

_____. *The Army of Frederick the Great*. Newton Abbot: David and Charles, 1974.

_____. *The Army of Maria Theresa: The Armed Forces of Imperial Austria, 1740–1780*. New York: Hippocrene, 1977.

_____. *The Fortress in the Age of Vauban and Frederick the Great, 1660–1789*. London: Routledge and Kegan Paul, 1985.

_____. *The Military Experience in the Age of Reason*. New York: Atheneum, 1988.

_____. *The Wild Goose and the Eagle: A Life of Marshal von Browne, 1705–1757*. London: Chatto and Windus, 1964.

Dukes, Paul. "New Perspectives: Alexander Leslie and the Smolensk War, 1632–1634." In *Scotland and the Thirty Years' War, 1618–1648*. Edited by Steve Murdoch. Leiden: Brill, 2001.

Ehrman, John. *The Navy in the War of William III, 1689–1697: Its State and Direction*. Cambridge: Cambridge University Press, 1953.

Elting, John R. *Swords around a Throne: Napoleon's Grande Armée*. New York: Macmillan, 1988.

Esper, Thomas. "Military Self-Sufficiency and Weapons Technology in Muscovite Russia." *Slavic Review* 28 (1969): 185–208.

_____. "The Replacement of the Longbow by Firearms in the English Army." *Technology and Culture* 6 (1965): 382–93.

Fallon, J.A. "Scottish Mercenaries in the Service of Denmark and Sweden, 1626–1632." Ph.D. diss., University of Glasgow, 1972.

Ferguson, Ronald T. "Blood and Fire: Contribution Policy of the French Armies in Germany (1668–1715)." Ph.D. thesis, University of Minnesota, 1970.

Firth, Charles. *Cromwell's Army: A History of the English Soldier during the Civil Wars, the Commonwealth, and the Protectorate*. Third edition, London: Methuen, 1921; reprint, London: Greenhill Books, 1992.

Fox, Frank. *Great Ships: The Battlefleet of King Charles II*. Greenwich: Conway Maritime Press, 1980.

Frost, Robert I. "Confessionalization in the Army in the Polish-Lithuanian Commonwealth, 1550–1667." In *Konfessionalisierung in Ostmitteleuropa*. Edited by J. Bahlicke and A. Strohmeyer. Stuttgart: Franz Steiner, 1999.

_____. "Scottish Soldiers, Poland-Lithuania and the Thirty Years' War." In *Scotland and the Thirty Years' War, 1618–1648*. Edited by Steve Murdoch. Leiden: Brill, 2001.

Gallaher, John G. "The Prussian Regiment of the Napoleonic Army." *The Journal of Military History* 55 (July 1991): 331–44.

Gilbert, Felix. "Machiavelli: The Renaissance of the Art of War." In *Makers of Modern Strategy from Machiavelli to the Nuclear Age*. Edited by Peter Paret. Princeton: Princeton University Press, 1986.

Glete, Jan. *Navies and Nations: Warships, Navies and State Building in Europe and America, 1500–1860*. 2 volumes. Stockholm: Almquist and Wiksell, 1993.

_____. *War and the State in Early Modern Europe: Spain, the Dutch Republic and Sweden as Fiscal-Military States, 1500–1660*. London: Routledge, 2002.

_____. "Warfare at Sea, 1450–1815." In *War in the Early Modern World, 1450–1815*. Edited by J. Black. Boulder: Westview Press, 1999.

_____. *Warfare at Sea, 1500–1650: Maritime Conflicts and the Transformation of Europe*. London and New York: Routledge, 2000.

Glozier, Matthew. "Scots in the French and Dutch Armies during the Thirty Years' War." In *Scotland and the Thirty Years' War, 1618–1648*. Edited by Steve Murdoch. Leiden: Brill, 2001.

Godley, Eveline. *The Great Condé: A Life of Louis II de Bourbon, Prince of Condé*. London: John Murray, 1915.

Goodman, David. *Spanish Naval Power, 1589–1665: Reconstruction and Defeat*. Cambridge: Cambridge University Press, 1997.

Gravett, Christopher. *German Medieval Armies, 1300–1500*. London: Osprey, 1986.

Griess, Thomas E., editor. *The Dawn of Modern Warfare*. Wayne, N.J.: Avery Publishing Group, 1984.

Griffith, Paddy. *The Art of War of Revolutionary France, 1789–1802*. London: Greenhill Books, 1998.

Grosjean, Alexia. "Scotland: Sweden's Closet Ally?" In *Scotland and the Thirty Years' War, 1618–1648*. Edited by Steve Murdoch. Leiden: Brill, 2001.

Guerlac, Henry. "Vauban: The Impact of Science on War." In *Makers of Modern Strategy: Form Machiavelli to the Nuclear Age.* Edited by P. Paret. Princeton: Princeton University Press, 1986.

Guilmartin, John Francis, Jr. *Galleons and Galleys.* London: Cassell, 2002.

_____. "Ballistics in the Black Powder Era." In *British Naval Armaments.* Edited by Robert D. Smith. London: Royal Armouries, 1989.

_____. *Gunpowder and Galleys: Changing Technology and Mediterranean Warfare at Sea in the Sixteenth Century.* Cambridge: Cambridge University Press, 1974.

_____. "Ideology and Conflict: The Wars of the Ottoman Empire, 1453– 1606." *Journal of Interdisciplinary History* 18 (1988): 721–47; reprinted in *The Origin and Prevention of Wars.* Edited by R.I. Rotberg and T.K. Rabb. Cambridge and New York: Cambridge University Press, 1989.

_____. "The Logistics of Warfare at Sea in the Sixteenth Century: The Spanish Perspective." In *Feeding Mars: Logistics in Western Warfare from the Middle Ages to the Present.* Edited by J. Lynn. Boulder: Westview Press, 1993.

Gush, George. *Renaissance Armies, 1480–1650.* Cambridge: Patrick Stephens, 1975.

Gwyn, Julian. "The Royal Navy in North America, 1712–1776." In *The British Navy and the Use of Naval Power in the Eighteenth Century.* Edited by J. Black and P. Woodfine. Atlantic Highlands: Humanities Press International, 1989.

Hale, John R. "Armies, Navies, and the Art of War." In *The New Cambridge Modern History*, Volume II. Edited by G.R. Elton. Cambridge: Cambridge University Press, 1958.

_____. "Armies, Navies, and the Art of War." In *The New Cambridge Modern History*, Volume III. Edited by R.B. Wernham. Cambridge: Cambridge University Press, 1968.

_____. *Artists and Warfare in the Renaissance.* New Haven: Yale University Press, 1990.

_____. "Brescia and the Venetian Militia System in the Cinquecento." In *Armi e cultura nel Bresciano, 1420–1870*. Edited by Ateneao di Brescia. Brescia: Ateneao di Brescia, 1981.

_____. "Francesco Tensini and the Fortification of Vicenza." *Studi Veneziani* 10 (1968): 231–89; reprinted in *Renaissance War Studies*. London: Hambledon Press, 1983.

_____. "Gunpowder and the Renaissance: An Essay in the History of Ideas." In *From the Renaissance to the Counter-Reformation: Essays in Honour of Garrett Mattingly*. Edited by C.H. Carter. London: Jonathan Cape, 1966; reprinted in *Renaissance War Studies*. London: Hambledon Press, 1983.

_____. "Men and Weapons: The Fighting Potential of Sixteenth Century Venetian Galleys." *War and Society: A Yearbook of Military History*. Edited by B. Bond and I. Roy. London: Croom Helm, 1975; reprinted in *Renaissance War Studies*. London: Hambledon Press, 1983.

_____. "Military Academies on the Venetian *Terraferma* in the Early Seventeenth Century." *Studi Veneziani* 15 (1973): 273–95; reprinted in *Renaissance War Studies*. London: Hambledon Press, 1983.

_____. *Renaissance Fortification: Art or Engineering?* London: Thames and Hudson, 1977.

_____. *Renaissance War Studies*. London: Hambledon Press, 1983.

_____. "Sixteenth Century Explanations of War and Violence." *Past and Present* 51 (May 1971): 3–26: reprinted in *Renaissance War Studies*. London: Hambledon Press, 1983.

_____. "The Early Development of the Bastion: An Italian Chronology, c.1450–c.1534." In *Europe and the Late Middle Ages*. Edited by J.R. Hale, J.R.L. Highfield, and B. Smalley. London: Faber, 1965; reprinted in *Renaissance War Studies*. London: Hambledon Press, 1983.

_____. "The End of Florentine Liberty: The Fortezza da Basso." In *Florentine Studies: Politics and Society in Renaissance Florence*. Edited by N.

Rubinstein. London: Faber, 1968; reprinted in *Renaissance War Studies*. London: Hambledon Press, 1983.

_____. "The First Fifty Years of a Venetian Magistracy: The *Provveditori alle Fortezze*." In *Renaissance Studies in Honor of Hans Baron*. Edited by A. Molho and J.A. Tedeschi. Dekalb: Northern Illinois University Press, 1971; reprinted in *Renaissance War Studies*. London: Hambledon Press, 1983.

_____. "The Military Education of the Officer Class in Early Modern Europe." In *Cultural Aspects of the Italian Renaissance: Essays in Honour of Paul Oskar Kristeller*. Edited by C.H. Clough. Manchester: Manchester University Press, 1976; reprinted in *Renaissance War Studies*. London: Hambledon Press, 1983.

_____. "To Fortify or Not to Fortify?: Machiavelli's Contribution to a Renaissance Debate." In *Essays in Honour of John Humphreys Whitfield*. Edited by H.C. Davis, J.M. Hatwell, D.G. Rees and G.W. Slowey. London: St. George's Press, 1975; reprinted in *Renaissance War Studies*. London: Hambledon Press, 1983.

_____. "Tudor Fortifications, 1485–1558." In *History of the King's Works*, Volume IV. Edited by Howard Colvin. London: Her Majesty's Stationery Office, 1982; reprinted in *Renaissance War Studies*. London: Hambledon Press, 1983.

_____. "War and Public Opinion in Renaissance Italy." In *Italian Renaissance Studies*. Edited by E.F. Jacob. London: Faber, 1960; reprinted in *Renaissance War Studies*. London: Hambledon Press, 1983.

_____. "War and Public Opinion in the Fifteenth and Sixteenth Centuries." *Past and Present* 22 (1962): 18–35.

_____. *War and Society in Renaissance Europe, 1450–1620*. Leicester: Leicester University Press, 1985.

Hall, A.R. *Ballistics in the Seventeenth Century*. Cambridge: Cambridge University Press, 1952.

Hall, Bert S. "'So Notable Ordynaunce': Christine de Pizan, Firearms, and Siege-craft in a Time of Transition." In *Culturhistorisch Kaleidoskoop: Een Huldealbum aangebodenaan Prof. Dr. Willy L. Braekman*. Edited by C. De Backer. Brussels: Stichting Mens en Kultuur, 1992.

_____. "The Changing Face of Siege Warfare: Technology and Tactics in Transition." In *The Medieval City under Siege*. Edited by I.A. Corfis and M. Wolfe. London: Boydell and Brewer, 1995.

_____. *Weapons and Warfare in Renaissance Europe: Gunpowder, Technology and Tactics*. Baltimore: Johns Hopkins University Press, 1997.

Hanlon, Gregory. *The Twilight of a Military Tradition: Italian Aristocrats and European Conflicts, 1560–1800*. New York: Holmes and Meier, 1998.

Harding, Richard. *Seapower and Naval Warfare*. Anapolis: Naval Institute Press, 1999.

_____. *The Evolution of the Sailing Navy, 1509–1815*. New York: St. Martin's Press, 1995.

Harford, Lee S., Jr. "The Bavarian Army under Napoleon, 1805–1813." Ph.D. diss., Florida State University, 1988.

Hattendorf, John, editor. *War at Sea in the Middle Ages and Renaissance*. London: Boydell and Brewer, 2003.

Haythornthwaite, Philip J. *The Armies of Wellington*. London: Arms and Armour Press, 1994.

Heath, Ian. *Armies of the Sixteenth Century: The Armies of England, Scotland, Ireland, the United Provinces, and the Spanish Netherlands*. London: Foundary, 2000.

_____. *The Irish Wars 1485–1603*. London: Osprey, 1993.

_____ and Angus McBride. *Byzantine Armies 1118–1461*. London: Osprey, 1995.

Hebbert, F.J. and George A. Rothrock. *Soldier of France: Sébastien Le Prestre de Vauban, 1633–1707*. New York: Peter Lang, 1989.

Heckenast, Gusztáv. "Equipment and Supply of Ference II Rákóczi's Army." In *From Hunyadi to Rákóczi: War and Society in Late Medieval and Early Modern Hungary.* Edited by J. Bak and B. Király. New York: Brooklyn College Press, 1982.

Hellie, R. *Enserfment and Military Change in Muscovy.* Chicago: University of Chicago Press, 1971.

_____. "The Petrine Army: Continuity, Change and Impact." *Canadian-American Slavic Studies* 8 (1974): 237–53.

_____. "Warfare, Changing Military Technology and the Evolution of Muscovite Society." In *Tools of War: Instruments, Ideas and Institutions of Warfare, 1445–1871.* Urbana: University of Illinois Press, 1987.

Higginbotham, Donald. *The War of American Independence: Military Attitudes, Policies, and Practice, 1763–1789.* New York: Macmillan, 1971.

Hill, James M. *Celtic Warfare, 1595–1763.* Edinburgh: John Donald, 1986.

Hochedlinger, Michael. *Austria's Wars of Emergence, 1683–1797.* London: Longman, 2003.

_____. "Mars Ennobled: The Ascent of the Military and the Creation of a Military Nobility in Mid-Eighteenth Century Austria." *German History* 17 (1999): 141–76.

Hollins, David. *Hungarian Hussar 1756–1815.* Botley: Osprey, 2003.

Holmes, Richard. *Redcoat: The British Solider in the Age of the Horse and Musket.* New York: W.W. Norton, 2002.

Hoof, J.P.C.M. van. "Fortifications in the Netherlands (c.1500–1940)." *Revue Internationale d'historie militaire* 58 (1984): 97–126.

Hooijmaaijers, Eelko. "Cornelis Cruys, a Dutch Rear-Admiral in Russian Service." In *Around Peter the Great: Three Centuries of Dutch-Russian Relations.* Edited by Carel Horstmeier, Hans van Koningsbrugge, Ilja Nieuwland, and Emmanuel Waegemans. Groningen: Institute for Northern and Eastern European Studies, 1997.

Hook, Adam. *The Conquistador 1492–1550*. Botley: Osprey, 2001.

Houlding, J.A. *Fit For Service: The Training of the British Army, 1715–1795*. Oxford: Clarendon Press, 1982.

Hughes, Basil Perronet. *Firepower: Weapons Effectiveness on the Battlefield, 1630–1850*. London: Armour and Armaments Press, 1974.

_____. *Open Fire: Artillery Tactics from Marlborough to Wellington*. Chichester: Anthony Bird, 1983.

Hughes, Lindsey. "Peter the Great: A Passion for Ships." In *Scotland and the Slavs: Cultures in Contact, 1500–2000*. Edited by Mark Cornwall and Murray Frame. Newtonville, Mass.: Oriental Research Partner, 2001.

Jenkins, E.H. *A History of the French Navy*. London: Macdonald and Jane's, 1973.

Jones, Colin. "New Military History for Old?: War and Society in Early Modern Europe." *European Studies Review* 12 (1982): 97–108.

Jones, James R. "The Dutch Navy and National Survival in the Seventeenth Century." *The International History Review* 10 (February 1988): 18–32.

_____. "Limitations of British Sea Power in the French Wars, 1689–1815." In *The British Navy and the Use of Naval Power in the Eighteenth Century*. Edited by J. Black and P. Woodfine. Atlantic Highlands: Humanities Press International, 1989.

Kagan, Frederick. *The Military History of Tsarist Russia*. New York: Palgrave, 2002.

Keep, John L. "Feeding the Troops: Russian Army Supply Policies during the Seven Years' War." *Canadian Slavic Papers* 29 (1987): 24–44.

_____. *Soldiers of the Tsar: Army and Society in Russia, 1462–1874*. Oxford: Clarendon Press, 1985.

Kemp, Anthony. *Weapons and Equipment of the Marlborough Wars*. Poole: Blandford Press, 1980.

Kennedy, Paul. *The Rise and Fall of British Naval Mastery*. London: Macmillan, 1976.

Kennett, Lee. *The French Armies in the Seven Years' War: A Study in Military Organization and Administration*. Durham: Duke University Press, 1967.

Kerby, John. "Peter the Great: He Gave Russia Her Army and Navy." *Army Quarterly and Defence Journal* 85 (December 1998): 437–40.

Konstam, Angus. *British Napoleonic Ship-of-the-Line*. Botley: Osprey, 2001.

_____. *Peter the Great's Army*. 2 volumes. London: Osprey, 1993.

_____. *Renaissance War Galley 1470–1590*. Botley: Osprey, 2002.

_____. *The Spanish Galleon 1530–1690*. Botley: Osprey, 2003.

Lambert, Andrew. *War at Sea in the Age of Sail*. London: Cassell, 2000.

Leach, Douglas Edward. *Arms for Empire: A Military History of the British Colonies in North America, 1607–1763*. New York: Macmillan, 1973.

_____. *Roots of Conflict: British Armed Forces and Colonial Americans, 1677–1763*. Chapel Hill: University of North Carolina Press, 1986.

LeDonne, John P. "Outlines of Russian Military Administration, 1762–1796: Part I, Troop Strength and Deployment." *Jahrbücher für Geschichte Osteuropas* 31 (1983): 321–47.

Lenihan, Padraig, editor. *Conquest and Resistance: War in Seventeenth-Century Ireland*. Leiden: Brill, 2001.

Lindegren, J. "The Swedish 'Military State', 1560–1720." *Scandinavian Journal of History* 10 (1985): 305–36.

Loades, David. *The Tudor Navy: An Administrative, Political, and Military History*. Cambridge: Scolar Press, 1992.

Lewis, Michael A. *Armada Guns: A Comparative Study of English and Spanish Armaments*. London: Allen and Unwin, 1961.

Lloyd, Christopher. "Armed Forces and the Art of War: Navies." In *The New Cambridge Modern History*, Volume VIII. Edited by A. Goodwin. Cambridge: Cambridge University Press, 1965.

Loewe, K. von. "Military Service in Early Sixteenth-Century Lithuania: A New Interpretation and Its Implications." *Slavic Review* 30 (1971): 249–56.

Love, Ronald S. "'All the King's Horsemen': The Equestrian Army of Henri IV, 1585–1598." *Sixteenth Century Journal* 22 (1991): 510–33.

Lund, Erik A. "The Generation of 1683: Habsburg General Officers and the Military Technical Corps, 1686–1723." *Mitteilungen des Österreichischen Staatsarchivs* 46 (1998): 189–213.

_____. *War for the Every Day: Generals, Knowledge, and Warfare in Early Modern Europe, 1680–1740*. Westport: Greenwood Press, 1999.

Lynn, John A. "A Quest for Glory: The Formation of Strategy under Louis XIV, 1661–1715." In *The Making of Strategy: Rulers, States, and War*. Edited by Williamson Murray, MacGregor Knox, and Alvin Bernstein. Cambridge: Cambridge University Press, 1994.

_____, editor. *Feeding Mars: Logistics in Western Warfare from the Middle Ages to the Present*. Boulder: Westview Press, 1993.

_____. "Food, Funds, and Fortresses: Resource Mobilization and Positional Warfare in the Wars of Louis XIV." In *Feeding Mars: Logistics in Western Warfare from the Middle Ages to the Present*. Edited by J. Lynn. Boulder: Westview Press, 1993.

_____. *Giant of the Grand Siècle: The French Army, 1610–1715*. Cambridge: Cambridge University Press, 1997.

_____. "How War Fed War: The Tax of Violence and Contributions during the *Grand Siècle*." *The Journal of Modern History* 65 (June 1993): 286–310.

_____. "Linear Warfare: Images and Ideals of Combat in the Age of Enlightenment." Chapter in *Battle: A History of Combat and Culture*. Boulder: Westview Press, 2003.

_____. "Recalculating French Army Growth during the *Grande Siècle*, 1610–1715." *French Historical Studies* 18 (1994): 881–906; reprinted in *The Military Revolution Debate: Readings on the Military Transformation of Early Modern Europe*. Edited by C.J. Rogers. Boulder: Westview, 1995.

_____. "Soldiers on the Rampage." *MHQ: The Quarterly Journal of Military History* 3 (Winter 1991): 92–101.

_____. *The Bayonets of the Republic: Motivation and Tactics in the Army of Revolutionary France, 1791–1794*. Urbana: University of Illinois Press, 1984.

_____. "The Pattern of Army Growth, 1445–1945." In *Tools of War: Instruments, Ideas, and Institutions of Warfare, 1445–1871*. Edited by John A.Lynn. Urbana: University of Illinois Press, 1990.

_____. "The Revolution on the Battlefield: Training and Tactics of the *Armée du Nord*, 1792–1794." Ph.D. diss., University of California at Los Angeles, 1973.

_____. "The Sun King's Star Wars." *MHQ: The Quarterly Journal of Military History* 7 (Summer 1995): 88–97.

_____. "The *trace italienne* and the Growth of Armies: The French Case." *The Journal of Modern History* 55 (1991): 297–330; reprinted in *The Military Revolution Debate: Readings on the Military Transformation of Early Modern Europe*. Edited by C.J. Rogers. Boulder: Westview, 1995.

_____. "Vauban." *MHQ: The Quarterly Journal of Military History* 1 (1989): 51–61.

Majewski, Wiesław. "The Polish Art of War in the Sixteenth and Seventeenth Centuries." In *A Republic of Nobles: Studies in Polish History to 1864*. Edited by J.K. Fedorowicz. Cambridge: Cambridge University Press, 1982.

Mallett, Michael. *Mercenaries and Their Masters: Warfare in Renaissance Italy*. London: Bodley Head, 1974.

_____. "Siegecraft in Late Fifteenth Century Italy." In *The Medieval City under Siege*. Edited by Ivy A. Corfis and Michael Wolfe. Woodbridge: Boydell Press, 1995.

_____ and J.R. Hale. *The Military Organization of a Renaissance State: Venice, c.1400 to 1617*. Cambridge and New York: Cambridge University Press, 1984.

Maltby, William. "Politics, Professionalism, and the Evolution of Sailing-Ship Tactics, 1650–1714." In *Tools of War: Instruments, Ideas, and Institutions of Warfare, 1445–1871*. Edited by John A.Lynn. Urbana: University of Illinois Press, 1990.

Martin, Ronald. "The Army of Louis XIV." In *The Reign of Louis XIV*. Edited by P. Sonnino. Atlantic Highlands: Humanities Press International, 1990.

_____. "The Marquis de Barbézieux as *Secrétaire d'état de la Guerre*." *Proceedings of the Annual Meeting of the Western Society for French History* 3 (1976): 60–67.

_____. "The Marquis de Chamlay, Friend and Confidential Advisor to Louis XIV: The Early Years, 1650–1691." Ph.D. diss., University of California at Santa Barbara, 1972.

McGowan, Alan. "The Dutch Influence on British Shipbuilding." In *1688: The Seaborne Alliance and Diplomatic Revolution*. Edited by Charles Wilson and David Proctor. Greenwich: Roundwood Press, 1989.

Mears, John A. "The Emergence of the Standing Professional Army in Seventeenth Century Europe." *Social Science Quarterly* 49 (June 1969): 106–15.

_____. "The Thirty Years' War, the 'General Crisis', and the Origins of a Standing Professional Army in the Habsburg Monarhcy." *Central European History* 21 (1988): 122–41.

Menning, Bruce W. "Russian Military Innovation in the Second Half of the Eighteenth Century." *War and Society* 2 (1984): 23–41.

_____. "Train Hard, Fight Easy: The Legacy of A.V. Suvorov and his 'Art of Victory'." *Air University Review* 38 (1986): 79–88.

Millar, Gilbert John. *Tudor Mercenaries and Auxiliaries, 1485–1547*. Charlottesville: University Press of Virginia, 1980.

Miller, Douglas. *Landsknechts*. London: Osprey, 1994.

_____. *The Swiss at War 1300–1500*. Botley: Osprey, 1998.

Moor, J.A. de. "Experience and Experiment: Some Reflections upon the Military Developments in Sixteenth and Seventeenth Century Western Europe." In *Exercise of Arms: Warfare in the Netherlands, 1568–1648*. Edited by Marco van der Hoeven. Leiden: Brill, 1997.

Moore, Anthony. *Army of Brandenburg-Prussia 1680–1715*. London: Gosling Press, 1993.

Murphey, Rhoads. *Ottoman Warfare, 1500–1700*. London: University College London Press, 1999.

Nickle, Barry H. "The Military Reforms of Prince Maurice of Orange." Ph.D. diss., University of Delaware, 1975.

Nicolle, David. *Armies of the Ottoman Turks 1300–1774*. London: Osprey, 1985.

_____. *Armies of the Ottoman Empire 1775–1820*. Botley: Osprey, 1998.

_____. *French Armies in the Hundred Years' War, 1328–1429*. Botley: Osprey, 2000.

_____. *Italian Medieval Armies, 1300–1500*. London: Osprey, 1983.

Nosworthy, Brent. *The Anatomy of Victory: Battle Tactics, 1689–1763*. New York: Hippocrene, 1990.

Ollard, Richad. *Man of War: Sir Robert Holmes and the Restoration Navy*. London: Hodder and Stoughton, 1969.

Oman, Charles. *A History of the Art of War in the Middle Ages*. 2 volumes. Second edition. London: Methuen, 1924.

_____. *A History of the Art of War in the Sixteenth Century*. London: Methuen, 1937.

Padfield, Peter. *Tide of Empires: Decisive Naval Campaigns in the Rise of the West*. 2 volumes. London: Routledge and Kegan Paul, 1979–82.

Palmer, R.R. "Frederick the Great, Buibert, Bülow: From Dynastic to National War." In *Makers of Modern Strategy from Machiavelli to the Nuclear Age.* Edited by Peter Paret. Princeton: Princeton University Press, 1986.

Parker, Geoffrey. *The Army of Flanders and the Spanish Road, 1567–1659: The Logistics of Spanish Victory and Defeat in the Low Countries Wars.* Cambridge and New York: Cambridge University Press, 1972.

_____. "The Artillery Fortress as an Engine of European Overseas Expansion, 1480–1750." In *Success is Never Final: Empire, War, and Faith in Early Modern Europe.* New York: Basic Books, 2002.

_____. "The Dreadnought Revolution of Tudor England." *Mariner's Mirror* 82 (1996): 269–300.

_____. "The Soldiers of the Thirty Years' War." In *Krieg und Politik 1618–1648: Europäische Probleme und Perspektiven.* Edited by Konrad von Repgen. Munich: R. Ouldenbourg, 1988.

_____. "Warfare." In *The New Cambridge Modern History*, Volume XIII. Edited by P. Burke. Cambridge: Cambridge University Press, 1979.

_____ and Angela Parker. *European Soldiers 1550–1650.* Cambridge: Cambridge University Press, 1977.

Parrott, David. "Richelieu, the *grands* and the French Army." In *Richelieu and His Age.* Edited by J. Bergin and L.W.B. Brockliss. Oxford: Oxford University Press, 1992.

_____. *Richelieu's Army: War, Government and Society in France, 1624–1642.* Cambridge and New York: Cambridge University Press, 2001.

_____. "The Administration of the French Army during the Ministry of Cardinal Richelieu." D.Phil. thesis, University of Oxford, 1985.

_____. "The Utility of Fortifications in Early Modern Europe: Italian Princes and Their Citadels, 1540–1640." *War in History* 7 (2000): 127–53.

Partington, J. *A History of Greek Fire and Gunpowder.* Cambridge: Cambridge University Press, 1960.

Pepper, Simon. "Military Architecture in Baroque Europe." In *The Triumph of the Baroque: Architecture in Europe, 1600–1750*. Edited by H. Millon. New York: Rizzoli, 1999.

_____. "Siege Law, Siege Ritual, and the Symbolism of Walled Cities in Renaissance Europe. In *City Walls: The Urban Enceinte in Global Perspective*. Edited by James D. Tracy. Cambridge and New York: Cambridge University Press, 2000.

_____ and Nicholas Adams. *Firearms and Fortifications: Military Architecture and Siege Warfare in Sixteenth-Century Siena*. Chicago: University of Chicago Press, 1986.

Perjés. Géza. "Army Provisioning, Logistics and Strategy in the Second Half of the 17th Century." *Acta Historica Academiae Scientiarum Hungaricae* 16 (1970): 1–52.

Phillips, Edward. *The Founding of Russia's Navy: Peter the Great and the Azov Fleet, 1688–1714*. Westport: Greenwood Press, 1981.

Phillips, Gervase. *The Anglo-Scots Wars, 1513–1550*. Woodbridge: Boydell, 1999.

Pierson, Peter. "The Development of Spanish Naval Strategy and Tactics in the Sixteenth Century." In *Politics, Religion and Diplomacy in Early Modern Europe: Essays in Honor of De Lamar Jensen*. Edited by Malcolm R. Thorp and Arthur J. Slavin. Kirksville: Sixteenth Century Journal Publishers, 1994.

Pritchard, James. *Louis XV's Navy, 1748–1762: A Study of Organization and Administration*. Kingston: McGill-Queen's University Press, 1987.

Quimby, Robert A. *The Background of Napoleonic Warfare: The Theory of Military Tactics in Eighteenth Century France*. New York: Columbia University Press, 1957.

Quintrell, Brian. "Charles I and his Navy in the 1630s." *The Seventeenth Century* 3 (1988): 159–79.

Raudzens, George. "In Search of Better Quantification for War History: Numerical Superiority and Casualty Rates in Early Modern Europe." *War and Society* 15 (1997): 1–30.

Redlich, Fritz. *De Praeda Militari: Looting and Booty, 1500–1815*. Wiesbaden: Franz Steiner Verlag, 1956.

_____. "Military Entrepreneurship and the Credit System in the 16th and 17th Centuries." *Kyklos* 10 (1957): 186–93.

_____. *The German Military Enterpriser and His Work Force*. 2 volumes. Wiesbaden: Franz Steiner Verlag, 1965.

Reger, William M. "In the Service of the Tsar: European Mercenary Officers and the Reception of Military Reform in Russia, 1654–1667." Ph.D. diss., University of Illinois at Urbana-Champaign, 1997.

Reid, Stuart. *British Redcoat 1740–1793*. London: Osprey, 1997.

_____. *King George's Army 1740–1793*. 3 volumes. London: Osprey, 1995–96.

Richards, John. *Landsknecht Soldiers 1486–1560*. Botley: Osprey, 2002.

Richmond, C.F. "English Naval Power in the Fifteenth Century." *History*, New series 52 (1967): 1–15.

_____. "The Keeping of the Seas during the Hundred Years' War, 1422–1440." *History*, New series 49 (1964): 283–98.

_____. "The War at Sea." in *The Hundred Years' War*. Edited by K. Fowler, London: Macmillan, 1971.

Richmond, H.W. *The Navy as an Instrument of Power, 1558–1727*. Cambridge: Cambridge University Press, 1953.

_____. *The Navy in the War of 1739–1748*. 3 volumes. Cambridge: Cambridge University Press, 1920.

Roberts, Keith. *Matchlock Musketeer 1585–1688*. Botley: Osprey, 2002.

Roberts, Michael. "Gustav Adolf and the Art of War." In *Essays in Swedish History*. Minneapolis: University of Minnesota Press, 1967.

Robson, Eric. "British Light Infantry in the Mid-Eighteenth Century: The Effect of American Conditions." *Army Quarterly* 63 (1952): 209–22.

_____. "The Armed Forces and the Art of War." In *The New Cambridge Modern History*, Volume VII. Edited by J.O. Lindsay. Cambridge: Cambridge University Press, 1957.

Rodger, N.A.M. *The Safeguard of the Sea: A Naval History of Britain, 660–1649*. New York: W.W. Norton and Company, 1997.

_____. *The Wooden World: An Anatomy of the Georgian Navy*. New York: W.W. Norton, 1986.

Rogers, H.C.B. *The British Army of the Eighteenth Century*. New York: Hippocrene Books, 1977.

Rose, Susan. *Medieval Naval Warfare, 1000–1500*. London: Routledge, 2002.

Ross, Steven. *From Flintlock to Rifle: Infantry Tactics, 1740–1866*. Rutherford: Fairleigh Dickinson University Press, 1979.

_____. "The Development of the Combat Division in Eighteenth Century French Armies." *French Historical Studies* 4 (1965): 84–94.

Roth, Chris. *The Armies of Agincourt*. Botley: Osprey, 1998.

Rothenberg, Gunther E. "Military Intelligence Gathering in the Second Half of the Eighteenth Century, 1740–1792." In *Go Spy the Land: Military Intelligence in History*. Edited by Keith Neilson and B.J.C. McKercher. Westport: Praeger, 1992.

_____. *The Art of Warfare in the Age of Napoleon*. Bloomington: Indiana University Press, 1978.

_____. *The Austrian Military Border in Croatia, 1522–1747*. Urbana: University of Illinois Press, 1960.

_____. "The Shield of the Dynasty: Reflections on the Habsburg Army, 1649–1918." *Austrian History Yearbook* 32 (2001): 169–206.

Rothero, Christopher. *The Armies of Agincourt*. London: Osprey, 1981.

_____. *The Armies of Crécy and Poitiers*. London: Osprey, 1981.

Rowlands, Guy. "Louis XIV, Aristocratic Power and the Elite Units of the French Army." *French History* 13 (1999): 303–31.

_____. *The Dynastic State and the Army under Louis XIV: Royal Service and Private Interest, 1661–1701*. Cambridge: Cambridge University Press, 2002.

Roy, Ian, editor. *Blaise de Monluc: The Habsburg-Valois Wars and the French Wars of Religion*. London: Longman, 1971.

Russell, Peter E. "Redcoats in the Wilderness: British Officers and Irregular Warfare in Europe and America, 1740 to 1760." *William and Mary Quarterly*, Third series 35 (1978): 629–52.

Scammell, G.V. "The Sinews of War: Manning and Provisioning English Fighting Ships, c.1550–1650." *Mariner's Mirror* 73 (1987): 351–68.

Schwoerer, Lois G. *No Standing Armies!: The Anti-Military Ideology in Seventeenth-Century England*. Baltimore: Johns Hopkins University Press, 1974.

Scott, Samuel F. "The French Revolution and the Line Army, 1787–1793." Ph.D. diss., University of Wisconsin, 1968.

_____. "The French Revolution and the Professionalization of the French Officer Corps, 1789–1793." In *On Military Ideology*. Edited by Morris Janowitz and Jaques van Doorn. Rotterdam: Rotterdam University Press, 1971.

_____. "The Regeneration of the Line Army during the French Revolution." *The Journal of Modern History* 42 (September 1970): 307–30.

_____. *The Response of the Royal Army to the French Revolution: The Role and Development of the Line Army, 1787–1793*. Oxford: Clarendon Press, 1978.

Scouller, Major R.E. *The Armies of Queen Anne*. Oxford: Oxford University Press, 1966.

Shanahan, William O. *Prussian Military Reforms, 1786–1813*. New York: AMS Press, 1966.

Sherborne, J.W. "Indentured Retinues and English Expeditions to France, 1369–1380." *The English Historical Review* 79 (1964): 718–46.

_____. The Hundred Years' War: The English Navy, Shipping and Manpower, 1369–1389." *Past and Present* 37 (1967): 163–75.

Showalter, Dennis. "Tactics and Recruitment in Eighteenth Century Prussia." *Studies in History and Politics* 3 (1983/84): 15–42.

_____. "Weapons and Ideas in the Prussian Army from Frederick the Great to Moltke the Elder." In *Tools of War: Instruments, Ideas, and Institutions of Warfare, 1445–1871*. Edited by John A. Lynn. Urbana: University of Illinois Press, 1990.

Shpakovsky, V., David Nicolle, and Angus McBride. *Medieval Russian Armies 1250–1500*. Botley: Osprey, 2002.

Silva Saturnino Monteiro, Silva da. "The Decline and Fall of Portuguese Seapower, 1583–1663." *The Journal of Military History* 65 (January 2001): 9–20.

Smith, Dianne L. "Muscovite Logistics, 1462–1598." *Slavonic and East European Review* 71 (January 1993): 35–65.

Smythe, Sir John. *Certain Discourses Military*. Edited by J.R. Hale. Ithaca: Cornell University Press, 1964.

Stapleton, John M., Jr. "Importing the Military Revolution: William III, the Glorious Revolution, and the Rise of the Standing Army in Britain, 1688–1712." M.A. thesis, Ohio State University, 1994.

Stein, Mark Lewis. "Seventeenth-Century Ottoman Forts and Garrisons on the Habsburg Frontier." Ph.D diss., University of Chicago, 2001.

Stevens, Carol B. "Evaluating Peter's Military Forces." In *Russia in the Reign of Peter the Great: Old and New Perspectives*. Edited by A. Cross. Cambridge: Cambridge University Press, 1998.

_____. *Soldiers of the Steppe: Army Reform and Social Change in Early Modern Russia*. DeKalb: Northern Illinois University Press, 1995.

Stone, Daniel. "Patriotism and Professionalism: The Polish Army in the Eighteenth Century." *Studies in History and Politics* 3 (1983/84): 61–72.

Storrs, Christopher. "The Army of Lombardy and the Resilience of Spanish Power in Italy in the Reign of Carlos II (1665–1700)." *War in History* 4–5 (1997–98): 371–97, 1–22.

Stoye, John W. "Soldiers and Civilians." In *The New Cambridge Modern History*, Volume VI. Edited by J.S. Bromley. Cambridge: Cambridge University Press, 1970.

Sturgill, Claude C. "Changing Garrisons: The French System of Etapes." *Canadian Journal of History* 20 (August 1985): 193–201.

Stradling, Robert A. *The Armada of Flanders: Spanish Maritime Policy and European War, 1568–1668*. Cambridge: Cambridge University Press, 1992.

_____. *The Spanish Monarchy and Irish Mercenaries: The Wild Geese in Spain, 1618–1668*. Dublin: Irish Academic Press, 1994.

Symcox, Geoffrey W. "Current Research on the Navy of Louis XIV: Problems and Perspective." In *Changing Interpretations and New Sources in Naval History: Papers from the Third U.S. Naval Academy History Symposium*. Edited by W. Love, Jr. New York: Garland, 1980.

_____. *The Crisis of French Naval Power, 1688–1697*. The Hague: Martinus Nijhoff, 1974.

_____. "The Navy of Louis XIV." In *The Reign of Louis XIV*. Edited by P. Sonnino. Atlantic Highlands: Humanities Press International, 1990.

Szabo, Franz A.J. "Unwanted Navy: Habsburg Naval Armaments under Maria Theresa." *Austrian History Yearbook* 17/18 (1981–82): 29–57.

Tallett, Frank. *War and Society in Early Modern Europe, 1494–1715*. London: Routledge, 1992.

Taylor, Frederick L. *The Art of War in Italy, 1494–1529*. Cambridge: Cambridge University Press, 1921.

Tedder, A.W. *The Navy of the Restoration*. Cambridge: Cambridge University Press, 1916.

Tincey, John. *Soldiers of the English Civil War*. 2 volumes. London: Osprey, 1989–90.

Trease, Geoffrey. *The Condottieri: Soldiers of Fortune*. New York: Holt, Rinehart, and Winston, 1971.

Trotter, Ben Scott. "Marshal Vauban and the Administration of Fortifications under Louis XIV (to 1691)." Ph.D. diss., Ohio State University, 1993.

Tunstall, B. *Naval Warfare in the Age of Sail: The Evolution of Fighting Tactics, 1650–1815*. London: Conway Maritime Press, 1990.

Vale, Malcolm. *War and Chivalry: Warfare and Aristocratic Culture in England, France and Burgundy at the End of the Middle Ages*. London: Duckworth, 1981.

Vauban, Sébastien Le Prestre de. *A Manual of Siegecraft and Fortification*. Ann Arbor: University of Michigan Press, 1968.

Vliet, A.P. van. "Foundation, Organization and Effects of the Dutch Navy (1568–1648)." In *Exercise of Arms: Warfare in the Netherlands, 1568–1648*. Edited by Marco van der Hoeven. Leiden: Brill, 1997.

Wagner, Eduard. *European Weapons and Warfare, 1618–1648*. Translated by Simon Pellar. London: Octopus Books, 1979.

Warner, Richard. "British Merchants and Russian Men-of-War: The Rise of the Russian Baltic Fleet." In *Peter the Great and the West: New Perspectives*. Edited by Lindsey Hughes. New York: Palgrave, 2001.

Weber, R.E.J. "The Introduction of the Single Line Ahead as a Battle Formation by the Dutch, 1665–1666." *Mariner's Mirror* 73 (1987): 5–19.

Weigley, Russell F. *The Age of Battles: The Quest for Decisive Warfare from Breitenfeld to Waterloo.* Bloomington: Indiana University Press, 1991.

Western, J.R. "Armed Forces and the Art of War: Armies." In *The New Cambridge Modern History*, Volume VIII. Edited by A. Goodwin. Cambridge: Cambridge University Press, 1965.

_____. *The English Militia in the Eighteenth Century.* London: Routledge and Kegan Paul, 1965.

_____. "War on a New Scale: Professionalism in Armies, Navies and Diplomacy." In *The Eighteenth Century.* Edited by A. Cobban. London: Thames and Hudson, 1969.

Weyland, Max. *Turenne: Marshal of France.* London: George G. Harrap, 1930.

White, Lorraine. "Spain's Early Modern Soldiers: Origins, Motivation and Loyalty." *War and Society* 19 (October 2001): 19–46.

Wijn, J.W. "Military Forces and Warfare, 1610–1648." In *The New Cambridge Modern History*, Volume IV. Edited by J.P. Cooper. Cambridge: Cambridge University Press, 1970.

Williams, Noel. *Redcoats and Courtesans: The Birth of the British Army, 1660–1690.* London: Brassey's, 1994.

Williams, Roger. *The Actions of the Low Countries.* Edited by D.W. Davies. Ithaca: Cornell University Press, 1964.

Wilson, John. *Bavarian Army 1680–1715: The Uniform and Organization Guide.* London: Gosling Press, 1993.

Wilson, Peter H. "European Warfare, 1450–1815." In *War in the Early Modern World, 1450–1815.* Edited by J. Black. Boulder: Westview Press, 1999.

_____. *German Armies: War and German Politics, 1648–1806.* London: University College London Press, 1998.

_____. "The German 'Soldier Trade' of the Seventeenth and Eighteenth Centuries: A Reassessment." *The International History Review* 18 (November 1996): 757–92.

_____. "The Politics of Military Recruitment in Eighteenth-Century Germany." *The English Historical Review* 117 (June 2003): 536–68.

Wimmer, Jan. "Jan Sobieski's Art of War." *Historia Militaris Polonica* 2 (1977): 17–38.

Wismes, Baron Armel de. "The French Navy under Louis XIV." In *Louis XIV and Absolutism.* Edited by R.M. Hatton. London: Macmillan Press, 1976.

Wood, James B. *The King's Army: Warfare, Soldiers, and Society during the Wars of Religion in France, 1562–1576.* Cambridge: Cambridge University Press, 1996.

Wright, John W. "Sieges and Customs of War at the Opening of the Eighteenth Century." *The American Historical Review* 39 (1934): 643–44.

Wrong, Charles J. "The French Infantry Officer at the Close of the *ancien régime.*" Ph.D. diss., Brown University, 1968.

PART IV
THE MILITARY
REVOLUTION,
1337–1815

Adams, Simon. "Tactics or Politics?: 'The Military Revolution' and the Habsburg Hegemony, 1525–1648." In *Tools of War: Instruments, Ideas, and Institutions of Warfare, 1445–1871*. Edited by John A.Lynn. Urbana: University of Illinois Press, 1990; reprinted in *The Military Revolution Debate: Readings on the Military Transformation of Early Modern Europe*. Edited by C.J. Rogers. Boulder: Westview, 1995.

Arnold, Tom. "Fortifications and Statecraft of the Gonzaga, 1530–1630." Ph.D. diss., Ohio State University, 1993.

_____. "Fortifications and the Military Revolution: The Gonzaga Experience, 1530–1630." In *The Military Revolution Debate: Readings on the Military Transformation of Early Modern Europe*. Edited by C.J. Rogers. Boulder: Westview, 1995.

_____. *Renaissance at War*. London: Cassell and Company, 2001.

Black, Jeremy. "A Military Revolution? A 1660–1792 Perspective." In *The Military Revolution Debate: Readings on the Military Transformation of Early Modern Europe*. Edited by C.J. Rogers. Boulder: Westview, 1995.

_____. *A Military Revolution?: Military Change and European Society, 1550–1800*. London: Macmillan, 1991.

_____. *Warfare in the Eighteenth Century*. London: Cassell, 1999.

Braddick, M.J. "An English Military Revolution?" *Historical Journal* 36 (1993): 965–75.

Childs, John. "The Military Revolution I: The Transition to Modern Warfare." In *The Oxford Illustrated History of Modern War*. Edited by Charles Townshend. New York: Oxford University Press, 1997.

_____. *Warfare in the Seventeenth Century*. London: Cassells, 2001.

Croxton, Derek. "A Territorial Imperative?: The Military Revolution, Strategy, and Peacemaking in the Thirty Years' War." *War in History* 5 (1998): 253–79.

De Vries, Kelly. "Gunpowder Weaponry and the Rise of the Early Modern State." *War in History* 3 (1998): 142–44.

Dorn, Harold. "The 'Military Revolution': Military History or History of Europe?" *Technology and Culture* 32 (1991): 656–58.

Downing, Brian M. *The Military Revolution and Political Change: Origins of Democracy and Autocracy in Early Modern Europe*. Princeton: Princeton University Press, 1992.

Duffy, Michael, editor. *The Military Revolution and the State, 1500–1800*. Exeter: Exeter University Press, 1980.

Eltis, David. *The Military Revolution in Sixteenth-Century Europe*. London: Tauris Academic Studies, 1995.

Frost, Robert I. "The Polish-Lithuanian Commonwealth and the 'Military Revolution.'" In *Poland and Europe: Historical Dimensions, Selected Essays from the 50th Anniversary International Congress of the Polish Arts and Sciences in America*. Edited by J.S. Pula and M.B. Biskupski. Boulder, Colo.: East European Monographs, 1994.

Guilmartin, John F., Jr. "The Military Revolution: Origins and First Tests Abroad." In *The Military Revolution Debate: Readings on the Military Transformation of Early Modern Europe*. Edited by C.J. Rogers. Boulder: Westview, 1995.

Hall, Bert S. and Kelly DeVries. "The Military Revolution Revisited." *Technology and Culture* 31 (1990): 500–7.

Jones, Colin. "The Military Revolution and the Professionalisation of the French Army under the Ancien Régime." In *The Military Revolution and the State, 1500–1800*. Exeter: University of Exeter Press, 1980; reprinted in *The Military Revolution Debate: Readings on the Military Transformation of Early Modern Europe*. Edited by C.J. Rogers. Boulder: Westview, 1995.

Kelenik, Jósef. "The Military Revolution in Hungary." In *Ottomans, Hungarians, and Habsburgs in Central Europe: The Military Confines in the Era of Ottoman Conquest*. Edited by Géza Dávid and Pál Fodor. Leiden: Brill, 2000.

Kingra, M.S. "The *Trace Italienne* and the Military Revolution during the Eighty Years' War, 1567–1648." *The Journal of Military History* 57 (1993): 431–46.

Loeber, Rolf and Geoffrey Parker. "The Military Revolution in Seventeenth-Century Ireland." In *Ireland from Independence to Occupation, 1641–1660*. Edited by Jane H. Ohlmeyer. Cambridge: Cambridge University Press, 1995.

Luh, Jurgen. *Ancien Régime Warfare and the Military Revolution: A Study*. Groningen: Instituut voor Noord en Oost-Europese Studies, 2000.

Lynn, John A. "Forging the Western Army in Seventeenth-Century France." In *The Dynamics of Military Revolution, 1300–2050*. Edited by MacGregor Knox and Williamson Murray. Cambridge and New York: Cambridge University Press, 2001.

_____. "The *trace italienne* and the Growth of Armies: The French Case." *The Journal of Modern History* 55 (1991): 297–330; reprinted in *The Military Revolution Debate: Readings on the Military Transformation of Early Modern Europe*. Edited by C.J. Rogers. Boulder: Westview, 1995.

_____. "Recalculating French Army Growth during the *Grande Siècle*, 1610–1715." *French Historical Studies* 18 (1994): 881–906; reprinted in *The Military Revolution Debate: Readings on the Military Transformation of Early Modern Europe*. Edited by C.J. Rogers. Boulder: Westview, 1995.

Moor, J.A. de. "Experience and Experiment: Some Reflections upon the Military Developments in Sixteenth and Seventeenth Century Western Europe." In *Exercise of Arms: Warfare in the Netherlands, 1568–1648*. Edited by Marco van der Hoeven. Leiden: Brill, 1997.

Nickle, Barry H. "The Military Reforms of Prince Maurice of Orange." Ph.D. diss., University of Delaware, 1975.

Palmer, M.A.J. "'The Military Revolution' Afloat: The Era of the Anglo-Dutch Wars and the Transition to Modern Warfare at Sea." *War in History* 4 (1997): 123–49.

Parker, Geoffrey. *The Military Revolution: Military Innovation and the Rise of theWest, 1500–1800*. Cambridge: Cambridge University Press, 1988.

_____. "The 'Military Revolution' in Seventeenth-Century Ireland." In *Success is Never Final: Empire, War, and Faith in Early Modern Europe*. New York: Basic Books, 2002.

_____. "The 'Military Revolution, 1560–1660'–A Myth?" *The Journal of Modern History* 48 (1976): 195–214; reprinted in *Spain and the Netherlands, 1559–1659: Ten Studies*. London: Collins, 1979; reprinted in *The Military Revolution Debate: Readings on the Military Transformation of Early Modern Europe*. Edited by C.J. Rogers. Boulder: Westview, 1995.

Parrott, David. "The Military Revolution in Early Modern Europe." *History Today* 42 (December 1992): 21–27.

_____. "Strategy and Tactics in the Thirty Years' War: The 'Military Revolution'." *Militärgeschichtliche Mitteilungen* 18 (1985): 7–25; reprinted in *The Military Revolution Debate: Readings on the Military Transformation of Early Modern Europe*. Edited by C.J. Rogers. Boulder: Westview, 1995.

_____. "The Utility of Fortifications in Early Modern Europe: Italian Princes and their Citadels, 1540–1640." *War in History* 7 (April 2000): 127–53.

Phillips, Gervase. *The Anglo-Scots Wars, 1513–1550*. Woodbridge: Boydell, 1999.

Plowright, J. "Revolution or Evolution?" *British Army Review* 90 (1988): 41–43.

Poe, M. "The Consequences of the Military Revolution in Muscovy: A Comparative Perspective." *Comparative Studies in Society and History* 38 (1996): 603–17.

Raudzens, George. "Military Revolution or Maritime Evolution? Military Superiorities or Transportation Advantages as Main Causes of European Colonial Conquests to 1788." *The Journal of Military History* 63 (July 1999): 631–42.

Roberts, Michael. "Gustav Adolf and the Art of War." In *Essays in Swedish History*. Minneapolis: University of Minnesota Press, 1967.

_____. *The Military Revolution, 1560–1660*. Belfast: Queen's University, 1955; reprinted in *Essays in Swedish History*. Edited by M. Roberts. Minneapolis: University of Minnesota Press, 1967; reprinted in *The Military Revolution Debate: Readings on the Military Transformation of Early Modern Europe*. Edited by C.J. Rogers. Boulder: Westview, 1995.

Rogers, Clifford. "As If a New Sun had Risen: England Fourteenth-Century Revolution in Military Affairs (RMA)." In *The Dynamics of Military Revolution, 1300–2050*. Edited by MacGregor Knox and Williamson Murray. Cambridge and New York: Cambridge University Press, 2001.

_____. "The Military Revolutions of the Hundred Years' War." *The Journal of Military History* 57 (April 1993): 241–78; reprinted in *The Military Revolution Debate: Readings on the Military Transformation of Early Modern Europe*. Edited by C.J. Rogers. Boulder: Westview, 1995.

_____, editor. *The Military Revolution Debate: Readings on the Military Transformation of Early Modern Europe*. Boulder: Westview, 1995.

Rothenberg, Gunther E. "Maurice of Nassau, Gustavus Adolphus, Raimondo Montecuccoli, and the "Military Revolution" of the Seventeenth Century." In *Makers of Modern Strategy from Machiavelli to the Nuclear Age*. Edited by Peter Paret. Princeton: Princeton University Press, 1986.

Stapleton, John M., Jr. "Importing the Military Revolution: William III, the Glorious Revolution, and the Rise of the Standing Army in Britain, 1688–1712." M.A. thesis, Ohio State University Press, 1994.

Storrs, Christopher and Hamish M. Scott. "The Military Revolution and the European Nobility, c.1600–1800." *War in History* 3 (1996): 1–41.

Thompson, I.A.A. "'Money, Money, and Yet More Money!': Finance, the Fiscal-State, and the Military Revolution, Spain, 1500–1650." In *The Military Revolution Debate: Readings on the Military Transformation of Early Modern Europe*. Edited by C.J. Rogers. Boulder: Westview, 1995.

Wheeler, James Scott. *The Making of a World Power: War and the Military Revolution in Seventeenth Century England*. Stroud: Sutton, 1999.

PART V
TRADE AND FINANCE,
1337–1815

Ashley, Maurice. *Financial and Commercial Policy under the Cromwellian Protectorate*. London: Jonathan Cape, 1934.

Attman, A. *The Struggle for Baltic Markets: Powers in Conflict, 1558–1618*. Gothenburg: Acta Regiae Societatis Scientarium et Litterarum Gothoburgensis, 1979.

Bonney, Richard. *The King's Debts: Finance and Politics in France, 1589–1661*. Oxford: Clarendon Press, 1981.

_____. "The Sinews of Power: The Finances of the French Monarchy from Henry IV to Louis XIV." *History Review* 12 (1992): 7–12.

Brewer, John. *Sinews of Power: War, Money and the English State, 1688–1783*. New York: Alfred Knopf, 1989.

Bullard, Melissa. *Filippo Strozzi and the Medici: Favour and Finance in Sixteenth Century Florence and Rome*. Cambridge and New York: Cambridge University Press, 1980.

Croft, Pauline. "English Commerce with Spain and the Armada War, 1558–1603." In *England, Spain and the Gran Armada, 1585–1604: Essays form the Anglo-Spanish Conferences, London and Madrid, 1988*. Edited by M.J. Rodriguiez-Salgado and S. Adams. Edinburgh: John Donald, 1991.

_____. "Trading with the Enemy, 1585–1604." *Historical Journal* 32 (1989): 281–302.

Davis, Ralph. *A Commercial Revolution: English Overseas Trade in the Seventeenth and Eighteenth Centuries.* London: Historical Association, 1967.

_____. *English Merchant Shipping and Anglo-Dutch Rivalry in the Seventeenth Century.* London: Her Majesty's Stationery Office, 1975.

_____. *The Rise of the Atlantic Economies.* Ithaca: Cornell University Press, 1973.

Dickson, P.G.M. *Finance and Government under Maria Theresa, 1740–1780.* 2 volumes. Oxford: Clarendon Press, 1987.

_____. *The Financial Revolution in England, 1688–1756.* London: Macmillan, 1967.

Ferguson, Ronald T. "Blood and Fire: Contribution Policy of the French Armies in Germany (1668–1715)." Ph.D. thesis, University of Minnesota, 1970.

Finkel, Caroline. "The Costs of Ottoman Warfare and Defence." *Byzantinische Forschungen* 16 (1990): 91–103.

George, Robert H. "The Financial Relations of Louis XIV and James II." *The Journal of Modern History* 3 (1931): 392–413.

Gilbert, Felix. *The Pope, His Banker and Venice.* Cambridge, Mass.: Harvard University Press, 1980.

Gross, Clyde L. "Louis XIV's Financial Relations with Charles II and the English Parliament." *The Journal of Modern History* 2 (June 1929): 177–204.

Hart, Marjolein C.'t. *The Making of a Bourgeois State: War, Politics and Finance during the Dutch Revolt.* Manchester: Manchester University Press, 1993.

Hill, C.E. *The Danish Sound Dues and the Command of the Baltic.* Durham: Duke University Press, 1926.

Israel, Jonathan I. *Dutch Primacy in World Trade, 1585–1740.* Oxford and New York: Oxford University Press, 1989.

_____. "England, the Dutch and the Struggle for Mastery of World Trade in the Age of the Glorious Revolution, 1688–1702." In *The World of Will-*

iam and Mary: Anglo-Dutch Perspectives on the Revolution of 1688–1689. Stanford: Stanford University Press, 1996; reprinted in *Conflicts of Empires: Spain, the Low Countries and the Struggle for World Supremacy, 1585–1713.* London: Hambledon Press, 1997.

_____. "England's Mercantilist Response to Dutch World Trade Primacy, 1647–1674." In *Conflicts of Empires: Spain, the Low Countries and the Struggle for World Supremacy, 1585–1713.* London: Hambledon Press, 1997.

_____. "Spain, the Spanish Embargoes, and the Struggle for Mastery of World Trade, 1585–1660." In *Empire and Entrepots: The Dutch, the Spanish and the Jews, 1585–1713.* London: Hambledon Press, 1990.

_____. "The Politics of International Trade Rivalry during the Thirty Years' War: Gabriel de Roy and Olivares' Mercantilist Projects, 1621–1645." *The International History Review* 8 (November 1986): 517–49.

Jackson, Gordon. "Anglo-Dutch Trade, c.1660–1760." In *1688: The Seaborne Alliance and Diplomatic Revolution.* Edited by Charles Wilson and David Proctor. Greenwich: Roundwood Press, 1989.

Jones, Dwyryd W. "Sequel to Revolution: The Economics of England's Emergence as a Great Power, 1688–1712." In *The Anglo-Dutch Moment: Essays on the Glorious Revolution and Its World Impact.* Edited by J.I. Israel. Cambridge: Cambridge University Press, 1991.

_____. "The Economic Consequences of William III." In *Knights Errant and True Englishmen: British Foreign Policy, 1600–1800.* Edited by J. Black. Edinburgh: John Donald, 1989.

_____. *War and Economy in the Age of William III and Marlborough.* Oxford: Basil Blackwell, 1988.

Jong, M.A.G. van. "Dutch Public Finance during the Eighty Years' War: The Case of the Province of Zeeland, 1585–1621." In *Exercise of Arms: Warfare in the Netherlands, 1568–1648.* Edited by Marco van der Hoeven. Leiden: Brill, 1997.

Lindblad, J.Thomas. *Sweden's Trade with the Dutch Republic, 1738–1795: A Quantitative Analysis of the Relationship between Economic Growth and International Trade in the Eighteenth Century*. Assen: Van Gorcum, 1982.

Lloyd, T.H. *England and the German Hanse, 1157–1611: A Study of their Trade and Commercial Diplomacy*. Cambridge: Cambridge University Press, 1991.

Lynn, John A. "A Missing Link in the Evolution of War Finance under Louis XIV." *Proceedings of the Annual Meeting of the Western Society for French History* 18 (1991): 130–35.

McLachlan, Jean O. *Trade and Peace with Old Spain, 1667–1750: A Study on the Influence of Commerce on Anglo-Spanish Diplomacy in the First Half of the Eighteenth Century*. Cambridge: Cambridge University Press, 1940; reprint, New York: Octagon, 1974.

Parker, Geoffrey. "War and Economic Change: The Economic Costs of the Dutch Revolt." In *Spain and The Netherlands, 1559–1659: Ten Studies*. London: Collins, 1979.

Ramsay, G.D. *The City of London in International Affairs at the Accession of Elizabeth Tudor*. Manchester: Manchester University Press, 1975.

_____. *The Queen's Merchants and the Revolt of the Netherlands: The End of the Antwerp Market*. Manchester: Manchester University Press, 1986.

_____. "The Settlement of the Merchant Adventurers at Stade, 1587–1611." In *Politics and Society in Reformation Europe: Essays for Sir Geoffrey Elton on his Sixty-Fifth Birthday*. Edited by E.I. Kouri and Tom Scott. London: Macmillan, 1987.

Redlich, Fritz. "Contributions in the Thirty Years' War." *Economic History Review* 12 (1959–60): 247–54.

Riley, James C. "French Finances, 1717–1768." *The Journal of Modern History* 59 (June 1987): 209–43.

_____. *The Seven Years' War and the Old Regime in France: The Economic and Financial Toll*. Princeton: Princeton University Press, 1986.

Roseveare, H. *The Financial Revolution, 1660–1760*. London: Longman, 1991.

Thompson, I.A.A. "'Money, Money, and Yet More Money!': Finance, the Fiscal-State, and the Military Revolution, Spain, 1500–1650." In *The Military Revolution Debate: Readings on the Military Transformation of Early Modern Europe*. Edited by C.J. Rogers. Boulder: Westview, 1995.

Trout, A.P. *Jean-Baptiste Colbert*. Boston: Twayne, 1978.

Wilson, Charles. *Anglo-Dutch Commerce and Finance in the Eighteenth Century*. Second edition. Cambridge: Cambridge University Press, 1966.

PART VI
INTERNATIONAL
RELATIONS THEORY

Anderson, Matthew S. "Eighteenth Century Theories of the Balance of Power." In *Studies in Diplomatic History: Essays in Memory of David Bayne Horn.* Edited by R.M. Hatton and M.S. Anderson. London: Longman, 1970.

Black, Jeremy. "The Theory of the Balance of Power in the First Half of the Eighteenth Century." *Review of International Studies* 9 (1983): 55–61.

_____. *Why Wars Happen.* London: Reaktron Books, 1998.

Blainey, Geoffrey. *The Causes of War.* New York: Free Press, 1973.

Blanning, Timothy. *The Origins of the French Revolutionary Wars.* London: Longman, 1986.

Dehio, Ludwig. *The Precarious Balance: The Politics of Power in Europe, 1494–1945.* London: Chatto and Windus, 1963.

Gilbert, Felix. "The 'New Diplomacy' of the Eighteenth Century." *World Politics* 4 (1951): 1–38.

_____. *To the Farewell Address: Ideas of Early American Foreign Policy.* Princeton: Princeton University Press, 1961.

Hatton, Ragnhild M. *War and Peace, 1680–1720.* London: Weidenfeld and Nicolson, 1969.

Hinsley, F.H. *Power and the Pursuit of Peace: Theory and Practice in the History of Relations between States.* Cambridge: Cambridge University Press, 1963.

Holsti, Kalevi J. *Peace and War: Armed Conflicts and International Order, 1648–1989*. Cambridge: Cambridge University Press, 1991.

Howe, P.C. "Revolutionary Perspectives on Old Regime Foreign Policy." *Consortium on Revolutionary Europe, Proceedings*. Tallahassee: Florida State University, 1987.

Jervis, Robert. *Perception and Misperception in International Politics*. Princeton: Princeton University Press, 1976.

Keens-Soper, Maurice. "The Practice of a States-System." *Studies in History and Politics* 2 (1981/82): 15–36.

Keohane, Robert O. and Joseph S. Nye. *Power and Interdependence*. New York: Little, Brown and Company, 1977.

Kennedy, Paul M. *The Rise and Fall of the Great Powers: Economic Change and Military Conflict from 1500 to 2000*. New York: Random House, 1987.

Levy, J.S. "Alliance Formation and War Behaviour: An Analysis of the Great Powers, 1495–1975." *Journal of Conflict Resolution* 25 (1981): 581–613.

_____. *War in the Modern Great Power System, 1495–1975*. Lexington: University of Kentucky Press, 1983.

Luard, Evan. *The Balance of Power: The System of International Relations, 1648–1815*. New York: St. Martin's Press, 1992.

Mattingly, Garrett. "No Peace Beyond What Line?" *Transactions of the Royal Historical Society*, Fifth series, 13 (1963): 145–62.

McNeill, William H. *The Pursuit of Power: Technology, Armed Force, and Society since A.D. 1000*. Chicago: University of Chicago Press, 1982.

Osiander, Andreas. *The States System of Europe, 1640–1990: Peacemaking and the Conditions of International Stability*. Oxford: Oxford University Press, 1994.

Parker, Geoffrey. "The Etiquette of Atrocity: The Laws of War in Early Modern Europe." In *Success is Never Final: Empire, War, and Faith in Early Modern Europe*. New York: Basic Books, 2002.

Repgen, Konrad. "What is a 'Religious War'?" In *Politics and Society in Reformation Europe: Essays for Sir Geoffrey Elton on his Sixty-Fifth Birthday.* Edited by E.I. Kouri and Tom Scott. London: Macmillan, 1987.

Savigear, Peter. "Intervention and the Balance of Power: An Eighteenth Century War of Liberation." *Studies in History and Politics* 2 (1981/82): 113–26.

Schroeder, Paul W. "Can Diplomatic History Guide Foreign Policy?" *The International History Review* 18 (May 1996): 358–70.

Taylor, A.J.P. *How Wars Begin.* New York: Atheneum, 1979.

Viner, J. "Power Versus Plenty as Objectives of Foreign Policy in the Seventeenth and Eighteenth Centuries." *World Politics* 1 (1948): 1–29.

Waltz, Kenneth. *Theory of International Politics.* Reading, Mass.: McGraw-Hill, 1979.

Wright, Quincy. *A Study of War.* Chicago: University of Chicago Press, 1964.

Wright, Moorhead, editor. *Theory and Practice of the Balance of Power, 1486–1914: Selected European Writings.* London: Dent, 1975.

PART VII
HISTORIOGRAPHY AND
BIBLIOGRAPHIES IN
DIPLOMATIC AND
MILITARY HISTORY

Beller, E.A. "Recent Studies on the Thirty Years' War." *The Journal of Modern History* 3 (March 1931): 72–85.

Black, Jeremy. "Britain as a Military Power, 1688–1815." *The Journal of Military History* 64 (January 2000): 159–78.

_____. "War and the World, 1450–2000." *The Journal of Military History* 63 (July 1999): 669–82.

DeConde, Alexander. "Historians, the War of American Independence, and the Persistence of the Exceptionalist Ideal." *The International History Review* 5 (August 1983): 399–430.

_____. "On the Nature of International History." *The International History Review* 10 (May 1988): 282–301.

Kaplan, Lawrence S. "The Treaty of Paris, 1783: A Historiographical Challenge." *The International History Review* 5 (August 1983):431–42.

Kubik, Timothy R.W. "Is Machiavelli's Canon Spiked? Practical Reading in Military History." *The Journal of Military History* 61 (January 1997): 7–30.

Rasor, E.L. *The Spanish Armada of 1588: Historiography and Annotated Bibliography.* Boulder: Greenwood Press, 1993.

Rodger, N.A.M. "Recent Books on the Royal Navy of the Eighteenth Century." *The Journal of Military History* 63 (July 1999): 683–703.

Schroeder, Paul W. "Napoleon Bonaparte." *The International History Review* 12 (May 1990): 324–29.

Young, William Anthony. "War and Diplomacy in the Age of Louis XIV: A Historical Study and Annotated Bibliography." D.A. diss., University of North Dakota, 2000.

PART VIII
FOURTEENTH AND
FIFTEENTH CENTURIES,
1337–1494

EUROPE, 1337–1494

Allmand, Christopher, editor. *The New Cambridge Medieval History, c.1415–c.1500*. Volume VII. Cambridge: Cambridge University Press, 1988.

Cheyney, Edward P. *The Dawn of a New Era, 1250–1453*. New York: Harper and Brothers, 1936.

Fernandez-Armesto, Felipe. *Before Columbus: Exploration and Colonization from the Mediterranean to the Atlantic, 1229–1492*. Philadelphia: University of Pennsylvania Press, 1987.

Gilmore, Myron P. *The World of Humanism, 1453–1517*. New York: Harper and Brothers, 1952.

Holmes, George. *Europe: Hierarchy and Revolt, 1320–1450*. Brighton: Harvester Press, 1975.

Housley, Norman. *Religious Warfare in Europe, 1400–1536*. New York: Oxford University Press, 2002.

Mollat, G. *The Popes at Avignon, 1305–1378*. London: Thomas Nelson and Sons, 1963.

Renouard, Yves. *The Avignon Papacy, 1305–1403*. London: Faber and Faber, 1970.

Rose, Susan. *Medieval Naval Warfare, 1000–1500*. London: Routledge, 2002.

Waley, Daniel. *Later Medieval Europe: From St. Louis to Luther*. London: Longmans, Green and Company, 1964.

HUNDRED YEARS' WAR, 1337–1453

Allmand, Christopher. *Henry V*. Berkeley: University of California Press, 1992.

_____. *Henry V*. London: Historical Association, 1968.

_____. "Henry V the Soldier, and the War in France." In *Henry V: The Practice of Kingship*. Edited by Gerald Leslie Harriss. Oxford: Clarendon Press, 1985.

_____. "Intelligence in the Hundred Years' War." In *Go Spy the Land: Military Intelligence in History*. Edited by Keith Neilson and B.J.C. McKercher. Westport: Praeger, 1992.

_____. *Lancastrian Normandy: The History of a Medieval Occupation, 1415–1450*. Oxford: Clarendon Press, 1983.

_____. "The Anglo-French Negotiations, 1439." *British Institute of Historical Research* 40 (1967): 1–33.

_____. *The Hundred Years' War: England and France at War, c. 1300–c.1450*. Cambridge and New York: Cambridge University Press, 1988.

_____. "The War and the Non-Combatant." In *The Hundred Years' War*. Edited by Kenneth Fowler. New York: St. Martin's Press, 1971.

Ayton, Andrew. "English Armies in the Fourteenth Century." In *Arms, Armies and Fortifications in the Hundred Years' War*. Edited by A. Curry and M. Hughes. Woodbridge: Boydell Press, 1994.

_____. *Knights and Warhorses: Military Service and the English Aristocracy under Edward III*. Woodbridge: Boydell Press, 1994.

_____. "The English Army and the Normandy Campaign of 1346." In *England and Normandy in the Middle Ages*. Edited by D. Bates and A. Curry. London: Hambledon Press, 1987.

Barber, Richard. *Edward, Prince of Wales and Aquitaine: A Biography of the Black Prince*. London: Allen Lane, 1978.

_____. *Life and Campaigns of the Black Prince*. London: Folio Society, 1979.

Bennett, Matthew. *Agincourt 1415: Triumph against the Odds*. London: Osprey, 1995.

_____. "The Development of Battle Tactics in the Hundred Years' War." In *Arms, Armies and Fortifications in the Hundred Years' War*. Edited by A. Curry and M. Hughes. Woodbridge: Boydell Press, 1994.

Buchan, Alice. *Joan of Arc and the Recovery of France*. London: English Universities Press, 1948.

Burne, Alfred H. *The Agincourt War: A Military History of the Latter Part of the Hundred Years' War from 1369 to 1453*. London: Eyre and Spottiswoode, 1956; reprint, Westport: Greenwood Press, 1976.

_____. "The Battle of Castillon, 1453." *History Today* 3 (1953): 249–56.

_____. *The Crecy War: A Military History of the Hundred Years' War from 1337 to the Peace of Bretigny, 1360*. London: Eyre and Spottiswoode, 1955.

Chaplais, P. *Essays in Medieval Diplomacy and Administration*. London: Hambledon Press, 1981.

Chrimes, S.B., C.D. Ross, and R.A. Griffiths, editors. *Fifteenth Century England, 1399–1509: Studies in Politics and Society*. Manchester: Manchester University Press, 1972.

Contamine, Philippe. "The French Nobility and the War." In *The Hundred Years' War*. Edited by Kenneth Fowler. New York: St. Martin's Press, 1971.

Curry, Anne, editor. *Agincourt 1415: Henry V, Sir Thomas Erpingham and the Triumph of the English Archers.* Stroud: Tempus, 2000.

_____. "English Armies in the Fifteenth Century." In *Arms, Armies and Fortifications in the Hundred Years' War.* Edited by A. Curry and M. Hughes. Woodbridge: Boydell Press, 1994.

_____. *The Battle of Agincourt: Sources and Interpretations.* Woodbridge: Boydell Press, 2000.

_____. *The Hundred Years' War.* London: Macmillan, 1993.

_____. *The Hundred Years' War, 1337–1453.* Botley: Osprey, 2002.

_____ and Michael Hughes, editors. *Arms, Armies and Fortifications in the Hundred Years' War.* Woodbridge: Boydell Press, 1994.

Cuttino, G.P. *English Diplomatic Administration, 1259–1339.* Second edition. Oxford: Oxford University Press, 1971.

_____. *English Medieval Diplomacy.* Bloomington: Indiana University Press, 1985.

DeVries, Kelly. *Infantry Warfare in the Early Fourteenth Century.* Woodbridge: Boydell Press, 1996.

_____. *Joan of Arc: A Military Leader.* Stroud: Sutton, 1999.

_____. "Perceptions of Victory and Defeat in the Southern Low Countries During the Hundred Years' War." Ph.D. diss., University of Toronto, 1987.

_____. "The Impact of Gunpowder Weaponry on Siege Warfare in the Hundred Years' War." In *The Medieval City under Siege.* Edited by Ivy A. Corfis and Michael Wolfe. Woodbridge: Boydell Press, 1995.

Dickinson, Joycelyne G. "The Congress of Arras, 1435." *History* 40 (1955): 31–41.

_____. *The Congress of Arras, 1435: A Study in Medieval Diplomacy.* Oxford: Clarendon Press, 1955.

Ferguson, John. *English Diplomacy 1422–1461*. Oxford: Clarendon Press, 1972.

Fowler, Kenneth. *Medieval Mercenaries*. Oxford: Blackwell, 2001.

_____. *The Age of Plantagenet and Valois*. London: Elek Press, 1967.

_____. *The King's Lieutenant: Henry of Grosmont, First Duke of Lancaster, 1310–1361*. London: Elek Press, 1969.

_____. "Truces." In *The Hundred Years' War*. Edited by Kenneth Fowler. New York: St. Martin's Press, 1971.

_____, editor. *The Hundred Years' War*. New York: St. Martin's Press, 1971.

Friel, Ian. "Winds of Change?: Ships and the Hundred Years' War." In *Arms, Armies and Fortifications in the Hundred Years' War*. Edited by A. Curry and M. Hughes. Woodbridge: Boydell Press, 1994.

Fryde, E.B. *The Great Revolt of 1381*. London: Historical Association, 1981.

Griffiths, Ralph A. *The Reign of Henry VI*. London: Ernest Benn, 1981.

Harari, Yuval Noah. "Inter-frontal Cooperation in the Fourteenth Century and Edward III's 1346 Campaign." *The Journal of Military History* 6 (November 1999): 379–95.

_____. "Strategy and Supply in Fourteenth-Century Western European Invasion Campaigns." *The Journal of Military History* 64 (April 2000): 297–334.

Hardy, Robert. "The Longbow." In *Arms, Armies and Fortifications in the Hundred Years' War*. Edited by A. Curry and M. Hughes. Woodbridge: Boydell Press, 1994.

Hewitt, H.J. "The Organization of War." In *The Hundred Years' War*. Edited by Kenneth Fowler. New York: St. Martin's Press, 1971.

_____. *The Black Prince's Expedition of 1355–1357*. Manchester: Manchester University Press, 1958.

_____. *The Organization of War under Edward III, 1338–1362*. Manchester: Manchester University Press, 1966.

Holmes, George. *The Later Middle Ages, 1272–1485*. New York: W.W. Norton, 1962.

Hughes, Michael. "The Fourteenth-Century French Raids on Hampshire and the Isle of Wright." In *Arms, Armies and Fortifications in the Hundred Years' War*. Edited by A. Curry and M. Hughes. Woodbridge: Boydell Press, 1994.

Jacob, E.F. *Henry V and the Invasion of France*. London: English Universities Press, 1947.

Jones, Michael. *Ducal Brittany, 1364–1399*. Oxford: Clarendon Press, 1970.

_____. "War and Fourteenth-Century France." In *Arms, Armies and Fortifications in the Hundred Years' War*. Edited by A. Curry and M. Hughes. Woodbridge: Boydell Press, 1994.

Keen, Maurice. *England in the Later Middle Ages: A Political History*. London: Methuen, 1973.

_____. "The End of the Hundred Years' War: Lancastrian France and Lancastrian England." In *England and Her Neighbors, 1066–1453: Essays in Honour of Pierre Chaplais*. Edited by M. Jones and M. Vale. London: Hambledon Press, 1989.

_____ and M.J. Daniel. "English Diplomacy and the Sack of Fougères in 1449." *History* 59 (October 1974): 375–91.

Kenyon, John R. "Coastal Artillery Fortification in England in the Late Fourteenth and Early Fifteenth Centuries." In *Arms, Armies and Fortifications in the Hundred Years' War*. Edited by A. Curry and M. Hughes. Woodbridge: Boydell Press, 1994.

Knight, Paul. *Henry V and the Conquest of France, 1416–1453*. Botley: Osprey, 1999.

Lander, J.R. "The Hundred Years' War and Edward IV's 1475 Campaign in France." In *Tudor Men and Institutions*. Edited by Arthur J. Slavin. Baton

Rouge: Louisiana State University Press, 1972; reprinted in *Crown and Nobility, 1450–1509*. London: Edward Arnold, 1976.

Le Patourel, John. "Edward III and the Kingdom of France." *History* 43 (1958): 173–89.

_____. "The Origins of the War." In *The Hundred Years' War*. Edited by Kenneth Fowler. New York: St. Martin's Press, 1971.

_____. "The Treaty of Brétigny, 1360." *Transactions of the Royal Historical Society*, Fifth series, 10 (1960): 19–39.

Lloyd, Alan. *The Hundred Years' War*. London: Granada, 1977.

Lucas, Henry Stephen. *John III, Duke of Brabant, and the French Alliance, 1345–1347*. Seattle: University of Washington Press, 1927.

_____. *The Low Countries and the Hundred Years' War, 1326–1347*. Ann Arbor: University of Michigan Press, 1929; reprint, Philadelphia: Porcupine Press, 1976.

Maddicott, John. "The Origins of the Hundred Years' War." *History Today* 36 (May 1986): 31–37.

McFarlane, K.B. "Anglo-Flemish Relations in 1415–1416." *Bodleian Library Quarterly* 7 (1932): 41–45.

_____. *Lancastrian Kings and Lollard Knights*. Oxford: Clarendon Press, 1972.

Newhall, R.A. *The English Conquest of Normandy, 1416–1424*. New Haven: Yale University Press, 1924.

Nicolle, David. *Crecy 1346: Triumph of the Longbow*. Botley: Osprey, 2000.

_____. *French Armies of the Hundred Years' War, 1328–1429*. Botley: Osprey, 2000.

_____. *Orleans 1429: France Turns the Tide*. Botley: Osprey, 2000.

Oman, Charles. *The Great Revolt of 1381*. Oxford: Clarendon Press, 1906.

Ormrod, W.M. *The Reign of Edward III*. New Haven: Yale University Press, 1990.

Packe, Michael. *King Edward III*. Edited by L.C.B. Seaman. London: Routledge and Kegan Paul, 1983.

Palmer, John. *England, France and Christendom, 1377–1399*. London: Routledge, 1972.

_____. "The Anglo-French Peace Negotiations, 1390–1396." *Transactions of the Royal Historical Society*, Fifth series, 16 (1966): 81–94.

_____. "England, France, the Papacy and the Flemish Succession." *The Journal of Medieval History* 2 (1976): 339–64.

_____. "English Foreign Policy, 1388–1399." In *The Reign of Richard II: Essays in Honour of May McKisack*. Edited by F.R.H. du Boulay and C.M. Barron. London: Athlone Press, 1971.

_____. "The War Aims of the Protagonists and the Negotiations for Peace." In *The Hundred Years' War*. Edited by Kenneth Fowler. New York: St. Martin's Press, 1971.

Perroy, Edouard. *The Hundred Years' War*. London: Eyre and Spottiswoode, 1965.

Phillpotts, C.J. "John of Gaunt and English Policy Towards France, 1389–1395." *The Journal of Medieval History* 16 (1990): 363–86.

_____. "The French Plan of Battle during the Agincourt Campaign." *The English Historical Review* 99 (1984): 59–66.

Pollard, A.J. *John Talbot and the War in France, 1427–1453*. London: Royal Historical Society, 1983.

Powicke, Michael. "The English Aristocracy and the War." In *The Hundred Years' War*. Edited by Kenneth Fowler. New York: St. Martin's Press, 1971.

Prestwich, Michael. *The Three Edwards: War and State in England, 1272–1377*. London: Weidenfeld and Nicolson, 1980.

Priestley, E.J. *The Battle of Shrewsbury, 1403*. Shrewsbury: Shrewsbury and Atcham Borough Council, 1979.

Richmond, C.F. "English Naval Power in the Fifteenth Century." *History* 52 (February 1967): 1–15.

_____. "The Keeping of the Seas during the Hundred Years' War, 1422–1440." *History* 49 (October 1964): 283–98.

_____. "The War at Sea." In *The Hundred Years' War*. Edited by Kenneth Fowler. New York: St. Martin's Press, 1971.

Rogers, Clifford J. "Edward III and the Dialectics of Strategy, 1327–1360." *Transactions of the Royal Historical Society*, Sixth series 4 (1994): 83–104.

_____. "The Age of the Hundred Years' War." In *Medieval Warfare: A History*. Edited by Maurice Keen. Oxford and New York: Oxford University Press, 1999.

_____. "The Military Revolutions of the Hundred Years' War." *The Journal of Military History* 57 (April 1993): 241–78; reprinted in *The Military Revolution Debate: Readings on the Military Transformation of Early Modern Europe*. Edited by C.J. Rogers. Boulder: Westview, 1995.

_____, editor. *The Wars of Edward III: Sources and Interpretations*. Woodbridge: Boydell and Brewer, 1999.

_____. *War Cruel and Sharp: English Strategy under Edward III, 1327–1360*. London: Boydell, 2000.

Roth, Chris. *The Armies of Agincourt*. Botley: Osprey, 1998.

Russell, P.E. *The English Intervention in Spain and Portugal in the Time of Edward III and Richard II*. Oxford: Clarendon Press, 1955.

Saul, Nigel. *Richard II*. New Haven: Yale University Press, 1997.

Seward, Desmond. *The Hundred Years' War: The English in France, 1337–1453*. New York: Atheneum, 1978.

Sherborne, J.W. "Indentured Retinues and English Expeditions to France, 1369–1380." *The English Historical Review* 79 (1964): 718–46.

_____. "The Battle of La Rochelle and the War at Sea, 1372–1375." *Bulletin of Historical Research* 42 (1969): 17–29.

_____. "The Cost of English Warfare with France in the Later Fourteenth Century." *Bulletin of Historical Research* 50 (1977): 135–50.

_____. The Hundred Years' War: The English Navy, Shipping and Manpower, 1369–1389." *Past and Present* 37 (1967): 163–75.

Smith, Robert D. "Artillery and the Hundred Years' War: Myth and Interpretation." In *Arms, Armies and Fortifications in the Hundred Years' War*. Edited by A. Curry and M. Hughes. Woodbridge: Boydell Press, 1994.

Sumption, Jonathan. *The Hundred Years' War: Trial by Battle*. Philadelphia: University of Pennsylvania Press, 1990.

_____. *The Hundred Years' War: Trial by Fire*. Philadelphia: University of Pennsylvania Press, 2000.

Templeman, G. "Edward III and the Beginnings of the Hundred Years' War." *Transactions of the Royal Historical Society*, Fifth series 2 (1952): 69–88.

Tuck, Anthony. *Crown and Nobility, 1272–1461*. Oxford: Basil Blackwell, 1985.

Tuck, J.A. "Richard II and the Hundred Years' War," In *Politics and Crisis in Fourteenth-Century England*. Edited by J. Taylor and W. Childs. Gloucester: Alan Sutton, 1990.

Vale, Malcolm. *Charles VII*. London: Eyre Methuen, 1974.

_____. *English Gascony, 1399–1453: A Study of War, Government and Politics during the Later Stages of the Hundred Years' War*. Oxford: Clarendon Press, 1970.

_____. *The Angevin Legacy and the Hundred Years' War, 1250–1340*. Oxford: Clarendon Press, 1990.

_____. *The Origins of the Hundred Years' War: The Angevin Legacy, 1250–1340*. Oxford: Clarendon Press, 1996.

_____. "The War in Aquitaine." In *Arms, Armies and Fortifications in the Hundred Years' War*. Edited by A. Curry and M. Hughes. Woodbridge: Boydell Press, 1994.

Vaughan, Richard. *John the Fearless: The Growth of Burgundian Power*. London: Longmans, Green and Company, 1966.

_____. *Philip the Bold: The Formation of the Burgundian State*. London: Longmans, Green and Company, 1962.

_____. *Philip the Good: The Apogee of Burgundy*. London: Longmans, Green and Company, 1970.

_____. *Valois Burgundy*. London: Allen Lane, 1975.

Wade Labarge, Margaret. *Gascony: England's First Colony, 1204–1453*. London: Hamish Hamilton, 1980.

_____. *Henry V: The Cautious Conqueror*. London: Secker and Warburg, 1975.

Wilkinson, B. *The Later Middle Ages in England, 1216–1485*. London: Longman, 1969.

Wolfe, Michael. "Siege Warfare and the *Bonnes Villes* of France during the Hundred Years' War." In *The Medieval City under Siege*. Edited by Ivy A. Corfis and Michael Wolfe. Woodbridge: Boydell Press, 1995.

Wolffe, Bertram P. *Henry VI*. London: Eyre Methuen, 1981.

FRENCH POWER IN EUROPE DURING THE LATE FIFTEENTH CENTURY, 1453–1494

Boehm, Laetitia. "Burgundy and the Empire in the Reign of Charles the Bold." *The International History Review* 1 (April 1979): 153–62.

Campion, Pierre. *Louis XI*. London: Cassell and Company, n.d.

Hare, Christopher. *Maximilian the Dreamer: Holy Roman Emperor, 1459–1519*. London: Stanley Paul and Company, 1913.

Kendall, Paul Murray. *Louis XI*. London: George Allen and Unwin, 1971.

Lewis, P.S. *Later Medieval France: The Polity*. London: Macmillan, 1968.

Potter, David. *A History of France, 1460–1660: The Emergence of a Nation State*. London: Macmillan, 1995.

Vaughan, Richard. *Charles the Bold: The Last Valois Duke of Burgundy*. London: Longman, 1973.

WARS OF THE ROSES, 1455–1485

Armstrong, C.A.J. "Politics and the Battle of St. Albans, 1455." *Bulletin of the Institute of Historical Research* 33 (1960): 1–72.

Bennett, Michael. *The Battle of Bosworth*. New York: St. Martin's Press, 1985.

Boardman, A.W. *The Battle of Towton*. Phoenix Mill: Sutton, 1994.

Carpenter, Christine. *The Wars of the Roses: Politics and the Constitution in England, c.1437–1509*. Cambridge: Cambridge University Press, 1997.

Chrimes, S.B. *Henry VII*. London: Eyre Methuen, 1972.

_____. *Lancastrians, Yorkists and Henry VII*. Second edition. London: Macmillan, 1966.

Cole, Hubert. *The Wars of the Roses*. London: Granada, 1973.

Cook, David R. *Lancastrians and Yorkists: The Wars of the Roses*. London: Longman, 1984.

Evans, H.T. *Wales and the Wars of the Roses*. Cambridge: Cambridge University Press, 1915.

Gillingham, John. *The Wars of the Roses: Peace and Conflict in Fifteenth-Century England*. London: Weidenfeld and Nicolson, 1981.

Goodman, Anthony. *The Wars of the Roses: Military Activity and English Society*. London: Routledge and Kegan Paul, 1981.

Gravett, Christopher. *Bosworth 1485*. Botley: Osprey, 2000.

_____. *Tewkesbury 1471: The Last Yorkist Victory*. Botley: Osprey, 2003.

_____. *Towton 1461: England's Bloodiest Battle*. Botley: Osprey, 2003.

Griffiths, Ralph A. *The Reign of Henry VI*. London: Ernest Benn, 1981.

_____ and Roger S. Thomas. *The Making of the Tudor Dynasty*. Stroud: Sutton, 1985.

Grummitt, David. "The Defence of Calais and the Development of Gunpowder Weaponry in England in the Late Fifteenth Century." *War in History* 7 (July 2000): 253–72.

Haigh, Philip A. *The Military Campaigns of the Wars of the Roses*. Phoenix Mill: Alan Sutton, 1995.

Hammond, P.W. *The Battles of Barnet and Tewkesbury*. Gloucester: Alan Sutton, 1990.

Head, C. "Pope Pius II and the Wars of the Roses," *Archivium Historiae Pontificae* 7 (1970): 139–78.

Hicks, Michael. *Wars of the Roses*. Botley: Osprey, 2003.

Kendall, Paul Murray. *Warwick the Kingmaker*. London: George Allen and Unwin, 1957.

Lander, J.R. *Conflict and Stability in Fifteenth-Century England*. Third edition. London: Hutchinson, 1977.

_____. *Crown and Nobility, 1450–1509*. London: Edward Arnold, 1976.

_____. *Government and Community: England, 1450–1509*. London: Edward Arnold, 1980.

_____. *Politics and Power in England, 1450–1509.* London: Edward Arnold, 1976.

_____. *The Wars of the Roses.* London: White Lion, 1965.

_____. "The Wars of the Roses." In *Crown and Nobility, 1450–1509.* London: Edward Arnold, 1976.

Oman, Charles. *Warwick the Kingmaker.* London: Macmillan, 1899.

Pollard, A.J. *The Wars of the Roses.* London: Macmillan, 1988.

Richmond, Colin. "The Battle of Bosworth." *History Today* 35 (August 1985): 17–22.

Ross, Charles. *Edward IV.* London: Eyre Methuen, 1974.

_____. *Richard III.* London: Eyre Methuen, 1981.

_____. *The Wars of the Roses: A Concise History.* London: Thames and Hudson, 1976.

Storey, R.L. *The End of the House of Lancaster.* London: Barrie and Rockliff, 1966.

Wise, Terence. *The Wars of the Roses.* London: Osprey, 1984.

Wolffe, Bertram. *Henry VI.* London: Eyre Methuen, 1981.

BALANCE OF POWER IN ITALY, 1350–1494

Abulafia, David. "The Inception of the Reign of King Ferrante I of Naples: The Events of Summer 1458 in the Light of Documentation from Milan." In *The French Descent into Renaissance Italy, 1494–1495: Antecedents and Effects.* Edited by D. Abulafia. Aldershot: Variorum, 1995.

Ady, Cecilia M. *Lorenzo dei Medici and Renaissance Italy.* London: English Universites Press, 1955.

Bayley, C.C. *War and Society in Renaissance Florence.* Toronto: University of Toronto Press, 1961.

Butters, Humfrey. "The Politics of Protection in Late Fifteenth-Century Italy: Florence and the Failed Sienese Exiles' Plot of May 1485." In *The French Descent into Renaissance Italy, 1494–1495: Antecedents and Effects*. Edited by D. Abulafia. Aldershot: Variorum, 1995.

Caferro, William. "Italy and the Companies of Adventure in the Fourteenth Century." *The Historian* 58 (Summer 1996): 794–810.

Dover, Paul M. "Letters, Notes and Whispers: Diplomacy, Ambassadors and Information in the Italian Renaissance Princely State." Ph.D. diss., Yale University, 2002.

Fubini, Riccardo. "Diplomacy and Government in the Italian City-States of the Fifteenth Century (Florence and Venice)." In *Politics and Diplomacy in Early Modern Italy: The Structure of Diplomatic Practice, 1450–1800*. Edited by Daniela Frigo. Cambridge: Cambridge University Press, 2000.

_____. "The Italian League and the Policy of the Balance of Power at the Accession of Lorenzo de' Medici." *The Journal of Modern History* 67 Supplemental Issue (December 1995): S166-S199.

Hook, Judith. *Lorenzo de' Medici: An Historical Biography*. London: Hamish Hamilton, 1984.

Ilardi, Vincent. "France and Milan: The Uneasy Alliance, 1452–1466." In *Gli Sforza a Milano e in Lombardia e i loro rapporti con gli stati italiani ed europei (1450–1530)*. Milan: Cisalpino-Goliardica, 1982; reprinted in *Studies in Italian Renaissance Diplomatic History*. London: Variorum, 1986.

_____. "Lombard Cattle and Diplomacy in the Fifteenth Century." In *Studies in Italian Renaissance Diplomatic History*. London: Variorum, 1986.

_____. "Quattrocento Politics in the Treccani Storia di Milano." *Bibliotheque d'Humanisme et Renaissance* 26 (1964): 162–190; reprinted in *Studies in Italian Renaissance Diplomatic History*. London: Variorum, 1986.

_____. *Studies in Italian Renaissance Diplomatic History*. London: Variorum, 1986.

_____. "The Assassination of Galeazzo Maria Sforza and the Reaction of Italian Diplomacy." In *Violence and Civil Disorder in Italian Cities, 1200–*

1500. Edited by Lauro Martines. Berkeley: University of California Press, 1972; reprinted in *Studies in Italian Renaissance Diplomatic History.* London: Variorum, 1986.

_____. "The Banker-Statesman and the Condottiere-Prince: Cosimo de'Medici and Francesco Sforza, 1450–1464." In *Studies in Italian Renaissance Diplomatic History.* London: Variorum, 1986.

_____. "The First Permanent Embassy Outside Italy: The Milanese Embassy at the French Court, 1464–1494." In *Politics, Religion and Diplomacy in Early Modern Europe: Essays in Honor of De Lamar Jensen.* Edited by Malcolm R. Thorp and Arthur J. Slavin. Kirksville: Sixteenth Century Journal Publishers, 1994.

_____. "The Italian League, Francesco Sforza, and Charles VII (1454–1461)." *Studies in the Renaissance* 6 (1959): 339–67; reprinted in *Studies in Italian Renaissance Diplomatic History.* London: Variorum, 1986.

_____. "The Political Role of the Gonzaga in the New Storia di Mantova." *Bibliotheque d'Humanisme et Renaissance* 27 (1966): 732–40; reprinted in *Studies in Italian Renaissance Diplomatic History.* London: Variorum, 1986.

_____. "The Visconti-Sforza Regime of Milan: Recently Published Sources." *Renaissance Quarterly* 31 (1978): 331–42; reprinted in *Studies in Italian Renaissance Diplomatic History.* London: Variorum, 1986.

_____. "Towards the Tragedia d'Italia: Ferrante and Galeazzo Maria Sforza: Friendly Enemies and Hostile Allies." In *The French Descent into Renaissance Italy, 1494–1495: Antecedents and Effects.* Edited by D. Abulafia. Aldershot: Variorum, 1995.

Kendall, Paul M. and Vincent Ilardi, editors. *Dispatches with Related Documents of Milanese Ambassadors in France and Burgundy, 1450–1483.* 3 volumes. Athens: Ohio University Press, 1970–81.

Laven, Peter. *Renaissance Italy.* New York: G.P. Putnam's, 1966.

Lubkin, Gregory. "Strategic Hospitality: Foreign Dignitaries at the Court of Milan, 1466–1476." *The International History Review* 8 (May 1986): 174–89.

Mallett, Michael. *Diplomacy and War in Later Fifteenth-Century Italy*. London: British Academy, 1981.

_____. "Mercenaries." In *Medieval Warfare: A History*. Edited by Maurice Keen. Oxford and New York: Oxford University Press, 1999.

_____. *Mercenaries and Their Masters: Warfare in Renaissance Italy*. London: Bodley Head, 1974.

_____. "Siegecraft in Late Fifteenth-Century Italy." In *The Medieval City under Siege*. Edited by Ivy A. Corfis and Michael Wolfe. Woodbridge: Boydell Press, 1995.

_____. "Venice and Its Condottieri, 1404–1454." In *Renaissance Venice*. Edited by J.R. Hale. Totowa: Rowman and Littlefield, 1973.

_____. "Venice and the War of Ferrara, 1482–1484." In *War, Culture and Society in Renaissance Venice: Essays in Honor of John Hale*. Edited by D.S. Chambers, C.H. Clough and M. Mallett. London: Hambledon Press, 1993.

Nicolle, David. *Italian Medieval Armies, 1300–1500*. London: Osprey, 1983.

Peyronnet, Georges. "The Distant Origins of the Italian Wars: Political Relations between France and Italy in the Fourteenth and Fifteenth Centuries." In *The French Descent into Renaissance Italy, 1494–1495: Antecedents and Effects*. Edited by D. Abulafia. Aldershot: Variorum, 1995.

Powell, Michael R. "The Military Capacity of the Milanese State under Ludovico il moro." Ph.D. diss., University of Warwick, 2000.

Russell, Joycelyne G. "The Humanists Converge: The Congress of Mantua (1459)." In *Diplomats at Work: Three Renaissance Studies*. Stroud: Alan Sutton, 1992.

Ryder, Alan. "The Angevin Bid for Naples, 1380–1480." In *The French Descent into Renaissance Italy, 1494–1495: Antecedents and Effects*. Edited by D. Abulafia. Aldershot: Variorum, 1995.

Setton, Kenneth M. *The Papacy and the Levant (1204–1571): Volume I, The Thirteenth and Fourteenth Centuries.* Philadelphia: American Philosophical Society, 1978.

_____. *The Papacy and the Levant (1204–1571): Volume II, The Fifteenth Century.* Philadelphia: American Philosophical Society, 1978.

Trease, Geoffrey. *The Condottieri: Soldiers of Fortune.* New York: Holt, Rinehart, and Winston, 1971.

Welch, Evelyn S. "Between Milan and Naples: Ippolita Maria Sforza, Duchess of Calabria." In *The French Descent into Renaissance Italy, 1494–1495: Antecedents and Effects.* Edited by D. Abulafia. Aldershot: Variorum, 1995.

SPAIN AND THE RECONQUEST

Cook, Weston F., Jr. "The Cannon Conquest of Nasrid Spain and the End of the Reconquista." *The Journal of Military History* 57 (1993): 43–70.

Fernandez-Armesto, Felipe. *Ferdinand and Isabella.* New York: Dorset, 1975.

Hillgarth, J.N. *The Spanish Kingdoms, 1250–1516.* 2 volumes. Oxford and New York: Oxford University Press, 1978.

Miller, Townsend. *Henry IV of Castile.* London: Victor Gollancz, 1972.

Nicolle, David. *Granada 1492: The Twilight of Moorish Spain.* Botley: Osprey, 1998.

Prescott, William H. *The Art of War in Spain: The Conquest of Granada, 1481–1492.* Edited by Albert D. McJoynt. London: Greenhill, 1995; reprinted from *A History of the Reign of Ferdinand and Isabella.* Third edition. New York: J.B. Alden, 1841.

MUSCOVY AND EASTERN EUROPE, 1350–1505

Croskey, Robert M. *Muscovite Diplomatic Practice in the Reign of Ivan III.* New York: Garland, 1987.

Fennell, J. *Ivan the Great of Moscow*. New York: St. Martin's Press, 1961.

Grey, Ian. *Ivan III and the Unification of Russia*. New York: Collier, 1964.

Halperin, Charles J. *Russia and the Golden Horde: The Mongol Impact on Medieval Russian History*. Bloomington: Indiana University Press, 1985.

Turnbull, Stephen. *Tannenberg 1410: Disaster for the Teutonic Knights*. Botley: Osprey, 2003.

OTTOMAN TURKS AND BYZANTIUM

Brockmann, Eric. *The Two Sieges of Rhodes, 1480–1522*. London: John Murray, 1969.

Ferenc, Szakály. "Phases of Turco-Hungarian Warfare before the Battle of Mohács (1365–1526)." *Acta Orientalia Academiae Scientiarum Hungaricae* 33 (1979): 65–111.

Fisher, S.N. *The Foreign Relations of Turkey, 1481–1512*. Urbana: University of Illinois Press, 1948.

Guilmartin, John F., Jr. "Ideology and Conflict: The Wars of the Ottoman Empire, 1453–1606." *Journal of Interdisciplinary History* 18 (1988): 721–47; reprinted in *The Origin and Prevention of Wars*. Edited by R.I. Rotberg and T.K. Rabb. Cambridge and New York: Cambridge University Press, 1989.

Har-El, S. *Struggle for Domination in the Middle East: The Ottoman-Mamluk War, 1485–1491*. Leiden: E.J. Brill, 1995.

Hess, Andrew. "The Evolution of the Ottoman Seaborne Empire in the Age of Oceanic Discoveries, 1453–1525." *American Historical Review* 75 (December 1970): 1892–1919.

Kianka, Frances. "Byzantine-Papal Diplomacy: The Role of Demetrius Cydones." *The International History Review* 7 (May 1985): 175–213.

Nicol, Donald M. *Byzantium and Venice: A Study in Diplomatic and Cultural Relations*. Cambridge: Cambridge University Press, 1988.

_____. *The End of the Byzantine Empire*. London: Edward Arnold, 1979.

Nicolle, David. *Constantinople 1453: The End of Byzantium*. Botley: Osprey, 2001.

_____. *Hungary and the Fall of Eastern Europe, 1000–1568*. London: Osprey, 1988.

Runciman, Steven. *The Fall of Constantinople, 1453*. Cambridge: Cambridge University Press, 1965.

Schwoebel, Robert. *The Shadow and the Crescent: the Renaissance Image of the Turk (1453–1517)*. Nieukoop: B. De Graff, 1967.

PART IX
EUROPE IN THE AGE OF
THE HABSBURG-VALOIS
WARS,
1494–1559

EUROPE, 1494–1559

Elton, Geoffrey, R. *Reformation Europe, 1517–1559*. New York: Harper and Row, 1963.

_____. *The Reformation, 1520–1559*. Volume II in *The New Cambridge Modern History*. Cambridge: Cambridge University Press, 1958.

Gilmore, Myron P. *The World of Humanism, 1453–1517*. New York: Harper and Brothers, 1952.

Hale, John R. "International Relations in the West: Diplomacy and War." In *The New Cambridge Modern History*, Volume I. Cambridge: Cambridge University Press, 1957.

_____. *Renaissance Europe: The Individual and Society, 1480–1520*. New York: Harper and Row, 1971.

Housley, Norman. *Religious Warfare in Europe, 1400–1536*. New York: Oxford University Press, 2002.

Jones, Martin. *Clash of Empires: Europe 1498–1560*. Cambridge: Cambridge University Press, 2000.

Potter, G.R., editor. *The Renaissance, 1493–1520*. Volume I in *The New Cambridge Modern History*. Cambridge: Cambridge University Press, 1957.

FRANCE, SPAIN, AND THE ITALIAN WARS, 1494–1519

Abulafia, David, editor. *The French Descent into Renaissance Italy, 1494–1495: Antecedents and Effects*. Aldershot: Variorum, 1995.

Ady, Cecilia M. "The Invasions of Italy." In *The New Cambridge Modern History*, Volume I. Cambridge: Cambridge University Press, 1957.

Baumgartner, Frederic J. *Louis XII*. New York: St. Martin's Press, 1994.

Blanchard, Joël. "Political and Cultural Implications of Secret Diplomacy: Commynes and Ferrara in the Light of Unpublished Documents." In *The French Descent into Renaissance Italy, 1494–1495: Antecedents and Effects*. Edited by David Abulafia. Aldershot: Variorum, 1995.

Brady, Thomas A., Jr. "Jacob Sturm and the Seizure of Brunswick-Wolfenbüttel by the Schmalkaldic League, 1542–1545." In *Politics, Religion and Diplomacy in Early Modern Europe: Essays in Honor of De Lamar Jensen*. Edited by Malcolm R. Thorp and Arthur J. Slavin. Kirksville: Sixteenth Century Journal Publishers, 1994.

Bridge, J.S.C. *A History of France from the Death of Louis XI*. 5 volumes. Oxford: Oxford University Press, 1921–36.

Chambers, David S. "Francesco II Gonzaga, Marquis of Mantua, 'Liberator of Italy.'" In *The French Descent into Renaissance Italy, 1494–1495: Antecedents and Effects*. Edited by David Abulafia. Aldershot: Variorum, 1995.

Clough, Cecil H. "The Romagna Campaign of 1494: A Significant Military Encounter." In *The French Descent into Renaissance Italy, 1494–1495: Antecedents and Effects*. Edited by David Abulafia. Aldershot: Variorum, 1995.

Fernández-Armesto, Felipe. *Columbus*. Oxford: Oxford University Press, 1991.

_____. *Ferdinand and Isabella*. New York: Dorset, 1975.

Gaury, Gerald de. *The Grand Captain: Gonzalo de Cordoba.* London: Longmans, Green and Company, 1955.

Gilbert, Felix. "Venetian Diplomacy before Pavia: From Reality to Myth." In *The Diversity of History: Essays in Honour of Sir Herbert Butterfield.* Edited by J.H. Elliott and H.G. Koenigsberger. Ithaca: Cornell University Press, 1970.

Guicciardini, Francesco. *The History of Italy.* Translated by S. Alexander. New York: Macmillan, 1969.

Hale, John R. *Machiavelli and Renaissance Italy.* London: The English Universities Press, 1961.

Hare, Christopher. *Maximilian the Dreamer: Holy Roman Emperor, 1459–1519.* London: Stanley Paul and Company, 1913.

Hillgarth, J.N. *The Spanish Kingdoms, 1250–1516.* 2 volumes. Oxford: Oxford University Press, 1978.

Kidwell, Carol. "Venice, the French Invasion and the Apulian Ports." In *The French Descent into Renaissance Italy, 1494–1495: Antecedents and Effects.* Edited by David Abulafia. Aldershot: Variorum, 1995.

Lucas, Ray. *Great Italian Wars 1494–1544: The Wargamer's Guide.* Hopewell: OMM Publishing, 2002.

Machiavelli, Niccolò. *The Prince.* Harmondsworth: Penguin, 1961.

Mallett, Michael. "Personalities and Pressures: Italian Involvement in the French Invasion of 1494." In *The French Descent into Renaissance Italy, 1494–1495: Antecedents and Effects.* Edited by David Abulafia. Aldershot: Variorum, 1995.

_____. *The Borgias: The Rise and Fall of a Renaissance Dynasty.* London: Bodley Head, 1969.

Nicolle, David. *Fornovo, 1495: France's Bloody Fighting Retreat.* London: Osprey, 1996.

Pepper, Simon. "Castles and Cannon in the Naples Campaign of 1494–1495." In *The French Descent into Renaissance Italy, 1494–1495: Antecedents and Effects*. Edited by David Abulafia. Aldershot: Variorum, 1995.

Santosuosso, Antonio. "Anatomy of Defeat in Renaissance Italy: The Battle of Fornovo in 1495." *The International History Review* 16 (May 1994): 221–50.

Seton-Watson, R.W. *Maximilian I, Holy Roman Emperor*. Westminster: Constable, 1902.

Shaw, Christine. *Julius II: The Warrior Pope*. Oxford: Blackwell, 1993.

_____. "The Roman Barons and the French Descent into Italy." In *The French Descent into Renaissance Italy, 1494–1495: Antecedents and Effects*. Edited by David Abulafia. Aldershot: Variorum, 1995.

Taylor, Frederick L. *The Art of War in Italy, 1494–1529*. Cambridge: Cambridge University Press, 1921.

CHARLES V, FRANCIS I, AND THE HABSBURG-VALOIS WARS, 1519–1559

Alvarez, Manuel Fernández. *Charles V: Elected Emperor and Hereditary Ruler*. London and New York: Thames and Hudson, 1975.

Armstrong, Edward. *The Emperor Charles V*. 2 volumes. Second edition. London: Macmillan and Company, 1910.

Baumgartner, Frederic J. *Henry II: King of France, 1547–1559*. Durham, N.C.: Duke University Press, 1988.

Blockmans, Wim. *Charles V, 1500–1558*. London: Edward Arnold, 2001.

Bonner, E.A. "The First Phase of the Politique of Henri II in Scotland: Its Genesis and the Nature of the 'Auld Alliance,' 1547–1554." Ph.D. diss., University of Sydney, 1992.

Brandi, Karl. *The Emperor Charles V: The Growth and Destiny of a Man and of a World-Empire*. Translated by C.V. Wedgwood. London: Jonathan Cape, 1939.

Chamberlin, E.R. *The Sack of Rome*. London: Batsford, 1979.

Chudoba, Bohdan. *Spain and the Empire, 1519–1643*. Chicago: University of Chicago Press, 1952; reprint, New York: Octagon, 1969.

Fernandez-Santamara, J. *The State, War and Peace: Spanish Political Thought in the Renaissance, 1516–1559*. Cambridge: Cambridge University Press, 1977.

Fichtner, Paula Sutter. *Ferdinand I of Austria: The Politics of Dynasticism in the Age of the Reformation*. New York: Columbia University Press, 1982.

Fischer-Galati, Stephen A. *Ottoman Imperialism and German Protestantism, 1521–1555*. Cambridge, Mass.: Harvard University Press, 1959.

Frey, Linda and Marsha Frey. "Fatal Diplomacy, 1541." *History Today* 40 (August 1990): 10–15.

Gorter-van Royen, L.V.G. "Denmark and Habsburg: The Netherlands between Dynastic and European Policies in the Beginning of the 16th Century." In *Baltic Affairs: Relations between the Netherlands and North-Eastern Europe, 1500–1800*. Edited by J. Lemmink and J.S.A.M. van Koningsbrugge. Nijmegen: Institute for Northern and Eastern European Studies, 1990.

Guicciardini, Francesco. *The History of Italy*. Translated by S. Alexander. New York: Macmillan, 1969.

Headley, John M. *The Emperor and His Chancellor: A Study in the Imperial Chancellery under Gattinara*. Cambridge: Cambridge University Press, 1983.

Hook, Judith. "Fortifications and the End of the Sienese State." *History* 62 (October 1977): 372–87.

_____. "Habsburg Imperialism and Italian Particularism: The Case of Charles V and Siena." *European Studies Review* 9 (1979): 283–312.

_____. *The Sack of Rome, 1527*. London: Macmillan, 1972.

Hoyer, Siegfried. "Arms and Military Organization in the German Peasant War." In *The German Peasant War of 1525: New Viewpoints.* Edited by B. Scribner and Gerhard Benecke. London: George Allen and Unwin, 1979.

Knecht, Robert J. *Francis I.* Cambridge: Cambridge University Press, 1982.

_____. "Francis I and Charles V: The Image of the Enemy." In *(Re)Constructing the Past.* Proceedings of the Colloquium on History and Legitimisation, 24–27 February 1999, Brussels, Belgium. Edited by Jan DeNolf and Barbara Simons. Brussels: Colloquium on History and Legitimisation, 2000.

_____. *French Renaissance Monarchy: Francis I and Henry II.* London: Longman, 1984.

_____. *Henry II: King of France, 1547–1559.* Durham: Duke University Press, 1988.

_____. *Renaissance Warrior and Patron: The Reign of Francis I.* Cambridge and New York: Cambridge University Press, 1994.

Koenigsberger, Helmut G. "Prince and States General: Charles V and the Netherlands (1506–1555)." *Transactions of the Royal Historical Society,* Sixth series 4 (1994): 127–51.

_____. "The Empire of Charles V." In *The New Cambridge Modern History,* Volume II. Second edition. Edited by G.R.Elton. Cambridge: Cambridge University Press, 1990.

Konstam, Angus. *Pavia, 1525: The Climax of the Italian Wars.* London: Osprey, 1996.

Lucas, Ray. *Great Italian Wars 1494–1544: The Wargamer's Guide.* Hopewell: OMM Publishing, 2002.

Lundell, Richard E. "The Mask of Dissimulation: Eustace Chapuys and Early Modern Diplomatic Technique, 1536–1545." Ph.D diss., University of Illinois at Urbana-Champaign, 2001.

Lundkvist, Sven. "The European Powers and Sweden in the Reign of Gustav Vasa." In *Politics and Society in Reformation Europe: Essays for Sir Geoffrey*

Elton on his Sixty-Fifth Birthday. Edited by E.I. Kouri and Tom Scott. London: Macmillan, 1987.

Maltby, William S. *The Reign of Charles V.* New York: Palgrave, 2002.

Miller, Douglas. *Landsknechts.* London: Osprey, 1994.

Parker, Geoffrey. "The Political World of Charles V." In *Charles V, 1500–1558 and His Times.* Edited by H. Soly. Antwerp: Metcatorfonds, 2000.

Pitts, Vincent J. *The Man Who Sacked Rome: Charles de Bourbon, Constable of France, 1490–1527.* New York: Peter Lang, 1994.

Potter, David. *War and Government in the French Provinces: Picardy, 1470–1560.* Cambridge: Cambridge University Press, 1993.

Rady, Martyn. *The Emperor Charles V.* London: Longman, 1988.

Richards, John. *Landsknecht Soldiers 1486–1560.* Botley: Osprey, 2002.

Rodriquez-Salgado, Maria J. *The Changing Face of Empire: Charles V, Philip II and Habsburg Authority, 1551–1559.* Cambridge and New York: Cambridge University Press, 1988.

_____. "The Habsburg-Valois Wars." In *The New Cambridge Modern History*, Volume II. Second edition. Edited by G.R.Elton. Cambridge: Cambridge University Press, 1990.

Russell, Joycelyne G. *Peacemaking in the Renaissance.* London: Duckworth, 1986.

_____. *The Field of Cloth of Gold: Men and Manners in 1520.* London: Routledge and Kegan Paul, 1969.

_____. "Women Diplomats: The Ladies' Peace of 1529." In *Diplomats at Work: Three Renaissance Studies.* Stroud: Alan Sutton, 1992.

Spooner, F.C. "The Habsburg-Valois Struggle." In *The New Cambridge Modern History*, Volume II. Cambridge: Cambridge University Press, 1958.

Tracy, James D. *Emperor Charles V, Impresario of War: Campaign Strategy, International Finance, and Domestic Politics.* Cambridge and New York: Cambridge University Press, 2002.

Tüchle, Hermann. "The Peace of Augsburg: New Order or Lull in the Fighting." In *Government in Reformation Europe, 1520–1560.* Edited by H.J. Cohn. London: Macmillan, 1971.

Tyler, Roland. *The Emperor Charles the Fifth.* London: George Allen and Unwin, 1956.

Vester, Mathew. "Territorial Politics in the Savoyard Domains, 1536–1580." Ph.D. thesis, University of California, Los Angeles, 1997.

_____. "The Piedmontese Restitution: Franco-Savoyard Diplomacy from 1515 to 1572." M.A. thesis, University of Virginia, 1992.

Yates, Frances. "Charles V and the Idea of the Empire." In *Astraea: The Imperial Theme in the Sixteenth Century.* London: Routledge and Kegan Paul, 1975.

TUDOR FOREIGN POLICY, 1485–1558

Barr, Niall. *Flodden 1513.* Stroud: Tempus, 2001.

Bennett, Michael. *Lambert Simnel and the Battle of Stoke.* New York: St. Martin's Press, 1987.

Bonner, Elizabeth. "The Recovery of St. Andrews Castle in 1547: French Naval Policy and Diplomacy in the British Isles." *The English Historical Review* 111 (1996): 578–98.

Bush, M. *The Government Policy of Protector Somerset.* London: Edward Arnold, 1975.

Chambers, David S. *Cardinal Bainbridge in the Court of Rome 1509–1514.* Oxford: Oxford University Press, 1965.

_____. "Cardinal Wolsey and the Papal Tiara." *Bulletin of the Institute of Historical Research* 38 (1965): 20–30.

Chrimes, S.B. *Henry VII.* London: Eyre Methuen, 1972.

Cruickshank, Charles. *Army Royal: Henry VIII's Invasion of France, 1513*. Oxford : Oxford University Press, 1969; reprinted as *Henry VIII and the Invasion of France*. Stroud: Sutton, 1990.

_____. *The English Occupation of Tournai, 1513–1519*. Oxford: Oxford University Press, 1971.

Currin, John M. "Henry VII and the Politics of Europe, 1485–1492: Diplomacy and War at the Accession of the Tudor Regime." Ph.D. diss., University of Minnesota, 1995.

_____. "'The King's Army into the Partes of Bretaigne': Henry VII and the Breton Wars, 1489–1491." *War in History* 7 (November 2000): 379–412.

Davies, C.S.L. "England and the French War, 1557–1559." In *The Mid-Tudor Polity, c.1540–1560*. Edited by J. Loach and R. Tittler. Totowa: Rowman and Littlefield, 1980.

_____. "Provisions for Armies, 1509–1550: A Study in the Effectiveness of Early Tudor Government." *Economic History Review*, Second series 17 (1964–65): 234–48.

_____. "The Administration of the Royal Navy Under Henry VIII: The Origins of the Navy Board." *The English Historical Review* 80 (April 1965): 268–88.

Dunlop, David. "The Politics of Peace-Keeping: Anglo-Scottish Relations from 1503 to 1511." *Renaissance Studies* 8 (1994): 138–161.

Eaves, Richard Glen. *Henry VIII and James V's Regency 1524–1528: A Study in Anglo-Scottish Diplomacy*. Lanham: University Press of America, 1987.

Elton, Geoffrey R. *Reform and Reformation: England, 1509–1558*. London: Edward Arnold, 1977.

_____. "War and the English in the Reign of Henry VIII." In *War, Strategy and International Politics: Essays in Honour of Sir Michael Howard*. Edited by L. Freedman, P. Hayes, and R. O'Neill. Oxford: Clarendon Press, 1992.

Engelbrecht, Jörg. "Anglo-German Relations in the Reign of Henry VIII." In *Henry VIII in History, Historiography and Literature*. Edited by Uwe Baumann. Frankfurt: Peter Lang, 1992.

Fissel, Mark. *English Warfare, 1511–1642*. London: Routledge, 2001.

Gunn, Steven. *Charles Brandon, Duke of Suffolk, 1484–1545*. Oxford: Blackwell, 1988.

_____. "The Duke of Suffolk's March on Paris in 1523." *The English Historical Review* 101 (1986): 596–634.

_____. "The French Wars of Henry VIII." In *Origins of War in Early Modern Europe*. Edited by J. Black. Edinburgh: John Donald, 1987.

_____. "Wolsey's Foreign Policy and the Domestic Crisis of 1527–1528." In *Cardinal Wolsey: Church, State and Art*. Edited by S.J. Gunn and P. Lindley. Cambridge: Cambridge University Press, 1991.

Gwyn, Peter. *The King's Cardinal: The Rise and Fall of Thomas Wolsey*. London: Barrie and Jenkins, 1990.

_____. "Wolsey's Foreign Policy: The Conferences at Calais and Bruges Reconsidered." *The Historical Journal* 23 (1980): 755–72.

Harbison, E. Harris. "French Intrique at the Court of Queen Mary." *The American Historical Review* 45 (April 1940): 533–51.

_____. *Rival Ambassadors at the Court of Queen Mary*. Princeton: Princeton University Press, 1940.

Head, David M. "Henry VIII's Scottish Policy." *The Scottish Historical Review* 61 (1982): 1–24.

Loach, Jennifer. *Edward VI*. Edited by G. Bernard and P. Williams. New Haven: Yale University Press, 1999.

Loades, David. *Mary Tudor: A Life*. Oxford: Basil Blackwell, 1989.

_____. *The Reign of Mary Tudor: Politics, Government and Religion in England, 1553–1558*. London: Ernest Benn, 1977.

Lockyer, Roger. *Henry VII*. London: Longman, 1968.

Loomie, Albert J. "Spanish Secret Diplomacy at the Court of St. James." In *Politics, Religion and Diplomacy in Early Modern Europe: Essays in Honor of De Lamar Jensen*. Edited by Malcolm R. Thorp and Arthur J. Slavin. Kirksville: Sixteenth Century Journal Publishers, 1994.

Lutz, Heinrich. "Cardinal Reginald Pole and the Path to Anglo-Papal Mediation at the Peace Conference of Marcq, 1553–1555." In *Politics and Society in Reformation Europe*. Edited by E.I. Kouri and Tom Scott. London: Macmillan, 1987.

McEntegart, Rory. "England and the League of Schmalkalden, 1531–1547: Faction, Foreign Policy and the English Reformation." Ph.D. diss., University of London, 1992.

_____. "Henry VIII and the Marriage to Anne of Cleves." In *Henry VIII: A European Court in England*. Edited by D. Starkey. New York: Cross River Press, 1991.

Mattingly, Garrett. *Catherine of Aragon*. London: Jonathan Cape, 1942.

Millar, Gilbert John. *Tudor Mercenaries and Auxiliaries, 1485–1547*. Charlottesville: University Press of Virginia, 1980.

Palmer, M.D. *Henry VIII*. London: Longman, 1971.

Palmer, William. *The Problem of Ireland in Tudor Foreign Policy, 1485–1603*. Woodbridge: Boydell Press, 1994.

Parmiter, Geoffrey de C. *The King's Great Matter: A Study of Anglo-Papal Relations, 1527–1534*. London: Longmans, 1967.

Phillips, Gervase. "Strategy and Its Limitations: The Anglo-Scots Wars, 1480–1550." *War in History* 6 (November 1999): 396–416.

_____. *The Anglo-Scots Wars, 1513–1550*. Woodbridge: Boydell, 1999.

_____. "The Army of Henry VIII: A Reassessment." *The Journal of the Society for Army Historical Research* 75 (1997): 9–23.

Potter, David. "Diplomacy in the Mid-Sixteenth Century: England and France, 1536–1550." Ph.D. diss., Cambridge University, 1973.

_____, editor. "Documents concerning the Negotiations of the Anglo-French Treaty of March 1550." *Camden Miscellany*, Fourth series, 29 (1984): 58–180.

_____. "Foreign Policy." In *The Reign of Henry VIII: Politics, Policy and Piety*. Edited by Diarmaid MacCulloch. New York: St. Martin's Press, 1995.

_____. "Foreign Policy in the Age of the Reformation: French Involvement in the Schmalkaldic War, 1544–1547." *The Historical Journal* 20 (1977): 525–44.

_____. "French Intrigue in Ireland during the Reign of Henri II, 1547–1559." *The International History Review* 2 (May 1983): 159–80.

_____. "The Duc de Guise and the Fall of Calais, 1557–1558." *The English Historical Review* 98 (1983): 481–512.

_____. "The Treaty of Boulogne and European Diplomacy, 1549–1550." *Bulletin of the Institute of Historical Research* 55 (May 1982): 50–65.

Russell, Joycelne G. "The Search for Universal Peace: The Conferences at Calais and Bruges in 1521." *Bulletin of the Institute of Historical Research* 44 (1971): 162–93.

Scarisbrick, J.J. *Henry VIII*. London: Eyre and Spottiswoode, 1972.

Storey, R.L. *The Reign of Henry VII*. London: Blandford, 1968.

Tjernagel, Neelak S. *Henry VIII and the Lutherans: A Study in Anglo-Lutheran Relations from 1521 to 1547*. St Louis: Concordia, 1965.

Wilkie, W.E. *The Cardinal Protectors of England: Rome and the Tudors before the Reformation*. Cambridge: Cambridge University Press, 1974.

THE TURKISH THREAT IN THE EARLY SIXTEENTH CENTURY

Alföldi, László. M. "The Battle of Mohács, 1526." In *From Hunyadi to Rákóczi: War and Society in Late Medieval and Early Modern Hungary.* Edited by János Bak and Béla K. Király Brooklyn: Columbia University Press, 1982.

Barta, Gábor. "A Forgotten Theatre of War 1526–1528 (Historical Events Preceding the Ottoman-Hungarian Alliance of 1528)." In *Hungarian-Ottoman Military and Diplomatic Relations in the Age of Süleyman the Magnificent.* Edited by Géza Dávid and Pál Fodor. Budapest: Loránd Eötvös University, Department of Turkish Studies and Hungarian Academy of Sciences, Institute of History, 1994.

Bradford, Ernle. *The Sultan's Admiral: The Life of Barbarossa.* New York: Harcourt, Brace and World, 1968.

Bridge, Antony. *Suleiman the Magnificent: Scourge of Heaven.* London: Granada, 1983.

Brockmann, Eric. *The Two Sieges of Rhodes, 1480–1522.* London: John Murray, 1969.

Brummett, Palmira. "Foreign Policy, Naval Strategy, and the Defence of the Ottoman Empire in the Early Sixteenth Century." *The International History Review* 11 (November 1989): 613–27.

_____. *Ottoman Seapower and Levantine Diplomacy in the Age of Discovery.* Albany: State University of New York Press, 1994.

Clot, A. *Suleiman the Magnificent: The Man, His Life, His Epoch.* London: Saqi Books, 1992.

Dávid, Géza and Pál Fodor, editors. *Hungarian-Ottoman Military and Diplomatic Relations in the Age of Süleyman the Magnificent.* Budapest: Loránd Eötvös University, Department of Turkish Studies and Hungarian Academy of Sciences, Institute of History, 1994.

_____, editors. *Ottomans, Hungarians, and Habsburgs in Central Europe: The Military Confines in the Era of Ottoman Conquest.* Leiden: Brill, 2000.

Elliott, John H. "Ottoman-Habsburg Rivalry: The European Perspective." In *Süleymân the Second and His Time.* Edited by Halil Inalcik and Cemal Kafadar. Istanbuhl: Isis Press, 1993.

Ferenc, Szakály. "Phases of Turco-Hungarian Warfare before the Battle of Mohács (1365–1526)." *Acta Orientalia Academiae Scientiarum Hungaricae* 33 (1979): 65–111.

Finlay, Robert. "Prophecy and Politics in Istanbul: Charles V, Sultan Suleyman, and the Habsburg Embassy of 1533–1534." *Journal of Early Modern History* 2 (1998): 249–72.

Fischer-Galati, Stephen A. *Ottoman Imperialism and German Protestantism, 1521–1555.* Cambridge, Mass.: Harvard University Press, 1959.

Fisher, S.N. *The Foreign Relations of Turkey, 1481–1512.* Urbana: University of Illinois Press, 1948.

Fodor, Pál. "Ottoman Policy towards Hungary, 1520–1541." *Acta Orientalia Academiae Scientiarum Hungaricae* 45 (1991): 271–345.

_____ and Géza Dávid. "Hungarian-Ottoman Peace Negotiations in 1512–1514." In *Hungarian-Ottoman Military and Diplomatic Relations in the Age of Süleyman the Magnificent.* Edited by Géza Dávid and Pál Fodor. Budapest: Loránd Eötvös University, Department of Turkish Studies and Hungarian Academy of Sciences, Institute of History, 1994.

Guilmartin, John F., Jr. "Ideology and Conflict: The Wars of the Ottoman Empire, 1453–1606." *Journal of Interdisciplinary History* 18 (1988): 721–47; reprinted in *The Origin and Prevention of Wars.* Edited by R.I. Rotberg and T.K. Rabb. Cambridge and New York: Cambridge University Press, 1989.

Hegyi, Klára. "Ottoman Military Force in Hungary." In *Hungarian-Ottoman Military and Diplomatic Relations in the Age of Süleyman the Magnificent.* Edited by Géza Dávid and Pál Fodor. Budapest: Loránd Eötvös University,

Department of Turkish Studies and Hungarian Academy of Sciences, Institute of History, 1994.

Hess, Andrew. "The Evolution of the Ottoman Seaborne Empire in the Age of Oceanic Discoveries, 1453–1525." *American Historical Review* 75 (December 1970): 1892–1919.

_____. *The Forgotten Frontier: A History of the Sixteenth-Century Ibero-African Frontier*. Chicago: University of Chicago Press, 1978.

_____. "The Ottoman Conquest of Egypt (1517) and the Beginning of the Sixteenth-Century World War." *International Journal of Middle East Studies* 4 (1973): 55–76.

_____. "The Road to Victory: The Significance of Mohács for Ottoman Expansion." In *From Hunyadi to Rákóczi: War and Society in Late Medieval and Early Modern Hungary*. Edited by J. Bak and B. Király. New York: Brooklyn College Press, 1982.

Imber, Colin H. "The Navy of Süleiman the Magnificent." *Archivum Ottomanicum* 6 (1980): 211–82.

Kubinyi, András. "The Battle of Szávaszentdemeter-Nagyolaszi (1523): Ottoman Advance and Hungarian Defence on the Eve of Mohács." In *Ottomans, Hungarians, and Habsburgs in Central Europe: The Military Confines in the Era of Ottoman Conquest*. Edited by Géza Dávid and Pál Fodor. Leiden: Brill, 2000.

Isom-Verhaaren, Christine. "Ottoman-French Interaction, 1480–1580: A Sixteenth-Century Encounter." Ph.D. diss., University of Chicago, 1997.

Kunt, M. and C. Woodhead, editors. *Süleyman the Magnificent and His Age: The Ottoman Empire in the Early Modern World*. London: Longman, 1995.

Merriman, Roger Bigelow. *Suleiman the Magnificent, 1520–1566*. Cambridge, Mass.: Harvard University Press, 1944.

Nicolle, David. *Hungary and the Fall of Eastern Europe, 1000–1568*. London: Osprey, 1988.

Perjés, Géza. *The Fall of the Medieval Kingdom of Hungary: Mohács 1526—Buda 1541*. Translated by Márió D. Fenyö. *War and Society in Central Europe* series, Volume 26. Boulder, Colo.: Social Science Monographs, 1989.

Rogers, J.M. and R.M. Ward. *Süleyman the Magnificent*. London: British Museum Publications, 1988.

Rothenberg, Gunther E. *The Austrian Military Border in Croatia, 1522–1747*. Urbana: University of Illinois Press, 1960.

Schwoebel, Robert. *The Shadow and the Crescent: the Renaissance Image of the Turk (1453–1517)*. Nieukoop: B. De Graff, 1967.

Setton, Kenneth M. *The Papacy and the Levant (1204–1571): Volume III, The Sixteenth Century*. Philadelphia: American Philosophical Society, 1984.

_____. *The Papacy and the Levant (1204–1571): Volume IV, The Sixteenth Century*. Philadelphia: American Philosophical Society, 1984.

Szakály, Ferenc. "Nándorfehérvár, 1521: The Beginning of the End of the Medieval Hungarian Kingdom." In *Hungarian-Ottoman Military and Diplomatic Relations in the Age of Süleyman the Magnificent*. Edited by Géza Dávid and Pál Fodor. Budapest: Loránd Eötvös University, Department of Turkish Studies and Hungarian Academy of Sciences, Institute of History, 1994.

PART X
SPANISH POWER AND EUROPE, 1559–1609

EUROPE, 1559–1609

Braudel, F. *The Mediterranean and the Mediterranean World in the Age of Philip II.* 2 volumes. London: Collins, 1972–73.

Davis, James C., editor. *Pursuit of Power: Venetian Ambassador's Reports on Spain, Turkey, and France in the Age of Philip II, 1560–1600.* New York: Harper and Row, 1970.

Elliott, John H. *Europe Divided, 1559–1598.* New York: Harper and Row, 1968.

Mallett, Michael. "Preparations for War in Florence and Venice in the Second Half of the Sixteenth Century." In *Florence and Venice: Comparisons and Relations.* Edited by Sergio Bertelli and others. Florence: La Nouva Italia, 1979.

Mattingly, Garrett. "International Diplomacy and International Law." In *The New Cambridge Modern History*, Volume III. Edited by R.B. Wernham. Cambridge: Cambridge University Press, 1971.

O'Connell, Marvin R. *The Counter Reformation, 1559–1610.* New York: Harper and Row, 1974.

Spitz, Lewis W. *The Protestant Reformation, 1517–1559.* New York: Harper and Row, 1985.

Vester, Mathew. "Territorial Politics in the Savoyard Domains, 1536–1580." Ph.D. thesis, University of California, Los Angeles, 1997.

Wernham, R.B., editor. *The Counter-Reformation and Price Revolution, 1559–1610.* Volume III in *The New Cambridge Modern History.* Cambridge: Cambridge University Press, 1971.

PHILIP II AND THE SPANISH EMPIRE, 1556–1598

Allen, Paul C. *Philip III and the Pax Hispanica, 1598–1621: The Failure of Grand Strategy.* New Haven: Yale University Press, 2000.

_____ "The Strategy of Peace: Spanish Foreign Policy and the '*Pax Hispanica*', 1598–1609." Ph.D. diss., Yale University, 1995.

Beeching, Jack. *The Galleys at Lepanto.* New York: Charles Scribner's Sons, 1982.

Boyden, James M. *The Courtier and the King: Ruy Gómez de Silva, Philip II, and the Court of Spain.* Berkeley: University of California Press, 1995.

Carter, Charles H. "The Nature of Spanish Government after Philip II." *Historian* 26 (November 1963): 1–18.

_____. *The Secret Diplomacy of the Habsburgs, 1598–1625.* New York: Columbia University Press, 1964.

Chudoba, Bohdan. *Spain and the Empire, 1519–1643.* Chicago: University of Chicago Press, 1952; reprint, New York: Octagon, 1969.

Estrada, Hugo O'Donnell y Duque de. "The Army of Flanders and the Invasion of England 1586–1588." In *England, Spain and the Gran Armada, 1585–1604: Essays from the Anglo-Spanish Conferences, London and Madrid, 1988.* Edited by M.J. Rodriguiez-Salgado and S. Adams. Edinburgh: John Donald, 1991.

Fernandez-Armesto, Felipe. *The Spanish Armada: The Experience of War in 1588.* Oxford: Oxford University Press, 1988.

Fichtner, Paula S. *Ferdinand I of Austria: The Politics of Dynasticism in the Age of the Reformation*. Boulder: East European Monographs, 1982.

González de León, Fernando. "The Road to Rocroi: The Duke of Alba, the Count Duke of Olivares and the High Command of the Spanish Army of Flanders in the Eighty Years' War, 1567–1659." Ph.D. diss., Johns Hopkins University, 1991.

_____ and Geoffrey Parker. "The Grand Strategy of Philip II and the Revolt of the Netherlands." In *The Origins and Development of the Dutch Revolt*. Edited by Graham Darby. London and New York: Routledge, 2001.

Goodman, D. *Power and Penury: Government, Technology and Science in Philip II's Spain*. Cambridge and New York: Cambridge University Press, 1988.

Gray, Randal. "Spinola's Galleys in the Narrow Seas, 1599–1603." *Mariner's Mirror* 64 (1978): 71–83.

Hess, Andrew C. "The Battle of Lepanto and Its Place in Mediterranean History." *Past and Present* Number 57 (1972): 53–73.

Jensen, De Lamar. *Diplomacy and Dogmatism: Bernardino de Mendoza and the French Catholic League*. Cambridge, Mass.: Harvard University Press, 1964.

_____. "Franco-Spanish Diplomacy and the Armada." In *From the Renaissance to the Counter-Reformation: Essays in Honour of Garrett Mattingly*. Edited by C.H. Carter. London: Jonathan Cape, 1966.

_____. "The Spanish Armada: The Worst-Kept Secret in Europe." *Sixteenth-Century Journal* 19 (1988): 621–41.

Jiménez, Carlos Gómez-Centurión. "The New Crusade: Ideology and Religion in the Anglo-Spanish Conflict." In *England, Spain and the Gran Armada, 1585–1604: Essays from the Anglo-Spanish Conferences, London and Madrid, 1988*. Edited by M.J. Rodriguiez-Salgado and S. Adams. Edinburgh: John Donald, 1991.

Kamen, Henry. *Philip of Spain*. New Haven: Yale University Press, 1997.

Kemp, Peter. *The Campaign of the Spanish Armada*. New York: Facts on File, 1988.

Koenigsberger, Helmut G. "Orange, Granvelle and Philip II." In *Politics and Society in Reformation Europe: Essays for Sir Geoffrey Elton on his Sixty-Fifth Birthday*. Edited by E.I. Kouri and Tom Scott. London: Macmillan, 1987.

_____. "The Statecraft of Philip II." *European Studies Review* 1 (1971): 1–21; reprinted in *Politicians and Virtuoosi: Essays in Early Modern History*. London: Hambledon Press, 1986.

_____. "Western Europe and the Power of Spain." In *The New Cambridge Modern History*, Volume III. Edited by R.B. Wernham. Cambridge: Cambridge University Press, 1968.

Konstam, Angus. *Lepanto 1571*. Botley: Osprey, 2003.

_____. *The Armada Campaign 1588: The Great Enterprise against England*. Botley: Osprey, 2001.

Lagomarsino, P. David. "Court Factions and the Formation of Spanish Policy Towards the Netherlands, 1559–1567." Ph.D. diss., Cambridge University, 1973.

Lewis, Michael. *The Spanish Armada*. London: B.T. Batsford, 1960.

Lynch, John. "Philip II and the Papacy." *Transactions of the Royal Historical Society*, Fifth series 2 (1961): 23–42.

Maltby, William S. *Alba: A Biography of Fernando Alvarez de Toledo, Third Duke of Alba, 1507–1582*. Berkeley: University of California Press, 1983.

Martin, Colin and Geoffrey Parker. *The Spanish Armada*. London: Hamish Hamilton, 1988.

Padfield, Peter. *Armada*. London: Victor Gollancz, 1988.

Parker, Geoffrey. "David or Goliath?: Philip II and His World in the 1580s." In *Spain, Europe and the Atlantic World: Essays in Honour of John H. Elliott*. Edited by R.L. Kagan and Geoffrey Parker. Cambridge and New York: Cambridge University Press, 1996; reprinted in *Success is Never Final:*

Empire, War, and Faith in Early Modern Europe. New York: Basic Books, 2002.

_____. "Lepanto (1571): The Costs of Victory." In *Spain and The Netherlands, 1559–1659: Ten Studies.* London: Collins, 1979.

_____. *Philip II.* London: Hutchinson, 1979.

_____. "Philip II, Paul Kennedy, and the Revolt of the Netherlands, 1572–76: A Case of Strategic Overstretch?" In *Clashes of Culture: Essays in Honour of Niels Steensgaard.* Edited by J.C.V. Johansen, E.L. Peterson, and H. Stevnsborg. Odense: Odense University Press, 1992.

_____. *Success is Never Final: Empire, War, and Faith in Early Modern Europe.* New York: Basic Books, 2002.

_____. *The Grand Strategy of Philip II.* New Haven: Yale University Press, 1998.

_____. "The Making of Strategy in Habsburg Spain: Philip II's 'Bid for Mastery,' 1556–1598." In *The Making of Strategy: Rulers, States, and War.* Edited by Williamson Murray, MacGregor Knox, and Alvin Bernstein. Cambridge: Cambridge University Press, 1994.

_____. *The World is Not Enough: The Imperial Vision of Philip II of Spain.* Waco, Texas: Markham Press, 2001.

_____. "The Worst-Kept Secret in Europe?: The European Intelligence Community and the Spanish Armada of 1588." In *Go Spy the Land: Military Intelligence in History.* Edited by Keith Neilson and B.J.C. McKercher. Westport: Praeger, 1992.

_____. "Was Parma Ready?: The Army of Flanders and the Spanish Armada in 1588." In *Beleid en Bestuur in de Oude Nederlanden: Liber Amicorum Prof. Dr. M. Baelde.* Edited by Hugo Soly and René Vermeir. Ghent: Vakgroep Nieuwe Geschiedenis U.G., 1993.

_____. "Why the Armada Failed." *History Today* 38 (May 1988): 26–33.

Petrie, Charles. *Don John of Austria.* London: Eyre and Spottiswoode, 1967.

Pickles, Tim. *Malta 1565: Last Battle of the Crusades*. Botley: Osprey, 1998.

Pierson, Peter. *Commander of the Armada: The Seventh Duke of Medina Sidonia*. New Haven: Yale University Press, 1989.

_____. *Philip II of Spain*. London and New York: Thames and Hudson, 1975.

Richardson, Kristin. "After the Armada: The Cuatro Villas de la Costa and Philip's Brittany Campaign." In *Politics, Religion and Diplomacy in Early Modern Europe: Essays in Honor of De Lamar Jensen*. Edited by Malcolm R. Thorp and Arthur J. Slavin. Kirksville: Sixteenth Century Journal Publishers, 1994.

Rodríguez-Salgado, M.J. "From Spanish Ruler to European Ruler: Philip II and the Creation of an Empire." Ph.D. thesis, Hull University, 1984.

_____. "Pilots, Navigation and Strategy in the *Gran Armada*." In *England, Spain and the Gran Armada, 1585–1604: Essays from the Anglo-Spanish Conferences, London and Madrid, 1988*. Edited by M.J. Rodriguiez-Salgado and Simon Adams. Edinburgh: John Donald, 1991.

_____ and Simon Adams, editors. *England, Spain and the Gran Armada, 1585–1604: Essays from the Anglo-Spanish Conferences, London and Madrid, 1988*. Edinburgh: John Donald, 1991.

_____, editors. "The Count of Feria's Dispatch to Philip II of 14 November 1558." *Camden Miscellany*, Fourth series, 29 (1984): 302–44.

Silke, John J. *Kinsale: The Spanish Intervention in Ireland at the End of the Elizabethan Wars*. New York: Fordham University Press, 1970.

Soto, Jose Luis Casado. "Atlantic Shipping in Sixteenth-Century Spain and the 1588 Armada." In *England, Spain and the Gran Armada, 1585–1604: Essays from the Anglo-Spanish Conferences, London and Madrid, 1988*. Edited by M.J. Rodriguiez-Salgado and Simon Adams. Edinburgh: John Donald, 1991.

Stradling, Robert A. *The Armada of Flanders: Spanish Maritime Policy and European War, 1568–1668*. Cambridge: Cambridge University Press, 1992.

Terrace, Edward S. "The Spanish Intervention in Brittany and the Failure of Philip II's Bid for European Hegemony, 1589–1598." Ph.D. diss., University of Illinois, 1997.

Thompson, I.A.A. "Spanish Armada Guns." *Mariner's Mirror* 61 (1975): 355–71.

_____. "The Appointment of the Duke of Medina Sidonia to the Command of the Spanish Armada." *Historical Journal* 12 (1969): 197–216.

_____. "The Armada and Administrative Reform: The Spanish Council of War in the Reign of Philip II." *The English Historical Review* 82 (1967): 698–725.

_____. "The Spanish Armada: Naval Warfare between the Mediterranean and Atlantic." In *England, Spain and the Gran Armada, 1585–1604: Essays from the Anglo-Spanish Conferences, London and Madrid, 1988.* Edited by M.J. Rodriguiez-Salgado and Simon Adams. Edinburgh: John Donald, 1991.

_____. *War and Government in Habsburg Spain, 1560–1620.* London: Athlone Press, 1976.

Tincey, John. *The Armada Campaign, 1588.* London: Osprey, 1988.

_____. *The Spanish Armada.* Botley: Osprey, 2000.

Waxman, Matthew C. "Strategic Terror: Philip II and Sixteenth-Century Warfare." *War in History* 4 (July 1997): 339–47.

Woodward, Geoffrey. *Philip II.* London: Longman, 1992.

THE DUTCH REVOLT, 1568–1609

Dalton, R.C. "Scotland's Involvement in the Revolt of the Dutch Republic, 1572–1603." Ph.D. diss., University of Guelph, 1978.

Darby, Graham, editor. *The Origins and Development of the Dutch Revolt.* London and New York: Routledge, 2001.

Den Tex, Jan. *Oldenbarnevelt.* 2 volumes. Cambridge: Cambridge University Press, 1973.

Deursen, A.T. van. "Holland's Experience of War during the Revolt of the Netherlands." In *Britain and the Netherlands: War and Society.* The Hague: Martinus Nijhoff, 1977.

Doedens, L.L. "'The Day the Nation was Born': The Battle of Heiligerlee, 1568." In *Exercise of Arms: Warfare in the Netherlands, 1568–1648.* Edited by Marco van der Hoeven. Leiden: Brill, 1997.

Fruin, R. *The Siege and Relief of Leyden in 1574.* The Hague: Martinus Nijhoff, 1927.

Geyl, Pieter. *The Revolt of the Netherlands (1555–1609).* London: Ernest Benn, 1958.

González de León, Fernando and Geoffrey Parker. "The Grand Strategy of Philip II and the Revolt of the Netherlands." In *The Origins and Development of the Dutch Revolt.* Edited by Graham Darby. London and New York: Routledge, 2001.

Griffiths, G. *William of Hornes, Lord of Heze, and the Revolt of the Netherlands (1576–1580).* Berkeley: University of California Press, 1954.

Henry, Grainne. *The Irish Military Community in Spanish Flanders, 1586–1621.* Dublin: Irish Academic Press, 1992.

Hoeven, Marco van der, editor. *Exercise of Arms: Warfare in the Netherlands (1568–1648).* Leiden: Brill, 1997.

Holt, Mack P. "Foreign Powers and the Dutch Revolt." *History Today* 34 (July 1984): 22–27.

Limm, Peter. *The Dutch Revolt, 1559–1648.* London: Longman, 1989.

Lombaerde, Piet. "The Fortifications of Ostend during the Great Siege of 1601–1604." *Fort* 127 (1999): 93–112.

Loo, I.J. van. "For Freedom and Fortune: The Rise of Dutch Privateering in the First Half of the Dutch Revolt, 1568–1609." In *Exercise of Arms: Warfare in the Netherlands, 1568–1648.* Edited by Marco van der Hoeven. Leiden: Brill, 1997.

Lovett, A.W. "A New Governor for the Netherlands: The Appointment of Don Luis de Requesens, Comendador Mayor de Castilla." *European Studies Review* 1 (1971): 89–103.

_____. "Francisco de Lixalde: A Spanish Paymaster in the Netherlands, 1567–1577." *Tijdschrift voor Geschiedenis* 84 (1971): 14–23.

Nickle, Barry H. "The Military Reforms of Prince Maurice of Orange." Ph.D. diss., University of Delaware, 1975.

Nimwegen, O. van. "Maurits van Nassau and Siege Warfare (1590–1597)." In *Exercise of Arms: Warfare in the Netherlands, 1568–1648.* Edited by Marco van der Hoeven. Leiden: Brill, 1997.

Parker, Geoffrey. "Corruption and Imperialism in the Spanish Netherlands: The Case of Francisco de Lixalde, 1567–1613." In *Spain and The Netherlands, 1559–1659: Ten Studies.* London: Collins, 1979.

_____. "July 26th, 1581: The Dutch Declaration of Independence." *History Today* 31 (July 1981): 3–6.

_____. "Mutiny and Discontent in the Spanish Army of Flanders, 1572–1607." In *Spain and The Netherlands, 1559–1659: Ten Studies.* London: Collins, 1979.

_____. "New Light on an Old Theme: Spain and the Netherlands, 1550–1650." *European History Quarterly* 15 (1985): 219–36.

_____. "Philip II, Paul Kennedy and the Revolt of the Netherlands, 1572–1576: A Case of Strategic Overstretch?" In *Clashes of Cultures: Essays in Honour of Niels Steensgaard.* Edited by Jens Christian V. Johansen and others. Odense: Odense University Press, 1992.

_____. *Spain and the Netherlands, 1559–1659: Ten Studies.* London: Collins, 1979.

_____. "Spain, Her Enemies and the Revolt of the Netherlands 1559–1648." *Past and Present* 49 (1970): 72–95; reprinted in *Spain and The Netherlands, 1559–1659: Ten Studies*. London: Collins, 1979.

_____. *Success is Never Final: Empire, War, and Faith in Early Modern Europe*. New York: Basic Books, 2002.

_____. *The Army of Flanders and the Spanish Road, 1567–1659: The Logistics of Spanish Victory and Defeat in the Low Countries Wars*. Cambridge and New York: Cambridge University Press, 1972.

_____. "The Decision-Making Process in the Government of the Catholic Netherlands under 'the Archdukes', 1596–1621." In *Spain and The Netherlands, 1559–1659: Ten Studies*. London: Collins, 1979.

_____. *The Dutch Revolt*. Ithaca: Cornell University Press, 1977.

_____. "The Dutch Revolt and the Polarization of International Politics." In *The General Crisis of the Seventeenth Century*. Edited by Geoffrey Parker and L.M. Smith. London: Routledge and Kegan Paul, 1978; reprinted in *Spain and The Netherlands, 1559–1659: Ten Studies*. London: Collins, 1979.

_____. "The Origins of the Dutch Revolt." *History Today* 34 (1984): 17–21.

_____. "Was Parma Ready?: The Army of Flanders and the Spanish Armada in 1588." In *Beleid en Bestuur in de Oude Nederlanden: Liber Amicorum Prof. Dr. M. Baelde*. Edited by Hugo Soly and Rene Vermeir. Ghent: Universiteit Gent, 1993.

_____. "Why Did the Dutch Revolt Last So Long?" In *Spain and The Netherlands, 1559–1659: Ten Studies*. London: Collins, 1979.

Puype, J.P. "Victory at Nieuwpoort, 2 July 1600." In *Exercise of Arms: Warfare in the Netherlands, 1568–1648*. Edited by Marco van der Hoeven. Leiden: Brill, 1997.

Rady, Martyn. *From Revolt to Independence: The Netherlands, 1550–1650*. London: Hodder and Stoughton, 1999.

Sutherland, Nicola M. "William of Orange and the Revolt of the Netherlands: A Missing Dimension." *Archiv für Reformationsgeschichte* 74 (1983): 201–30; reprinted in *Princes, Politics and Religion, 1547–1589*. London: Hambledon Press, 1984.

Swart, K.W. *William the Silent and the Revolt of the Netherlands*. London: Historical Association, 1978.

Tjaden, A.J. "Frederic II of Denmark, Lord of Holland and Zealand?: Diplomats in Action (1584–1587)." In *Baltic Affairs: Relations between the Netherlands and North-Eastern Europe, 1500–1800*. Edited by J.Ph.S Lemmink and J.S.A.M. van Koningsbrugge. Nijmegen: Institute for Northern and Eastern European Studies, 1990.

Wedgwood, Cicely Veronica. *William the Silent: William of Nassau, Prince of Orange, 1533–1584*. London: Jonathan Cape, 1944.

Zwitzer, H.L. "The Eighty Years' War." In *Exercise of Arms: Warfare in the Netherlands, 1568–1648*. Edited by Marco van der Hoeven. Leiden: Brill, 1997.

QUEEN ELIZABETH I AND ENGLISH FOREIGN POLICY, 1558–1603

Adams, Simon. *The Armada Campaign of 1588*. London: Historical Association, 1988.

_____. "The Battle that Never Was: The Downs and the Armada Campaign." In *England, Spain and the Gran Armada, 1585–1604: Essays from the Anglo-Spanish Conferences, London and Madrid, 1988*. Edited by M.J. Rodriguiez-Salgado and Simon Adams. Edinburgh: John Donald, 1991.

_____. "The Lurch into War." *History Today* 38 (May 1988): 18–25.

_____. "The Queen Embattled: Elizabeth I and the Conduct of Foreign Policy. In *Queen Elizabeth I: Most Politick Princess*. Edited by Simon Adams. London: History Today, 1984.

_____. "The Outbreak of the Elizabethan Naval War against the Spanish Empire: The Embargo of May 1585 and Sir Francis Drake's West Indies

Voyage." In *England, Spain and the Gran Armada, 1585–1604: Essays from the Anglo-Spanish Conferences, London and Madrid, 1988.* Edited by M.J. Rodriguiez-Salgado and Simon Adams. Edinburgh: John Donald, 1991.

_____. "The Protestant Cause: Religious Alliance with the West European Calvinist Communities as a Political Issue in England, 1585–1630." Ph.D. diss., Oxford University, 1973.

Ambler, R.W. "'Wise and Experimented': Sir William Pelham, Elizabethan Soldier and Landlord, c.1560–1587." In *The Medieval Military Revolution: State Society and Military Change in Medieval and Early Modern Europe.* Edited by Andrew Ayton. London and New York: I.B. Tauris Publishers, 1995.

Andrews, Kenneth R. "Caribbean Rivalry and the Anglo-Spanish Peace of 1604." *History* 59 (February 1974): 1–17.

_____. *Drake's Voyages: A Re-Assessment of Their Place in Elizabethan Maritime Expansion.* London: Weidenfeld and Nicolson, 1967.

_____. *Elizabethan Privateering: English Privateering during the Spanish War, 1585–1603.* Cambridge: Cambridge University Press, 1964.

Barker, Felix. "If the Armada had Landed." *History Today* 38 (May 1988): 34–41.

_____. "Sir Philip Sidney and the Forgotten War of 1586." *History Today* 36 (November 1986): 40–46.

Bayne, C.G. *Anglo-Roman Relations, 1558–1564.* Oxford: Oxford University Press, 1913.

Bell, Gary M. "Elizabethan Diplomacy: The Subtle Revolution." In *Politics, Religion and Diplomacy in Early Modern Europe: Essays in Honor of De Lamar Jensen.* Edited by Malcolm R. Thorp and Arthur J. Slavin. Kirksville: Sixteenth Century Journal Publishers, 1994.

Black, J.B. *Elizabeth and Henry IV.* Oxford: Oxford University Press, 1914.

_____. "Queen Elizabeth, the Sea Beggars and the Capture of Brille, 1572." *The English Historical Review* 46 (1931): 30–47.

Borman, T. "Untying the Knot?: The Survival of the Anglo-Dutch Alliance, 1587–1597." *European History Quarterly* 27 (1997): 307–37.

Boyton, Linda. *The Elizabethan Militia, 1558–1638.* London: Routledge and Kegan Paul, 1976.

Cruickshank, Charles. *Elizabeth's Army.* Second edition. Oxford and New York: Oxford University Press, 1966.

Dawson, Jane. "Mary Queen of Scots, Lord Darnley, and Anglo-Scottish Relations in 1565." *The International History Review* 8 (February 1986): 1–24.

_____. "William Cecil and the British Dimension of Early Elizabethan Foreign Policy." *History* 74 (1989): 196–216.

Doran, Susan. *Elizabeth I and Foreign Policy, 1558–1603.* London: Routledge, 2000.

_____. *Monarchy and Matrimony: The Courtships of Elizabeth I.* London: Routledge, 1996.

_____. "Religion and Politics at the Court of Elizabeth I: The Habsburg Marriage Negotiations of 1559–1567." *The English Historical Review* 104 (October 1989): 908–26.

Dunthorne, Hugh. "Scots in the Wars of the Low Countries, 1572–1648." In *Scotland and the Low Countries, 1124–1994.* Edited by Grant G. Simpson. East Linton: Tuckwell Press, 1996.

Falls, Cyril. *Elizabeth's Irish Wars.* London: Methuen and Company, 1950.

_____. *Mountjoy: Elizabethan General.* London: Odhams Press, 1955.

Fissel, Mark. *English Warfare 1511–1642.* London: Routledge, 2001.

Haigh, Christopher. *Elizabeth I.* London: Longman, 1988.

Haynes, Alan. *Invisible Power: The Elizabethan Secret Services, 1570–1603.* Stroud: Alan Sutton, 1992.

Konstam, Angus. *Elizabethan Sea Dogs 1560–1605.* Botley: Osprey, 2000.

_____. *The Armada Campaign 1588: The Great Enterprise against England*. Botley: Osprey, 2001.

Kouri, E.I. *England and the Attempts to Form a Protestant Alliance in the Late 1560s: A Case Study in European Diplomacy*. Helsinki: Suomalainen Tiedeakatemia, 1981.

_____. "For True Faith or National Interest?: Queen Elizabeth I and the Protestant Powers." In *Politics and Society in Reformation Europe: Essays for Sir Geoffrey Elton on his Sixty-Fifth Birthday*. Edited by E.I. Kouri and Tom Scott. London: Macmillan, 1987.

Lenman, Bruce. *England's Colonial Wars, 1550–1688*. London: Longman, 2000.

Lloyd, Howell A. *The Rouen Campaign, 1590–1592: Politics, Warfare, and the Early-Modern State*. Oxford: Clarendon Press, 1973.

Lock, Julian. "How Many Tercios has the Pope? The Spanish War and the Sublimination of Elizabethan Anti-Popery." *History* 81 (1996): 197–214.

Loomie, Albert J. "Sir Robert Cecil and the Spanish Embassy." *Bulletin of the Institute of Historical Research* 42 (1969): 492–514.

_____. *Toleration and Diplomacy: The Religious Issue in Anglo-Spanish Relations, 1603–1605*. Philadelphia: American Philosophical Society, 1963.

MacCaffrey, Wallace T. *Elizabeth I*. London: Edward Arnold, 1993.

_____. *Elizabeth I: War and Politics, 1588–1603*. Princeton: Princeton University Press, 1992.

_____. *Queen Elizabeth and the Making of Policy, 1572–1588*. Princeton: Princeton University Press, 1981.

_____. "The Anjou Match and the Making of Elizabethan Foreign Policy." In *The English Commonwealth, 1547–1640: Essays in Politics and Society Presented to Joel Hurstfield*. Edited by Peter Clark, Alan G.R. Smith, and Nicholas Tyacke. Leicester: Leicester University Press, 1979.

_____. "The Newhaven Expedition, 1562–1563." *Historical Journal* 40 (1997): 1–21.

_____. *The Shaping of the Elizabethan Regime*. London: Jonathan Cape, 1969.

Mackie, J. Duncan. "James VI and I and the Peace with Spain, 1604." *Scottish Historical Review* 23 (1926): 241–49.

Maltby, William S. *The Black Legend in England: The Development of Anti-Spanish Sentiment, 1558–1660*. Durham: Duke University Press, 1971.

Mattingly, Garrett. *The Defeat of the Spanish Armada*. London: Jonathan Cape, 1959; published in the United States as *The Spanish Armada*. New York: Houghton Mifflin, 1959.

McGurk, John. *The Elizabethan Conquest of Ireland*. Manchester: Manchester University Press, 1997.

Mears, Natalie. "Love-Making and Diplomacy: Elizabeth I and the Anjou Marriage Negotiations, c. 1578–1582." *History* 86 (October 2001): 442–66.

Morgan, Hiram. "Hugh O'Neill and the Nine Years' War in Tudor Ireland." *Historical Journal* 36 (1993): 21–37.

_____. *Tyrone's Rebellion: The Outbreak of the Nine Years' War in Tudor Ireland*. Woodbridge: Boydell Press, 1993.

Morgan, Walter. *The Expedition In Holland, 1572–1574: The Revolt of the Netherlands: The Early Struggle for Independence*. Edited by Duncan Caldecott-Baird. London: Seeley, 1976.

Neale, John E. "Elizabeth and the Netherlands, 1586–1587." *The English Historical Review* 45 (July 1930): 373–96.

Nolan, John S. "The Militarization of the Elizabethan State." *The Journal of Military History* 58 (July 1994): 391–420.

Oosterhoff, F.G. *Leicester and the Netherlands, 1586–1587*. Utrecht: HES, 1988.

Palmer, William. *The Problem of Ireland in Tudor Foreign Policy, 1485–1603*. Woodbridge: Boydell Press, 1994.

Parker, Geoffrey. "If the Armada Had Landed." *History* 61 (October 1976): 358–68; reprinted in *Spain and The Netherlands, 1559–1659: Ten Studies*. London: Collins, 1979.

_____. "Of Providence and Protestant Winds: The Spanish Armada of 1588 and the Dutch Armada of 1688." In *Success is Never Final: Empire, War, and Faith in Early Modern Europe*. New York: Basic Books, 2002.

_____. "Treason and Plot in Elizabethan Diplomacy: The 'Fame of Sir Edward Stafford' Reconsidered." In *Success is Never Final: Empire, War, and Faith in Early Modern Europe*. New York: Basic Books, 2002.

Platt, F. Jeffrey. "The Elizabethan 'Foreign Office'." *The Historian* 56 (Summer 1994): 725–40.

Ramsay, G.D. "The Foreign Policy of Elizabeth I." In *The Reign of Elizabeth I*. Edited by Christopher Haigh. Athens: University of Georgia Press, 1984.

Read, Conyers. *Lord Burghley and Queen Elizabeth*. New York: Alfred Knopf, 1960.

_____. *Mr Secretary Cecil and Queen Elizabeth*. London: Jonathan Cape, 1955.

_____. *Mr Secretary Walsingham and the Policy of Queen Elizabeth*. 3 volumes. Oxford: Clarendon Press, 1925.

_____. "Queen Elizabeth's Seizure of the Duke of Alba's Pay-Ships." *Journal of Modern History* 5 (1933): 433–64.

Rodríguez-Salgado, M.J. "The Anglo-Spanish War: The Final Episode in the 'Wars of the Roses'?" In *England, Spain and the Gran Armada, 1585–1604: Essays from the Anglo-Spanish Conferences, London and Madrid, 1988*. Edited by M.J. Rodriguiez-Salgado and Simon Adams. Edinburgh: John Donald, 1991.

_____ and Simon Adams, editors. *England, Spain and the Gran Armada, 1585–1604: Essays from the Anglo-Spanish Conferences, London and Madrid, 1988*. Edinburgh: John Donald, 1991.

Silke, John J. *Kinsale: The Spanish Intervention in Ireland at the End of the Elizabethan Wars*. New York: Fordham University Press, 1970.

Slavin, Arthur J. "Daniel Rogers in Copenhagen, 1588: Mission and Memory." In *Politics, Religion and Diplomacy in Early Modern Europe: Essays in Honor of De Lamar Jensen*. Edited by Malcolm R. Thorp and Arthur J. Slavin. Kirksville: Sixteenth Century Journal Publishers, 1994.

Stewart, Richard W. "The 'Irish Road': Military Supply and Arms for Elizabeth's Army during the O'Neill Rebellion in Ireland, 1598–1601." In *War and Government in Britain, 1598–1650*. Edited by Mark C. Fissel. Manchester: Manchester University Press, 1991.

Sutherland, Nicola M. "Queen Elizabeth and the Conspiracy of Amboise, March 1560." *The English Historical Review* 81 (1966): 474–89; reprinted in *Princes, Politics and Religion, 1547–1589*. London: Hambledon Press, 1984.

_____ "The Foreign Policy of Queen Elizabeth, the Sea Beggars and the Capture of Brill, 1572." In *Princes, Politics and Religion, 1547–1589*. London: Hambledon Press, 1984.

_____. "The Origins of Queen Elizabeth's Relations with the Huguenots, 1559–1562." *Proceedings of the Huguenot Society of London* 20 (1964): 626–48; reprinted in *Princes, Politics and Religion, 1547–1589*. London: Hambledon Press, 1984.

Thorp, Malcolm R. "Catholic Conspiracy in Early Elizabethan Foreign Policy." *The Sixteenth-Century Journal* 15 (1984): 431–38.

_____. "William Cecil and the Antichrist: A Study in Anti-Catholic Ideology." In *Politics, Religion and Diplomacy in Early Modern Europe: Essays in Honor of De Lamar Jensen*. Edited by Malcolm R. Thorp and Arthur J. Slavin. Kirksville: Sixteenth Century Journal Publishers, 1994.

Tincey, John. *The Spanish Armada*. Botley: Osprey, 2000.

Wernham, R.B. *After the Armada: Elizabethan England and the Struggle for Western Europe, 1588–1595*. Oxford: Clarendon Press, 1984.

_____. "Elizabethan War Aims and Strategy." In *Essays Presented to Sir John Neale*. Edited by S.T. Bindoff and others. London: University of London Press, 1961.

_____. "English Policy and the Revolt of the Netherlands." In *Britain and the Netherlands*. Edited by J.S. Bromley and E.H. Kossman. London: Chatto and Windus, 1960.

_____. "Queen Elizabeth and the Portuguese Expedition of 1589." *The English Historical Review* 66 (1951): 1–26, 194–218.

_____. "Queen Elizabeth I, the Emperor Rudolph II and Archduke Ernest, 1593–1594." In *Politics and Society in Reformation Europe: Essays for Sir Geoffrey Elton on his Sixty-Fifth Birthday*. Edited by E.I. Kouri and Tom Scott. London: Macmillan, 1987.

_____. *The Making of Elizabethan Foreign Policy, 1558–1603*. Berkeley: University of California Press, 1980.

_____. *The Return of the Armadas*. Oxford: Oxford University Press, 1994.

Williams, Roger. *The Actions of the Low Countries*. Edited by D.W. Davies. Ithaca: Cornell University Press, 1964.

Wilson, Charles. *Queen Elizabeth and the Revolt of the Netherlands*. London: Macmillan, 1970.

Wormald, Jenny. *Mary Queen of Scots: A Study in Failure*. London: George Philip, 1988.

FRENCH WARS OF RELIGION, 1559–1610

Armstrong, Edward. *The French Wars of Religion: Their Political Aspects*. London: Percival and Company, 1892.

Buisseret, David. *Henry IV*. London: George Allen and Unwin, 1984.

_____. *Sully and the Growth of Centralized Government in France, 1598–1610*. London: Eyre and Spottiswoode, 1968.

Davies, J.M. "Neither Politique nor Patrior?: Henry, Duc de Montmorency and Philip II, 1582–1589." *Historical Journal* 34 (1991): 539–66.

_____. "The Duc de Montmorency, Philip II and the House of Savoy: A Neglected Aspect of the Sixteenth-Century French Civil Wars." *The English Historical Review* 105 (1990): 870–92.

Dickerman, E.H. "A Neglected Aspect of the Spanish Armada: The Catholic League's Picard Offensive." *Canadian Journal of History* 11 (1976): 19–23.

Hayden, J. Michael. "Continuity in the France of Henry IV and Louis XIII: French Foreign Policy, 1598–1615." *The Journal of Modern History* 45 (March 1973): 1–23.

Holt, Mack. *The Duke of Anjou and the Politique Struggle during the Wars of Religion.* Cambridge and New York: Cambridge University Press, 1986.

_____. *The French Wars of Religion, 1562–1629.* Cambridge and New York: Cambridge University Press, 1995.

Jensen, De Lamar. "French Diplomacy and the Wars of Religion." *The Sixteenth Century Journal* 5 (October 1974): 23–46.

Knecht, Robert J. *Catherine de' Medici.* London: Longman, 1998.

_____. *The French Civil Wars, 1562–1598.* Harlow: Pearson, 2000.

_____. *The French Religious Wars, 1562–1598.* Botley: Osprey, 2002.

_____. *The French Wars of Religion, 1559–1598.* London: Longman, 1989.

Lee, Maurice. *James I and Henri IV: An Essay in English Foreign Policy, 1603–1610.* Urbana: University of Illinois Press, 1970.

Lucas, Ray. *French Wars of Religion 1562–1598.* Hopewell, OMM Publishing, 2002.

Mousnier, Roland. *The Assassination of Henry IV: The Tyrannicide Problem and the Consolidation of the French Absolute Monarchy in the Early Seventeenth Century.* London: Faber and Faber, 1973.

Shimizu, J. *Conflict of Loyalties: Politics and Religion in the Career of Gaspard de Coligny, Admiral of France, 1519–1572*. Geneva: Droz, 1970.

Soman, A., editor. *The Massacre of St. Bartholomew: Reappraisals and Documents*. The Hague: Martinus Nijhoff, 1974.

Sutherland, Nicola M. *Princes, Politics and Religion, 1547–1589*. London: Hambledon Press, 1984.

_____. *The French Secretaries of State in the Age of Catherine de Medici*. London: Athlone Press, 1962.

_____. *The Massacre of Saint Bartholomew and the European Conflict, 1559–1572*. Basingstoke: Macmillan, 1973.

_____. "The Massacre of St. Bartholomew and the Problem of Spain." In *Princes, Politics and Religion, 1547–1589*. London: Hambledon Press, 1984.

_____. "The Role of Coligny in the French Civil Wars." In *Actes due Colloque l'Amiral de Coligny et son Temps*. Paris: Société de l'Histoire du Protestantisme Français, 1974.

Thompson, James Westfall. *The Wars of Religion in France, 1559–1576: The Huguenots, Catherine de Medici, and Philip II*. Chicago: University of Chicago Press, 1909.

Vester, Mathew. "Territorial Politics in the Savoyard Domains, 1536–1580." Ph.D. thesis, University of California, Los Angeles, 1997.

_____. "The Piedmontese Restitution: Franco-Savoyard Diplomacy from 1515 to 1572." M.A. thesis, University of Virginia, 1992.

Whitehead, A.W. *Gaspard de Coligny: Admiral of France*. London: Methuen, 1904.

Wood, James B. *The King's Army: Warfare, Soldiers, and Society during the Wars of Religion in France, 1562–1576*. Cambridge: Cambridge University Press, 1996.

_____. "The Royal Army during the Early Wars of Religion, 1559–1576." In *Society and Institutions in Early Modern France: Essays Presented to J. Russell Major*. Edited by M.P. Holt. Athens: University of Georgia Press, 1991.

AUSTRIAN HABSBURGS AND THE HOLY ROMAN EMPIRE, 1558–1612

Evans, R.J.W. "Bohemia, the Emperor, and the Porte, 1550–1600." *Oxford Slavonic Papers*, New series 3 (1970): 85–106.

_____. *Rudolf II and His World: A Study in Intellectual History, 1576–1612*. Oxford: Clarendon Press, 1973.

Fichtner, Paula Sutter. "Dynastic Marriage in Sixteenth-Century Habsburg Diplomacy and Statecraft: An Interdisciplinary Approach." *The American Historical Review* 81 (1976): 243–65.

_____. *Emperor Maximilian II*. New Haven: Yale University Press, 2001.

_____. *Ferdinand I of Austria: The Politics of Dynasticism in the Age of the Reformation*. New York: Columbia University Press, 1982.

Rothenberg, Gunther E. *The Austrian Military Border in Croatia, 1522–1747*. Urbana: University of Illinois Press, 1960.

TURKISH THREAT TO EUROPE, 1559–1648

Bayerle, Gustav. *Ottoman Diplomacy in Hungary: Letters from the Pashas of Buda, 1590–1593*. Bloomington: Indiana University Press, 1972.

Bradford, Ernle. *The Great Siege*. London: Hodder and Stoughton, 1961.

Dávid, Géza and Pál Fodor, editors. *Ottomans, Hungarians, and Habsburgs in Central Europe: The Military Confines in the Era of Ottoman Conquest*. Leiden: Brill, 2000.

Finkel, Caroline. "French Mercenaries in the Habsburg-Ottoman War of 1593–1606." *Bulletin of the School of Oriental and African Studies* 55 (1992): 451–71.

_____. *The Administration of Warfare: The Ottoman Military Campaigns in Hungary, 1593–1606*. Vienna: Verlag des Verbandes der Wissenschaftlichen Gesellschaften Österreichs, 1988.

Fodor, Pál. "Prelude to the 'Long War' (1593–1606): Some Notes on the Ottoman Foreign Policy in 1591–1593." In *Great Ottoman Turkish Civilization*, Volume I. Edited by Kemal Çiçek, Ercüment Kuran, Nejat Güyünc and Iber Ortayli. Ankara: Türkiye, 2000.

Guilmartin, John F., Jr. "Ideology and Conflict: The Wars of the Ottoman Empire, 1453–1606." *Journal of Interdisciplinary History* 18 (1988): 721–47; reprinted in *The Origin and Prevention of Wars*. Edited by R.I. Rotberg and T.K. Rabb. Cambridge and New York: Cambridge University Press, 1989.

Hegyi, K. "The Ottoman Military Force in Hungary." In *Hungarian-Ottoman Military and Diplomatic Relations in the Age of Süleyman the Magnificent*. Edited by G. Dávid and P. Fodor. Budapest: Lorand Eötvös University, 1994.

Hess, Andrew. "The Battle of Lepanto and Its Place in Mediterranean History." *Past and Present* Number 57 (1972): 53–73.

_____. *The Forgotten Frontier: A History of the Sixteenth-Century Ibero-African Frontier*. Chicago: University of Chicago Press, 1978.

_____. "The Moriscos: An Ottoman Fifth Column in Sixteenth Century Spain." *American Historical Review* 74 (1968): 1–25.

Isom-Verhaaren, Christine. "Ottoman-French Interaction, 1480–1580: A Sixteenth-Century Encounter." Ph.D. diss., University of Chicago, 1997.

Ivanics, Mária. "The Role of the Crimean Tartars in the Habsburg-Ottoman War (1595–1606)." In *Great Ottoman Turkish Civilization*, Volume I. Edited by Kemal Çiçek, Ercüment Kuran, Nejat Güyünc and Iber Ortayli. Ankara: Türkiye, 2000.

Konstam, Angus. *Lepanto 1571*. Botley: Osprey, 2003.

Kortepeter, Carl Max. "Gazi Giray II, Khan of the Crimea, and Ottoman Policy in Eastern Europe and the Caucasus, 1588–1594." *The Slavic and East European Review* 44 (January 1966): 139–66.

_____. "Ottoman Imperial Policy and the Economy of the Black Sea Region in the Sixteenth Century." *Journal of the American Oriental Society* 86 (April-June 1966): 86–113.

_____. *Ottoman Imperialism during the Reformation: Europe and the Caucasus*. New York: New York University Press, 1972.

Kurat, A.N. "The Turkish Expedition to Astrakhan in 1569 and the Problem of the Don-Volga Canal." *Slavonic and East European Review* 40 (1961–62): 7–23.

Murphey, Rhoads. "The Functioning of the Ottoman Army under Murad IV (1623–1639): Key to Understanding the Relationship between Center and Periphery." Ph.D. thesis, University of Chicago, 1979.

Pickles, Tim. *Malta 1565: Last Battle of the Crusades*. Botley: Osprey, 1998.

Rothenberg, Gunther E. *The Austrian Military Border in Croatia, 1522–1747*. Urbana: University of Illinois Press, 1960.

Setton, Kenneth M. *The Papacy and the Levant (1204–1571): Volume III, The Sixteenth Century*. Philadelphia: American Philosophical Society, 1984.

_____. *The Papacy and the Levant (1204–1571): Volume IV, The Sixteenth Century*. Philadelphia: American Philosophical Society, 1984.

Stein, Mark Lewis. "Seventeenth-Century Ottoman Forts and Garrisons on the Habsburg Frontier." Ph.D. diss., University of Chicago, 2001.

Tenenti, Alberto. *Piracy and the Decline of Venice, 1580–1615*. London: Longman, Green and Company, 1967.

NORTHERN AND EASTERN EUROPE IN THE SIXTEENTH CENTURY

Grey, Ian. *Ivan the Terrible*. London: History Book Club, 1964.

Kirchner, Walther. "A Milestone in European History: The Danish-Russian Treaty of 1562." *Slavonic and East European Review* 22 (August 1944): 39–48.

Pavlov, Andrei and Maureen Perrie. *Ivan the Terrible*. London: Pearson, 2003.

Roberts, Michael. *The Early Vasas: A History of Sweden, 1523–1611*. Cambridge: Cambridge University Press, 1968.

PART XI
EUROPE IN THE AGE OF
THE THIRTY YEARS' WAR,
1609–1648

EUROPE, 1609–1648

Anderson, Alison Deborah. *On the Verge of War: International Relations and the Jülich-Kleve Succession Crises (1609–1614)*. Boston: Humanities Press, 1999.

_____. "The Jülich-Kleve Succession Crisis (1609–1620): A Study in International Relations." Ph.D. thesis, University of Illinois, 1992.

Beller, E.A. "The Thirty Years' War." In *The New Cambridge Modern History*, Volume IV. Edited by J.P. Cooper. Cambridge: Cambridge University Press, 1970.

Bonney, Richard. *The Thirty Years' War, 1618–1648*. Botley: Osprey, 2002.

Bussmann, Klaus and Heinz Schilling. *1648—War and Peace in Europe*. 3 volumes. Münster: Landschaftsverband Westfälen-Lippe, Westfälisches Landesmuseum für Kunst und Kulturgeschichte, 1999.

Carter, Charles H. "The Ambassadors of Early Modern Europe: Patterns of Diplomatic Representation in the Early Seventeenth Century." In *From the Renaissance to the Counter-Reformation: Essays in Honour of Garrett Mattingly*. Edited by C.H. Carter. London: Jonathan Cape, 1966.

Cooper, J.P. "Sea-Power." In *The New Cambridge Modern History*, Volume IV. Edited by J.P. Cooper. Cambridge: Cambridge University Press, 1970.

_____, editor. *The Decline of Spain and the Thirty Years' War, 1609–1648/ 1659.* Volume IV in *The New Cambridge Modern History.* Cambridge: Cambridge University Press, 1970.

Croxton, Derek. "A Territorial Imperative?: The Military Revolution, Strategy, and Peacemaking in the Thirty Years' War." *War in History* 5 (1998): 253–79.

_____. "The Peace of Westphalia of 1648 and the Origins of Sovereignty." *The International History Review* 21 (September 1999): 569–91.

_____. "'The Prosperity of Arms is Never Continual': Military Intelligence, Surprise, and Diplomacy in 1640s Germany." *The Journal of Military History* 64 (October 2000): 981–1004.

_____ and Anuschka Tischer. *The Peace of Westphalia: A Historical Dictionary.* Westport: Greenwood Press, 2002.

Darby, Graham. *The Thirty Years' War.* London: Hodder and Stoughton, 2001.

Elliott, John H. "War and Peace in Europe, 1618–1648." In *1648—War and Peace in Europe,* Volume I. Edited by Klaus Bussmann and Heinz Schilling. Münster: Landschaftsverband Westfälen-Lippe, Westfälisches Landesmuseum für Kunst und Kulturgeschichte, 1999.

Friedrich, Carl J. *The Age of Baroque, 1610–1660.* New York: Harper and Brothers, 1952.

Gindely, Anton. *History of the Thirty Years' War.* 2 volumes. New York: G.P. Putnam's Sons, 1892.

Guthrie, William P. *Battles of the Thirty Years' War: From White Mountain to Nordlingen, 1618–1635.* Westport: Greenwood Press, 2001.

_____. "Naval Actions of the Thirty Years' War," *Mariner's Mirror* 87 (August 2001): 262–80.

_____. *The Later Thirty Years' War: From the Battle of Wittstock to the Treaty of Westphalia.* Westport: Greenwood Press, 2003.

Gutmann, Myron P. "The Origins of the Thirty Years' War." *Journal of Interdisciplinary History* 18 (Spring 1988): 749–70.

Kleinman, Ruth. "Charles Emanuel I of Savoy and the Bohemian Election of 1619." *European Studies Review* 5 (1975): 3–29.

Lee, Stephen. *The Thirty Years' War*. London: Routledge, 1991.

Langer, Herbert. *The Thirty Years' War*. Poole: Blandford Press, 1980.

Limm, Peter. *The Thirty Years' War*. London: Longman, 1984.

Maland, David. *Europe at War, 1600–1650*. London: Macmillan, 1980.

Mortimer, Geoff. "Did Contemporaries Recognize a 'Thirty Years' War'?" *The English Historical Review* 116 (2001): 124–36.

_____. *Eyewitness Accounts of the Thirty Years' War, 1618–1648*. New York: Palgrave, 2002.

Oresko, Robert. "The House of Savoy and the Thirty Years' War." In *1648—War and Peace in Europe*, Volume I. Edited by Klaus Bussmann and Heinz Schilling. Münster: Landschaftsverband Westfälen-Lippe, Westfälisches Landesmuseum für Kunst und Kulturgeschichte, 1999.

_____ and David Parrott. "*Reichsitalien* and the Thirty Years' War." In *1648—War and Peace in Europe*, Volume I. Edited by Klaus Bussmann and Heinz Schilling. Münster: Landschaftsverband Westfälen-Lippe, Westfälisches Landesmuseum für Kunst und Kulturgeschichte, 1999.

Osborne, Toby. *Dynasty and Diplomacy in the Court of Savoy: Political Culture and the Thirty Years' War*. Cambridge and New York: Cambridge University Press, 2002.

_____. "The Diplomatic Career of Abbot Scaglia during the Thirty Years' War." D.Phil., University of Oxford, 1996.

Pagès, Georges. *The Thirty Years' War, 1618–1648*. London: Adam and Charles Black, 1970.

Parker, Geoffrey. *Europe in Crisis, 1598–1648*. Brighton: Harvester Press, 1980.

_____. *Success is Never Final: Empire, War, and Faith in Early Modern Europe*. New York: Basic Books, 2002.

_____. "The Soldiers of the Thirty Years' War." In *Krieg und Politik 1618–1648: Europäische Probleme und Perspektiven*. Edited by Konrad Repgen. Munich: R. Oldenbourg Verlag, 1988.

_____, editor. *The Thirty Years' War*. London: Routledge, Kegan and Paul, 1984.

Parrott, David. "Strategy and Tactics in the Thirty Years' War: The 'Military Revolution'." *Militärgeschichtliche Mitteilungen* 18 (1985): 7–25; reprinted in *The Military Revolution Debate: Readings on the Military Transformation of Early Modern Europe*. Edited by C.J. Rogers. Boulder: Westview, 1995.

_____. "The Mantuan Succession and the Thirty Years' War." In *1648—War and Peace in Europe*, Volume I. Edited by Klaus Bussmann and Heinz Schilling. Münster: Landschaftsverband Westfälen-Lippe, Westfälisches Landesmuseum für Kunst und Kulturgeschichte, 1999.

_____. "The Mantuan Succession, 1627–1631: A Sovereignty Dispute in Early Modern Europe." *The English Historical Review* 112 (1997): 20–65.

Polišenský, Josef V. *The Thirty Years' War*. London: B.T. Batsford, 1971.

_____. *The Tragic Triangle: The Netherlands, Spain and Bohemia 1617–1621*. Prague: Charles University, 1991.

_____. *War and Society in Europe, 1618–1648*. Cambridge: Cambridge University Press, 1978.

Rabb, Theodore K., editor. *The Thirty Years' War*. Second edition. New York: University Press of America, 1972.

Repgen, Konrad. "Negotiating the Peace of Westphalia: An Overview with an Examination of the Major Problems." In *1648—War and Peace in Europe*, Volume I. Edited by Klaus Bussmann and Heinz Schilling. Münster: Landschaftsverband Westfälen-Lippe, Westfälisches Landesmuseum für Kunst und Kulturgeschichte, 1999.

Setton, Kenneth M. *Venice, Austria, and the Turks in the Seventeenth Century.* Philadelphia: American Philosophical Society, 1991.

Steiger, Heinhard. "Concrete Peace and General Order—The Legal Meaning of the Treaties of the 24th of October 1648." In *1648—War and Peace in Europe*, Volume I. Edited by Klaus Bussmann and Heinz Schilling. Münster: Landschaftsverband Westfälen-Lippe, Westfälisches Landesmuseum für Kunst und Kulturgeschichte, 1999.

Steinberg, S.H. *The "Thirty Years' War" and the Conflict for European Hegemony, 1600–1660.* London: Edward Arnold, 1966.

Sutherland, Nicola M. "The Origins of the Thirty Years' War and the Structure of European Politics." *The English Historical Review* 107 (1992): 587–625.

Trevor-Roper, Hugh. "The Outbreak of the Thirty Years' War." In *Renaissance Essays*. Edited by H. Trevor-Roper. London: Secker and Warburg, 1985.

Wedgwood, Cicely Veronica. *The Thirty Years' War.* London: Jonathan Cape, 1938.

Wijn, J.W. "Military Forces and Warfare, 1610–1648." In *The New Cambridge Modern History*, Volume IV. Edited by J.P. Cooper. Cambridge: Cambridge University Press, 1970.

SPANISH HABSBURGS, 1598–1648

Allen, Paul C. *Philip II and the Pax Hispanica, 1598–1621: The Failure of Grand Strategy.* New Haven: Yale University Press, 2000.

_____. "The Strategy of Peace: Spanish Foreign Policy and the '*Pax Hispanica*', 1598–1609. Ph.D. diss., Yale University, 1995.

Brightwell, Peter. "Spain and Bohemia: The Decision to Intervene, 1619." *European Studies Review* 12 (1982): 117–41.

_____. "Spain and the Origins of the Thirty Years' War." Ph.D. diss., Cambridge University, 1967.

_____. "Spain, Bohemia and Europe, 1619–1621." *European Studies Review* 12 (1982): 371–99.

_____. "The Spanish Origins of the Thirty Years' War." *European Studies Review* 9 (1979): 409–31.

_____. "The Spanish System and the Twelve Years' Truce." *The English Historical Review* 89 (April 1974): 270–92.

Carter, Charles H. "Belgian 'Autonomy' under the Archdukes, 1598–1621." *The Journal of Modern History* 36 (September 1964): 245–59.

_____. "Gondomar: Ambassador to James I." *The Historical Journal* 6 (1964): 189–208.

_____. "The Nature of Spanish Government after Philip II." *The Historian* 26 (1963): 1–18.

_____. *The Secret Diplomacy of the Habsburgs, 1598–1625.* New York: Columbia University Press, 1964.

Chudoba, Bohdan. *Spain and the Empire, 1519–1643.* Chicago: University of Chicago Press, 1952; reprint, New York: Octagon, 1969.

Elliott, John H. "Foreign Policy and Domestic Crisis: Spain, 1598–1659." In *Krieg und Politik, 1618–1648.* Edited by Konrad Repgen. Munich: R. Oldenbourg Verlag, 1988.

_____. "Managing Decline: Olivares and the Grand Strategy of Imperial Spain." In *Grand Strategies in War and Peace.* Edited by Paul Kennedy. New Haven: Yale University Press, 1991.

_____. *Richelieu and Olivares.* Cambridge: Cambridge University Press, 1984.

_____. "Self-Perception and Decline in Early Seventeenth-Century Spain." In *Spain and Its World, 1500–1700.* Princeton: Princeton University Press, 1988.

_____. *The Count-Duke of Olivares: The Statesman in the Age of Decline.* New Haven: Yale University Press, 1986.

_____. *The Revolt of the Catalans: A Study in the Decline of Spain*. Cambridge: Cambridge University Press, 1963.

_____. "The Statecraft of Olivares." In *The Diversity of History: Essays in Honour of Sir Herbert Butterfield*. Edited by J.H. Elliott and H.G. Koenigsberger. Ithaca: Cornell University Press, 1970.

_____. "The Year of the Three Ambassadors." In *History and Imagination: Essays in Honour of H.R. Trevor-Roper*. Edited by H. Lloyd-Jones, V. Pearl, and B. Worden. Oxford: Duckworth, 1981.

Gonzalez de Leon, Fernando. "The Road to Rocroi: The Duke of Alba, the Count Duke of Olivares and the High Command of the Spanish Army of Flanders in the Eighty Years' War, 1567–1659." Ph.D. diss., Johns Hopkins University, 1991.

Israel, Jonathan I. "A Conflict of Empires: Spain and the Netherlands, 1618–1648." *Past and Present* (August 1977): 34–74.

_____. "A Spanish Project to Defeat the Dutch without Fighting: The Rhine-Maas Canal, 1624–1629." In *Conflicts of Empires: Spain, the Low Countries and the Struggle for World Supremacy, 1585–1713*. London: Hambledon Press, 1997.

_____. "Art and Diplomacy: Gerard Ter Borch and the Münster Peace Negotiations, 1646–1648." In *Conflicts of Empires: Spain, the Low Countries and the Struggle for World Supremacy, 1585–1713*. London: Hambledon Press, 1997.

_____. "Garrisons and Empire: Spain's Strongholds in North-West Germany, 1589–1659." In *Conflicts of Empires: Spain, the Low Countries and the Struggle for World Supremacy, 1585–1713*. London: Hambledon Press, 1997.

_____. "Olivares, the Cardinal-Infante and Spain's Strategy in the Low Countries (1635–1643): The Road to Rocroi." In *Spain, Europe and the Atlantic World: Essays in Honour of John H. Elliott*. Edited by R.L. Kagan and Geoffrey Parker. Cambridge: Cambridge University Press, 1995; reprinted in *Conflicts of Empires: Spain, the Low Countries and the Struggle for World Supremacy, 1585–1713*. London: Hambledon Press, 1997.

_____. "The Court of Albert and Isabella, 1598–1621." In *Conflicts of Empires: Spain, the Low Countries and the Struggle for World Supremacy, 1585–1713*. London: Hambledon Press, 1997.

_____. *The Dutch Republic and the Hispanic World, 1606–1661*. Oxford: Clarendon Press, 1982.

_____. "The Politics of International Trade Rivalry during the Thirty Years' War: Gabriel de Roy and Olivares' Mercantilist Projects, 1621–1645." *The International History Review* 8 (November 1986): 517–49.

Parker, Geoffrey. "New Light on an Old Theme: Spain and the Netherlands, 1550–1650." *European History Quarterly* 15 (1985): 219–37.

_____. *The Army of Flanders and the Spanish Road, 1567–1659: The Logistics of Spanish Victory and Defeat in the Low Countries Wars*. Cambridge and New York: Cambridge University Press, 1972.

_____. "The Decision-Making Process in the Government of the Catholic Netherlands under 'the Archdukes', 1596–1621." In *Spain and The Netherlands, 1559–1659: Ten Studies*. London: Collins, 1979.

_____. "The Treaty of Lyon (1601) and the Spanish Road." In *Success is Never Final: Empire, War, and Faith in Early Modern Europe*. New York: Basic Books, 2002.

Parrott, David. "The Causes of the Franco-Spanish War of 1635–1659." In *The Origins of War in Early Modern Europe*. Edited by J. Black. Edinburgh: John Donald, 1987.

Phillips, Carla Rahn. *Six Galleons for the King of Spain: Imperial Defense in the Early Seventeenth Century*. Baltimore: Johns Hopkins University Press, 1986.

Polišenský, Josef V. *The Tragic Triangle: The Netherlands, Spain and Bohemia 1617–1621*. Prague: Charles University, 1991.

Reeve, L.J. "Quiroga's Paper of 1631: A Missing Link in Anglo-Spanish Diplomacy during the Thirty Years' War." *The English Historical Review* 101 (October 1986): 913–25.

Sanchez, Magdalena Sofie. "Dynasty, State and Diplomacy in the Spain of Philip III." Ph.D. diss., Johns Hopkins University, 1988.

Stradling, Robert A. "A Spanish Statesman of Appeasement: Medina de las Torres and Spanish Policy, 1639–1670." *Historical Journal* 19 (1976): 1–31; reprinted in *Spain's Struggle for Europe, 1598–1668*. London: Hambledon Press, 1994.

_____. "Catastrophe and Recovery: The Defeat of Spain, 1639–1643." *History* 64 (June 1979): 205–19; reprinted in *Spain's Struggle for Europe, 1598–1668*. London: Hambledon Press, 1994.

_____. "Filling the Ranks: Spanish Mercenary Recruitment and the Crisis of the 1640s." In *Spain's Struggle for Europe, 1598–1668*. London: Hambledon Press, 1994.

_____. "Olivares and the Origins of the Franco-Spanish War, 1627–1635." *The English Historical Review* 101 (1986): 68–94; reprinted in *Spain's Struggle for Europe, 1598–1668*. London: Hambledon Press, 1994.

_____. *Philip IV and the Government of Spain, 1621–1665*. Cambridge: Cambridge University Press, 1988.

_____. "Prelude to Disaster: The Precipitation of the War of the Mantuan Succession, 1627–1629." *Historical Journal* 33 (1990): 769–85; reprinted in *Spain's Struggle for Europe, 1598–1668*. London: Hambledon Press, 1994.

_____. "Spain's Military Failure and the Supply of Horses." *History* 69 (1984): 208–21; reprinted in *Spain's Struggle for Europe, 1598–1668*. London: Hambledon Press, 1994.

_____. *The Armada of Flanders: Spanish Maritime Policy and European War, 1568–1668*. Cambridge: Cambridge University Press, 1992.

_____. "The Spanish Dunkirkers, 1621–1648: A Record of Plunder and Destruction." *Tijdschrift voor Geschiedenis* 93 (1980): 541–58; reprinted in *Spain's Struggle for Europe, 1598–1668*. London: Hambledon Press, 1994.

_____. *The Spanish Monarchy and Irish Mercenaries: The Wild Geese in Spain, 1618–1668*. Dublin: Irish Academic Press, 1994.

_____. "'The Two Great Luminaries of our Planet': Spain and France in the Policy of Olivares." In *Spain's Struggle for Europe, 1598–1668*. London: Hambledon Press, 1994.

Thompson, I.A.A. *War and Government in Habsburg Spain, 1560–1620*. London: Athlone Press, 1976.

White, Arthur W., Jr. "Suspension of Arms: Anglo-Spanish Mediation in the Thirty Years' War, 1621–1625." Ph.D. diss., Tulane University, 1978.

Williams, Patrick. "Philip III and the Restoration of Spanish Government, 1598–1603." *The English Historical Review* 88 (1973): 751–69.

DUTCH REPUBLIC, 1609–1648

Den Tex, Jan. *Oldenbarnevelt*. 2 volumes. Cambridge: Cambridge University Press, 1973.

Geyl, Pieter. *Orange and Stuart, 1641–1672*. London: Weidenfeld and Nicolson, 1969.

_____. *The Netherlands in the Seventeenth Century*. 2 volumes. London: Ernest Benn, 1964.

Faber, Dirk E.A. and Renger E. de Bruin. "Utrecht's Opposition to the Münster Peace Process." In *1648—War and Peace in Europe*, Volume I. Edited by Klaus Bussmann and Heinz Schilling. Münster: Landschaftsverband Westfälen-Lippe, Westfälisches Landesmuseum für Kunst und Kulturgeschichte, 1999.

Glozier, Matthew. "Scots in the French and Dutch Armies during the Thirty Years' War." In *Scotland and the Thirty Years War, 1618–1648*. Edited by Steve Murdoch. Leiden: Brill, 2001.

Israel, Jonathan I. "A Conflict of Empires: Spain and the Netherlands, 1618–1648." *Past and Present* (August 1977): 34–74.

_____. "A Spanish Project to Defeat the Dutch without Fighting: The Rhine-Maas Canal, 1624–1629." In *Conflicts of Empires: Spain, the Low*

Countries and the Struggle for World Supremacy, 1585–1713. London: Hambledon Press, 1997.

_____. "Art and Diplomacy: Gerard Ter Borch and the Münster Peace Negotiations, 1646–1648." In *Conflicts of Empires: Spain, the Low Countries and the Struggle for World Supremacy, 1585–1713.* London: Hambledon Press, 1997.

_____. "Garrisons and Empire: Spain's Strongholds in North-West Germany, 1589–1659." In *Conflicts of Empires: Spain, the Low Countries and the Struggle for World Supremacy, 1585–1713.* London: Hambledon Press, 1997.

_____. *The Dutch Republic and the Hispanic World, 1606–1661.* Oxford: Clarendon Press, 1982.

Limm, Peter. *The Dutch Revolt, 1559–1648.* London: Longman, 1989.

Parker, Geoffrey. "New Light on an Old Theme: Spain and the Netherlands, 1550–1650." *European History Quarterly* 15 (1985): 219–37.

_____. *The Army of Flanders and the Spanish Road, 1567–1659: The Logistics of Spanish Victory and Defeat in the Low Countries Wars.* Cambridge and New York: Cambridge University Press, 1972.

Polišenský, Josef V. *The Tragic Triangle: The Netherlands, Spain and Bohemia 1617–1621.* Prague: Charles University, 1991.

Rady, Martyn. *From Revolt to Independence: The Netherlands, 1550–1650.* London: Hodder and Stoughton, 1999.

Vogel, H.Ph. "Arms Production and Exports in the Dutch Republic, 1600–1650." In *Exercise of Arms: Warfare in the Netherlands, 1568–1648.* Edited by Marco van der Hoeven. Leiden: Brill, 1997.

Zwitzer, H.L. "The Eighty Years' War." In *Exercise of Arms: Warfare in the Netherlands, 1568–1648.* Edited by Marco van der Hoeven. Leiden: Brill, 1997.

AUSTRIAN HABSBURGS AND GERMANY, 1609–1648

Asch, Ronald G. *The Thirty Years' War: The Holy Roman Empire and Europe, 1618–1648*. New York: St. Martin's Press, 1997.

Barker, Thomas M. *The Military Intellectual and Battle: Raimondo Montecuccoli and the Thirty Years' War*. Albany: State University of New York Press, 1975.

Benecke, Gerhard. *Germany in the Thirty Years' War*. London: Edward Arnold, 1978.

Bireley, Robert. *Religion and Politics in the Age of the Counter-Reformation: Emperor Ferdinand II, William Lamormaini, S.J., and the Formation of Imperial Policy*. Chapel Hill: University of North Carolina Press, 1981.

――――――. "The Peace of Prague (1635) and the Counterreformation in Germany." *The Journal of Modern History* 48 On Demand Supplement (March 1976): 31–70.

――――――. "The Thirty Years' War as Germany's Religious War." In *Krieg und Politik, 1618–1648: Europäische Probleme und Perspektiven*. Edited by Konrad Repgen. Munich: R. Oldenburg, 1988.

Chudoba, Bohdan. *Spain and the Empire, 1519–1643*. Chicago: University of Chicago Press, 1952; reprint, New York: Octagon, 1969.

Mann, Golo. *Wallenstein: His Life Narrated*. New York: Holt, Rinehart and Winston, 1971.

Mears, John A. "The Thirty Years' War, the 'General Crisis', and the Origins of a Standing Professional Army in the Habsburg Monarchy." *Central European History* 21 (1988): 122–41.

Polišenský, Josef V. "A Note on Scottish Soldiers in the Bohemian War 1619–1622." In *Scotland and the Thirty Years War, 1618–1648*. Edited by Steve Murdoch. Leiden: Brill, 2001.

_____. "Gallants to Bohemia." *Slavonic and East European Review* 25 (1946–47): 391–404.

_____. *The Thirty Years' War*. London: B.T. Batsford, 1971.

_____. *The Tragic Triangle: The Netherlands, Spain and Bohemia 1617–1621*. Prague: Charles University, 1991.

Pursell, Brennan Conrad. "The Constitutional Causes of the Thirty Years' War: Friedrich V, the Palatine Crisis, and European Politics, 1618–1632." Ph.D. diss., Harvard University, 2000.

Setton, Kenneth M. *Venice, Austria, and the Turks in the Seventeenth Century*. Philadelphia: American Philosophical Society, 1991.

Watson, Francis. *Wallenstein: Soldier under Saturn*. London: Chatto and Windus, 1938.

Wedgwood, Cicely Veronica. *The Thirty Years' War*. London: Jonathan Cape, 1938.

SWEDEN, DENMARK, POLAND, AND RUSSIA, 1600–1648

Ahnlund, Nils. *Gustavus Adolphus the Great*. New York: History Book Club, 1940.

Czaplinski, Władisław. "Polish-Danish Diplomatic Relations, 1598–1648." *Poland at the 11th International Congress of the Historical Sciences in Stockholm*. Warsaw: Panstwowe Wydawn ictwo Naukowe, 1960.

Dukes, Paul. "New Perspectives: Alexander Leslie and the Smolensk War, 1632–1634." In *Scotland and the Thirty Years War, 1618–1648*. Edited by Steve Murdoch. Leiden: Brill, 2001.

Dunning, Chester. *Russia's First Civil War: The Time of Troubles and the Founding of the Romanov Dynasty*. University Park: Pennsylvania State University Press, 2001.

Dupuy, Trevor N. *The Military Life of Gustavus Adolphus: Father of Modern War.* New York: Franklin Watts, 1969.

Fallon, J.A. "Scottish Mercenaries in the Service of Denmark and Sweden, 1626–1632." Ph.D. diss., University of Glasgow, 1972.

Frost, Robert I. "Poland-Lithuania and the Thirty Years' War." In *War and Peace in Europe, 1618–1648, Volume I: Politics, Religion, Law and Society.* Edited by K. Bussman and H. Schilling. Münster: Westfälisches Landes Museum, 1998.

_____. "Scottish Soldiers, Poland-Lithuania and the Thirty Years' War." In *Scotland and the Thirty Years War, 1618–1648.* Edited by Steve Murdoch. Leiden: Brill, 2001.

Gajecky, George and O. Baran. *The Cossacks in the Thirty Years' War.* 2 volumes. Rome: P.P. Basiliani, 1969–83.

Grosjean, Alexia. "Scotland: Sweden's Closest Ally?" In *Scotland and the Thirty Years War, 1618–1648.* Edited by Steve Murdoch. Leiden: Brill, 2001.

_____. "Scots and the Swedish State: Diplomacy, Military Service and Ennoblement, 1611–1660." Ph.D. thesis, University of Aberdeen, 1998.

Lockhart, Paul Douglas. "Denmark and the Empire: A Reassessment of Danish Foreign Policy under King Christian IV." *Scandinavian Studies* 64 (1992): 390–416.

_____. *Denmark in the Thirty Years' War, 1618–1648: King Christian IV and the Decline of the Oldenburg State.* Selinsgrove: Susquehanna University Press, 1996.

_____. "Religion and Princely Liberties: Denmark's Intervention in the Thirty Years' War, 1618–1625." *The International History Review* 17 (February 1995): 1–22.

Murdoch, Steve. "Scotland, Denmark-Norway and the House of Stuart, 1603–1660: A Diplomatic and Military Analysis." Ph.D. thesis, University of Aberdeen, 1998.

Polišenský, Josef V. "Denmark-Norway and the Bohemian Cause in the Early Part of the Thirty Year' War." In *Festgabe für L.L. Hammerich: Aus Anlasss Seines Siebzigsten Geburtstags*. Edited by L. Hammerich. Copenhagen: Naturmetodens Sproginstitut, 1962.

Porshnev, B.F. *Muscovy and Sweden in the Thirty Years' War, 1630–1635*. Edited by Paul Dukes. Cambridge: Cambridge University Press, 1995.

Ringmar, E. *Identity, Interest and Action: A Cultural Explanation of Sweden's Intervention in the Thirty Years' War*. Cambridge: Cambridge University Press, 1996.

Roberts, Michael. *Gustavus Adolphus: A History of Sweden, 1611–1632*. 2 volumes. London: Longmans, Green and Company, 1953–58.

_____. *Gustavus Adolphus and the Rise of Sweden*. London: The English Universities Press, 1973.

_____. "Oxenstierna in Germany, 1633–1636." In *From Oxenstierna to Charles XII: Four Studies*. Cambridge: Cambridge University Press, 1991.

_____. "The Political Objectives of Gustavus Adolphus in Germany, 1630–1632." *Transactions of the Royal Historical Society*, Fifth series, 7 (1957): 19–46; reprinted in *Essays in Swedish History*. Minneapolis: University of Minnesota Press, 1967.

RICHELIEU, MAZARIN, AND FRANCE, 1610–1648

Baxter, Douglas Clark. *Servants of the Sword: French Intendants of the Army, 1630–1670*. Urbana: University of Illinois Press, 1976.

Bergin, J.A. and L.W.B. Brockliss, editors. *Richelieu and His Age*. Oxford: Oxford University Press, 1992

Bonney, Richard. *Political Change in France under Richelieu and Mazarin, 1624–1661*. Oxford: Oxford University Press, 1978.

_____. "The Paradox of Mazarin." *History Today* 32 (February 1982): 18–24.

Burckhardt, Carl J. *Richelieu and His Age.* 3 volumes. London: George Allen and Unwin, 1940–71.

Church, William F. *Richelieu and Reason of State.* Princeton: Princeton University Press, 1972.

Clarke, Jack A. *Huguenot Warrior: The Life and Times of Henri de Rohan, 1579–1638.* The Hague: Martinus Nijhoff, 1966.

Croxton, Derek. "Peacemaking in Early Modern Europe: Cardinal Mazarin and the Congress of Westphalia, 1643–1648." Ph.D. thesis, University of Illinois, 1996.

_____. *Peacemaking in Early Modern Europe: Cardinal Mazarin and the Congress of Westphalia, 1643–1648.* Selinsgrove: Susquehanna University Press, 1999.

Dethan, Georges. *The Young Mazarin.* London: Thames and Hudson, 1977.

Glozier, Matthew. "Scots in the French and Dutch Armies during the Thirty Years' War." In *Scotland and the Thirty Years War, 1618–1648.* Edited by Steve Murdoch. Leiden: Brill, 2001.

Godley, Eveline. *The Great Condé: A Life of Louis II de Bourbon, Prince of Condé.* London: John Murray, 1915.

Hassall, Arthur. *Mazarin.* London: Macmillan, 1903.

Hayden, J. Michael. "Continuity in the France of Henry IV and Louis XIII: French Foreign Policy, 1598–1615." *The Journal of Modern History* 45 (March 1973): 1–23.

Kleinman, Ruth. *Anne of Austria, Queen of France.* Columbus: Ohio State University Press, 1985.

Knecht, Robert J. *Richelieu.* London: Longman, 1991.

Lodge, Richard. *Richelieu.* London: Macmillan, 1896.

Moote, A. Lloyd. *Louis XIII: The Just*. Berkeley: University of California Press, 1989.

Osborne, Toby. "*Chimères, monopoles* and *stratagèmes*: French Exiles in the Spanish Netherlands during the Thirty Years' War." *The Seventeenth Century* 15 (2000): 149–74.

Pagès, Georges. *The Thirty Years' War, 1618–1648*. London: Adam and Charles Black, 1970.

Parker, David. *The Making of French Absolutism*. London: Edward Arnold, 1983.

Parrott, David. "French Military Organization in the 1630s: The Failure of Richelieu's Ministry." *Seventeenth-Century French Studies* 9 (1987): 151–67.

_____. "Richelieu, the *Grands*, and the Army." In *Richelieu and His Age*. Edited by Joseph Bergin and Laurence Brockliss. Oxford: Clarendon Press, 1992.

_____. *Richelieu's Army: War, Government and Society in France, 1624–1642*. Cambridge: Cambridge University Press, 2001.

_____. "Strategy and Tactics in the Thirty Years' War: The Military Revolution." *Militärgeschichtliche Mitteilungen* 38 (1985): 7–25.

_____. "The Administration of the French Army during the Ministry of Cardinal Richelieu." Ph.D. diss., Oxford University, 1985.

_____. "The Causes of the Franco-Spanish War of 1635–1659." In *The Origins of War in Early Modern Europe*. Edited by J. Black. Edinburgh: John Donald, 1987.

_____. "The Mantuan Succession, 1627–1631: A Sovereignty Dispute in Early Modern Europe." *The English Historical Review* 112 (1997): 20–65.

Ranum, Orest. *Richelieu and the Councillors of Louis XIII*. Oxford: Clarendon Press, 1983.

Tapié, Victor-L. *France in the Age of Louis XIII and Richelieu*. New York: Praeger, 1974.

Treasure, Geoffrey. *Cardinal Richelieu and the Development of Absolutism*. New York: St. Martin's Press, 1972.

_____. *Mazarin: The Crisis of Absolutism in France*. London: Routledge, 1995.

_____. *Richelieu and Mazarin*. London: Routledge, 1998.

Weber, Hermann. "'*Une Bonne Paix*': Richelieu's Foreign Policy and the Peace of Christendom." In *Richelieu and His Age*. Edited by Joseph. Bergin and Laurence Brockliss. Oxford: Oxford University Press, 1992.

Wedgwood, Cicely Veronica. *Richelieu and the French Monarchy*. London: English Universities Press, 1949.

Weyland, Max. *Turenne: Marshal of France*. London: George G. Harrap, 1930.

Wilkinson, Richard. *France and the Cardinals, 1610–1661*. London: Hodder and Stoughton, 1995.

Woodley, Jocelyn. "The Development of the French Diplomatic System under Richelieu, 1624–1642." M.Phil. thesis, Cambridge University, 1989.

EARLY STUARTS AND THE ENGLISH CIVIL WAR, 1603–1652

Adair, John. *Cheriton, 1644: The Campaign and the Battle*. Kineton: Roundwood Press, 1973.

_____. *Roundhead General: A Military Biography of Sir William Waller*. London: MacDonald, 1969.

Adams, Simon. "Foreign Policy and the Parliaments of 1621 and 1624." In *Faction and Parliament*. Edited by Keith M. Sharpe. Oxford: Oxford University Press, 1978.

_____. "Spain or the Netherlands?: The Dilemmas of Early Stuart Foreign Policy." In *Before the English Civil War*. Edited by H. Tomlinson. London: Macmillan, 1983.

_____. "The Road to La Rochelle: English Foreign Policy and the Hugue-nots, 1610–1629." *Proceedings of the Huguenot Society of London* 22 (1975): 414–29.

Albion, Gordon. *Charles I and the Court of Rome: A Study in Seventeenth-Century Diplomacy.* London: Burns, Oates, and Washbourne, 1935.

Andrews, Kenneth R. "Caribbean Rivalry and the Anglo-Spanish Peace of 1604." *History* 59 (1974): 1–17.

_____. *Ships, Money, and Politics: Seafaring and Naval Enterprise in the Reign of Charles I.* Cambridge: Cambridge University Press, 1991.

Ashley, Maurice. *Cromwell's Generals.* London: Jonathan Cape, 1954.

_____. *Rupert of the Rhine.* London: Granada, 1976.

_____. *The Battle of Naseby and the Fall of King Charles I.* Gloucester: Alan Sutton, 1992.

_____. *The English Civil War: A Concise History.* London: Thames and Hudson, 1974.

_____. *The Greatness of Oliver Cromwell.* London: Hodder and Stoughton, 1957.

Asquith, Stuart. *New Model Army 1645–1660.* London: Osprey, 1992.

Barratt, John. *Cavaliers: The Royalist Army at War, 1642–1646.* Stroud: Sutton, 2000.

Baumber, Michael. "The Navy and the Civil War in Ireland, 1643–1646." *Mariner's Mirror* 75 (1989): 265–69.

Beller, E.A. "The Military Expedition of Sir Charles Morgan to Germany, 1627–1629." *The English Historical Review* 43 (1928): 528–39.

_____. "The Mission of Sir Thomas Roe to the Conference at Hamburg, 1638–1640." *The English Historical Review* 41 (1926): 61–77.

_____. "The Negotiations of Sir Stephen Le Sieur." *The English Historical Review* 40 (1925): 22–33.

Bennett, Martyn. *The English Civil War, 1640–1649.* London: Longman, 1995.

_____. *The Civil Wars in Britain and Ireland, 1638–1651.* Oxford: Blackwell, 1997.

Bigby, Dorothy A. *Anglo-French Relations 1641 to 1649.* London: University of London Press, 1933.

Brown, M.J. *Itinerant Ambassador: The Life of Sir Thomas Roe.* Lexington: University Press of Kentucky, 1970.

Burke, J. "The New Model Army and the Problem of Siege Warfare." *Irish Historical Review* 27 (May 1990): 1–29.

Burne, Alfred and Peter Young. *The Great Civil War: A Military History of the First Civil War, 1642–1646.* London: Eyre, 1959.

Cant, Reginald. "The Embassy of the Earl of Leicester to Denmark in 1632." *The English Historical Review* 54 (1939): 252–62.

Carlton, C. *Going to the Wars: The Experience of the British Civil Wars, 1638–1651.* London: Routledge, 1992.

Carter, Charles H. "Gondomar: Ambassador to James I." *Historical Journal* 7 (1964): 189–208.

Cogswell, Thomas. "England and the Spanish Match." In *Conflict in Early Stuart England: Studies in Religion and Politics, 1603–1642.* Edited by Richard Cust and Ann Hughes. London: Longman, 1989.

_____. "Foreign Policy and Parliament: The Case of La Rochelle, 1625–1626." *The English Historical Review* 99 (1984): 241–67.

_____. "Prelude to Ré: The Anglo-French Struggle over La Rochelle, 1624–1627." *History* 71 (February 1986): 1–21.

_____. *The Blessed Revolution: English Politics and the Coming of War, 1621–1624.* Cambridge and New York: Cambridge University Press, 1989.

Coward, Barry. *Oliver Cromwell.* London: Addison, Wesley, Longman, 1991.

Dunthorne, Hugh. "Scots in the Wars of the Low Countries, 1572–1648." In *Scotland and the Low Countries, 1124–1994*. Edited by Grant G. Simpson. East Linton: Tuckwell Press, 1996.

Durston, Christopher. *Charles I*. London: Routledge, 1998.

_____. *James I*. London: Routledge, 1993.

Firth, Charles. *Cromwell's Army: A History of the English Soldier during the Civil Wars, the Commonwealth, and the Protectorate*. Third edition, London: Methuen, 1921; reprint, London: Greenhill Books, 1992.

Fissel, Mark C. *English Warfare, 1511–1642*. London: Routledge, 2001.

_____. *The Bishops' Wars: Charles I's Campaigns against Scotland, 1638–1640*. Cambridge: Cambridge University Press, 1994.

Fraser, Antonia. *Cromwell: The Lord Protector*. New York: Alfred A. Knopf, 1973.

Gardiner, Samuel Rawson. *History of the Great Civil War, 1642–1649*. 4 volumes. London: Longmans, 1898–1901; reprint, London: Windrush Press, 1987.

Gaunt, Peter. *Oliver Cromwell*. Oxford: Basil Blackwell, 1996.

_____. *The British Wars, 1637–1651*. London: Routledge, 1997.

_____. *The English Civil Wars 1642–1651*. Botley: Osprey, 2003.

Gentles, Ian. "The Choosing of Officers for the New Model Army." *Bulletin of the Institute of Historical Research* 67 (1994): 264–85.

_____. *The New Model Army in England, Ireland, and Scotland, 1645–1653*. Oxford: Basil Blackwell, 1992.

Gillingham, John. *Cromwell: Portrait of a Soldier*. London: Weidenfeld and Nicolson, 1976.

Gregg, Pauline. *King Charles I*. Berkeley: University of California Press, 1981.

Grosjean, Alexia. "Scots and the Swedish State: Diplomacy, Military Service and Ennoblement, 1611–1660." Ph.D. thesis, University of Aberdeen, 1998.

Harrington, Peter. *English Civil War Fortifications 1642–1651*. Botley: Osprey, 2003.

_____. "English Civil War Fortifications." *Fort: The International Journal of Fortification and Military Architecture* 15 (1987): 39–60.

Haythornthwaite, Philip J. *English Civil War, 1642–1651: An Illustrated Military History*. Poole: Blandford, 1983.

Henneke, Christian E. "The Art of Diplomacy under the Early Stuarts, 1603–1642." Ph.D. diss., University of Virginia, 1999.

Hirst, Derek. *Authority and Conflict: England, 1603–1658*. Cambridge, Mass.: Harvard University Press, 1986.

Holmes, Clive. *The Eastern Association in the English Civil War*. Cambridge: Cambridge University Press, 1974.

Hutton, Ronald. *The Royalist War Effort, 1642–1646*. London: Longman, 1982.

Kenyon, John. *The Civil Wars of England*. New York: Alfred A. Knopf, 1988.

_____ and J. Ohlmeyer, editors. *The Civil Wars: A Military History of England, Scotland, and Ireland, 1638–1660*. Oxford: Oxford University Press, 1998.

Kishlansky, Mark A. *The Rise of the New Model Army*. Cambridge: Cambridge University Press, 1979.

Knachel, Philip A. *England and the Fronde: The Impact of the English Civil War and Revolution on France*. Ithaca: Cornell University Press, 1967.

Lake, Peter. "Constitutional Consensus and Puritan Opposition in the 1620s: Thomas Scott and the Spanish Match." *Historical Journal* 25 (1982): 805–25.

Lee, Maurice. *James I and Henri IV: An Essay in English Foreign Policy, 1603–1610*. Urbana: University of Illinois Press, 1970.

Lenman, Bruce. *England's Colonial Wars, 1550–1668*. London: Longman, 2000.

Lockyer, Roger. *Buckingham: The Life and Political Career of George Villiers, First Duke of Buckingham, 1592–1628*. London: Longman, 1981.

——————. *James VI and I*. London: Addison, Wesley, and Longman, 1998.

——————. *The Early Stuarts: A Political History of England, 1603–1642*. Second edition. London: Addison, Wesley, and Longman, 1999.

Loomie, Albert J. *Toleration and Diplomacy: The Religious Issue in Anglo-Spanish Relations, 1603–1605*. Philadelphia: American Philosophical Society, 1963.

Mackie, J. Duncan. "James VI and I and the Peace with Spain, 1604." *Scottish Historical Review* 23 (1926): 241–49.

McCabe, A. "England's Foreign Policy in 1619." *Mitteilungen des Instituts für Österreichische Geschichte* 58 (1950): 457–77.

Mowat, Robert B. "The Mission of Sir Thomas Roe to Vienna, 1641–1642." *The English Historical Review* 25 (1910): 264–75.

Murdoch, Steve. "Diplomacy in Transition: Stuart-British Diplomacy in Northern Europe, 1618–1648." In *Ships, Guns and Bibles in the North Sea and Baltic States, c. 1350-c. 1770*. Edited by A.I. Macinnes, T. Riis, and F. Pedersen. East Linton: Tuckwell Press, 2000.

——————. "Scotland, Denmark-Norway and the House of Stuart, 1603–1660: A Diplomatic and Military Analysis." Ph.D. thesis, University of Aberdeen, 1998.

——————. "Scottish Ambassadors and British Diplomacy, 1618–1648." In *Scotland and the Thirty Years' War, 1618–1648*. Edited by Steve Murdoch. Leiden: Brill, 2001.

——————. "The House of Stuart and the Scottish Professional Soldier 1613–1640: A Conflict of Nationality and Identities." In *War: Identities in Conflct 1300–2000*. Edited by Bertrand Taithe and Tim Thornton. Stroud: Sutton, 1998.

_____, editor. *Britain, Denmark-Norway, and the House of Stuart, 1603–1660: A Diplomatic and Military Analysis.* East Linton: Tuckwell Press, 2000.

_____, editor. *Scotland and the Thirty Years' War, 1618–1648.* Leiden: Brill, 2001.

Newman, P.R. *The Battle of Marston Moor.* Chichester: Anthony Bird, 1981.

Ohlmeyer, Jane H. "Ireland Independent: Confederate Foreign Policy and International Relations during the mid-Seventeenth Century." In *Ireland from Independence to Occupation 1641–1660.* Edited by J.H. Olhmeyer. Cambridge: Cambridge University Press, 1984.

Osborne, Toby. "Abbot Scaglia, the Duke of Buckingham and Anglo-Savoyard Relations during the 1620s." *European History Quarterly* 30 (2000): 5–32.

Quintrell, Brian. *Charles I, 1625–1640.* London: Longman, 1993.

_____. "Charles I and his Navy in the 1630s." *The Seventeenth Century* 3 (1988): 159–79.

Reeve, L.J. *Charles I and the Road to Personal Rule.* Cambridge and New York: Cambridge University Press, 1989.

Reid, Stuart. *Auldearn 1645: The Marquis of Montrose's Scottish Campaign.* Botley: Osprey, 2003.

_____. *Scots Armies of the English Civil Wars.* Botley: Osprey, 1999.

Roy, Ian. "The Royalist Army in the First Civil War." Ph.D. diss., Oxford University, 1963.

_____. "The Royalist Council of War, 1642–1646." *Bulletin of Historical Research* 35 (1962): 150–68.

Ruigh, Robert. *The Parliament of 1624: Politics and Foreign Policy.* Cambridge, Mass.: Harvard University Press, 1971.

Russell, Conrad. *The Fall of the British Monarchies, 1637–1642.* Oxford: Clarendon Press, 1991.

Sharpe, Kevin. *The Personal Rule of Charles I.* New Haven: Yale University Press, 1992.

Springell, Francis C. and William Crowne, editors. *Connoisseur and Diplomat: The Earl of Arundel's Embassy to Germany in 1636 as Recounted in William Crowne's Diary.* London: Maggs Brothers, 1963.

Stearn, Stephen. "The Caroline Military System: The Expedition to Cadiz and Rhé, 1625–1627." Ph.D. diss., University of California, 1967.

Tincey, John. *Edgehill 1642: The First Battle of the English Civil War.* Botley: Osprey, 2001.

_____. *Soldiers of the English Civil War.* 2 volumes. London: Osprey, 1989–90.

_____ and Graham Turner. *Marston Moor 1644: The Beginning of the End.* Botley: Osprey, 2003.

Turner, Graham. *First Newbury 1643.* Botley: Osprey, 2003.

Wedgwood, Cicely Veronica. *Oliver Cromwell.* London: Duckworth, 1939.

_____. *The Great Rebellion: The King's Peace, 1637–1641.* London: Collins, 1955.

_____. *The Great Rebellion: The King's War, 1641–1647.* London: Collins, 1958.

Wheeler, James Scott. "Logistics of the Cromwellian Conquest of Scotland, 1650–1651." *War and Society* 10 (1992): 1–18.

_____. *The Irish and British Wars, 1637–1654: Triumph, Tragedy, and Failure.* London and New York: Routledge, 2002.

White, Arthur W., Jr. "Suspension of Arms: Anglo-Spanish Mediation in the Thirty Years' War, 1621–1625." Ph.D. diss., Tulane University, 1978.

Woolrych, Austin. *Battles of the English Civil War: Marston Moor, Naseby, Preston.* London: B.T. Batsford, 1961.

Worthington, David. "Alternative Diplomacy? Scottish Exiles at the Courts of the Habsburgs and their Allies, 1618–1648." In *Scotland and the Thirty Years' War, 1618–1648*. Edited by Steve Murdoch. Leiden: Brill, 2001.

Young, John R. "The Scottish Parliament and European Diplomacy, 1641–1647: The Palatine, the Dutch Republic, and Sweden." In *Scotland and the Thirty Years' War, 1618–1648*. Edited by Steve Murdoch. Leiden: Brill, 2001.

Young, Peter. *Edgehill, 1642: The Campaign and the Battle*. Kineton: Round-wood Press, 1967.

_____. *Marston Moor, 1644: The Campaign and the Battle*. Kineton: Roundwood Press, 1970.

_____. *Naseby, 1645: The Campaign and the Battle*. London: Century, 1985.

_____. *The English Civil War Armies*. London: Osprey, 1992.

_____ and Alfred H. Burne. *The Great Civil War*. London: Eyre and Spot-tiswoode, 1959.

_____ and Wilfrid Emberton. *Sieges of the Great Civil War, 1642–1646*. London: Bell and Hyman, 1978.

_____ and Richard Holmes. *The English Civil War: A Military History of the Three Civil Wars, 1642–1651*. London: Eyre Methuen, 1974.

_____ and Margaret Toynbee. *Cropredy Bridge, 1644*. Kineton: Round-wood Press, 1970.

_____ and Norman Tucker, editors. *The Civil War: Military Memoirs of Richard Atkyns and John Gwyn*. London: Longmans, Green and Company, 1967.

Zaller, R. "James I and the Palatinate." *Albion* 6 (1974): 144–75.

PART XII
EUROPE AND THE WARS OF
LOUIS XIV,
1648–1715

EUROPE, 1648–1715

André, Louis. "Louis XIV and Foreign Affairs." In *Louis XIV: A Profile*. Edited by J.B. Wolf. New York: Hill and Wang, 1972.

Ashley, Maurice. *Louis XIV and the Greatness of France*. London: English Universities Press, 1946.

Baxter, Stephen B. *William III and the Defense of European Liberty, 1650–1702*. New York: Harcourt, Brace and World, 1966; published in the United Kingdom as *William III*. London: Longmans, Green and Company, 1966.

Black, Jeremy. "Louis XIV's Foreign Policy Reassessed." *Seventeenth-Century French Studies* 10 (1988): 199–212.

Bluche, François. *Louis XIV*. New York: Franklin Watts, 1990.

Bromley, John S., editor. *The Rise of Great Britain and Russia, 1688–1715/1725*. Volume VI in *The New Cambridge Modern History*. Cambridge: Cambridge University Press, 1970.

Burke, Peter. *The Fabrication of Louis XIV*. New Haven: Yale University Press, 1992.

Campbell, Peter R. *Louis XIV*. London: Longman, 1993.

Carsten, F.L., editor. *The Ascendancy of France, 1648–1688*. Volume V in *The New Cambridge Modern History*. Cambridge: Cambridge University Press, 1961.

Claydon, Tony. *William III*. London and New York: Longman, 2002.

Franken, M.A.M. "The General Tendencies and Structural Aspects of the Foreign Policy and Diplomacy of the Dutch Republic in the Latter Half of the Seventeenth Century." *Acta Historiae Neerlandica* 3 (1968): 1–42.

Geyl, Pieter. *Orange and Stuart, 1641–1672*. London: Weidenfeld and Nicolson, 1969.

_____. *The Netherlands in the Seventeenth Century*. 2 volumes. London: Ernest Benn, 1963–64.

Goubert, Pierre, *Louis XIV and Twenty Million Frenchmen*. London: Allen Lane, 1970.

Hatton, Ragnild M. *Europe in the Age of Louis XIV*. London: Thames and Hudson, 1969.

_____, editor. *Louis XIV and Absolutism*. London: Macmillan, 1976.

_____, editor. *Louis XIV and Europe*. London: Macmillan, 1976.

_____. "Louis XIV and His Fellow Monarchs." In *Louis XIV and the Craft of Kingship*. Edited by J.C. Rule. Columbus: Ohio State University Press,1969; reprinted in *Louis XIV and Europe*. Edited by R.M. Hatton. London: Macmillan, 1976.

_____. *Louis XIV and His World*. London: Thames and Hudson, 1972.

_____. "Louis XIV: Recent Gains in Historical Knowledge." *The Journal of Modern History* 45 (1973): 277–91.

_____ and J.S. Bromley. *William III and Louis XIV: Essays 1680–1720 by and for Mark A. Thomson*. Liverpool: Liverpool University Press, 1967.

Hochedlinger, Michael. *Austria's Wars of Emergence, 1683–1797*. London: Longman, 2003.

Israel, Jonathan I. *The Dutch Republic and the Hispanic World, 1606–1661.* Oxford: Clarendon Press, 1982.

Jones, George H. *The Mainstream of Jacobitism.* Cambridge, Mass.: Harvard University Press, 1954.

Jones, James R. *Court and Country: England, 1658–1714.* London: Edward Arnold, 1978.

Klaits, Joseph. *Printed Propaganda under Louis XIV: Absolute Monarchy and Public Opinion.* Princeton: Princeton University Press, 1976.

Lenman, Bruce. *Britain's Colonial Wars, 1688–1783.* London: Pearson Education, 2001.

_____. *England's Colonial Wars, 1550–1668.* London: Longman, 2000.

_____. *The Jacobite Risings in Britain, 1689–1746.* London: Eyre Methuen, 1980.

Lossky, Andrew. "France in the System of Europe in the Seventeenth Century." *Proceedings of the Annual Meeting of the Western Society for French History* 1 (1974): 32–48.

_____. "International Relations in Europe." In *The New Cambridge Modern History*, Volume VI. Edited by J.S. Bromley. Cambridge: Cambridge University Press, 1970.

_____. *Louis XIV and the French Monarchy.* New Brunswick: Rutgers University Press, 1994.

Lottin, A. "Louis XIV and Flanders." In *Conquest and Coalescence: The Shaping of the State in Early Modern Europe.* Edited by Mark Greengrass. London: Edward Arnold, 1991.

Lynn, John A. "A Quest for Glory: The Formation of Strategy under Louis XIV, 1661–1715." In *The Making of Strategy: Rulers, States, and War.* Edited by Williamson Murray, MacGregor Knox, and Alvin Bernstein. Cambridge: Cambridge University Press, 1994.

_____. *The French Wars, 1667–1714: The Sun King at War*. Botley: Osprey, 2002.

_____. *The Wars of Louis XIV, 1667–1714*. London: Addison, Wesley, Longman, 1999.

_____. "Vauban." *MHQ: The Quarterly Journal of Military History* 1 (1989): 51–61.

Maurice, C. Edmund. *Life of Frederick William: The Great Elector of Brandenburg*. London: George Allen and Unwin, 1926; reprint, Westport: Greenwood Press, 1981.

McKay, Derek. *The Great Elector*. Harlow: Pearson, 2001.

Mettam, Roger. *Power and Faction in Louis XIV's France*. Oxford: Basil Blackwell, 1988.

Nathan, James. "Force, Order and Diplomacy in the Age of Louis XIV." *The Virginia Quarterly Review* 69 (Autumn 1993): 633–49.

Nussbaum, Frederick L. *The Triumph of Science and Reason, 1660–1685*. New York: Harper and Brothers, 1953.

O'Connor, John T. "The Diplomatic History of the Reign." In *The Reign of Louis XIV*. Edited by P. Sonnino. Atlantic Highlands: Humanities Press International, 1990.

Ogg, David. *Louis XIV*. London: Home University Press, 1933.

Oresko, Robert. "The House of Savoy in Search for a Royal Crown in the Seventeenth Century." In *Royal and Republican Sovereignty in Early Modern Europe: Essays in Memory of Ragnhild Hatton*. Edited by R. Oresko, G.C. Gibbs, and H.M. Scott. Cambridge: Cambridge University Press, 1997.

P|rvev, Ivan. *Habsburgs and Ottomans between Vienna and Belgrade (1683–1739)*. New York: Columbia University Press, 1995.

Roider, Karl. "Origins of Wars in the Balkans, 1660–1792." In *The Origins of Wars in Early Modern Europe*. Edited by J. Black. Edinburgh: John Donald, 1987.

Rule, John C. *Louis XIV and the Craft of Kingship*. Columbus: Ohio State University Press, 1969.

Schevill, Ferdinand. *The Great Elector*. Chicago: University of Chicago Press, 1947.

Setton, Kenneth M. *Venice, Austria, and the Turks in the Seventeenth Century*. Philadelphia: American Philosophical Society, 1991.

Shennan, J.H. *Louis XIV*. London: Routledge, 1986.

Sonnino, Paul. "The Origins of Louis XIV's Wars." In *The Origins of War in Early Modern Europe*. Edited by J. Black. Edinburgh: John Donald, 1987.

_____, editor. *The Reign of Louis XIV*. Atlantic Highlands: Humanities Press International, 1990.

Spielman, John P. *Leopold I of Austria*. London: Thames and Hudson, 1976.

Storrs, Christopher. *War, Diplomacy and the Rise of Savoy, 1690–1720*. Cambridge: Cambridge University Press, 1999.

Stoye, John W. *Europe Unfolding, 1648–1688*. New York: Harper and Row, 1969.

Sturdy, David J. *Louis XIV*. New York: St. Martin's Press, 1998.

Symcox, Geoffrey W. *Victor Amadeus II of Savoy: Absolutism in the Savoyard State, 1675–1730*. London: Thames and Hudson, 1983.

Tapié, Victor-L. "Louis XIV's Methods in Foreign Policy." In *Louis XIV and Europe*. London: Macmillan 1976.

Thomson, Mark A. "Parliament and Foreign Policy, 1689–1714." 38 *History* (1953): 234–43; reprinted in *William III and Louis XIV: Essays 1680–1720 by and for Mark A. Thomson*. Edited by R.M. Hatton and J.S. Bromley. Liverpool: Liverpool University Press, 1968.

Treasure, Geoffrey. *Louis XIV*. London: Longman, 2001.

Wilkinson, Richard. *Louis XIV, France and Europe, 1661–1715*. London: Hodder and Stoughton, 1993.

Wines, Roger. "The Imperial Circles, Princely Diplomacy and Imperial Reform, 1681–1714." *The Journal of Modern History* 39 (March 1967): 1–29.

Wolf, John B. *Louis XIV*. New York: W.W. Norton and Company, 1968.

_____. "Louis XIV, Soldier-King." In *Louis XIV and the Craft of Kingship*. Edited by J.C. Rule. Columbus: Ohio State University Press, 1969.

_____. *The Emergence of the Great Powers, 1685–1715*. New York: Harper and Brothers, 1951.

_____. "The Reign of Louis XIV: A Selected Bibliography of Writings since the War of 1914–1918." *The Journal of Modern History* 36 (1964): 127–44.

Young, William Anthony. "War and Diplomacy in the Age of Louis XIV: A Historical Study and Annotated Bibliography." D.A. diss., University of North Dakota, 2000.

Zeller, Gaston. "French Diplomacy and Foreign Policy in Their European Setting." In *The New Cambridge Modern History*, Volume V. Edited by F.L. Carsten. Cambridge: Cambridge University Press, 1961.

FRENCH EXPANSIONISM AND THE WARS AGAINST SPAIN AND THE DUTCH REPUBLIC, 1648–1678/79

Bérenger, Jean. "An Attempted Rapprochement between France and the Emperor: The Secret Treaty for the Partition of the Spanish Succession of 19 January 1668." In *Louis XIV and Europe*. Edited by R.M. Hatton. London: Macmillan, 1976.

Bonney, Richard. "The French Civil War, 1649–1653." *European Studies Review* 8 (1978): 71–100.

Ekberg, Carl J. "Abel Servien, Cardinal Mazarin, and the Formulation of French Foreign Policy, 1653–1659." *The International History Review* 3 (July 1981): 317–29.

_____. "From Dutch War to European War: A Study in French High Politics during 1673." Ph.D. diss., Rutgers University, 1970.

_____. "From Dutch to European War: Louis XIV and Louvois are Tested." *French Historical Studies* 8 (Spring 1974): 393–408.

_____. *The Failure of Louis XIV's Dutch War*. Chapel Hill: University of North Carolina Press, 1979.

_____. "The Great Captain's Greatest Mistake: Turenne's German Campaign of 1673." *Military Affairs* 41 (October 1977): 114–18.

Godley, Eveline. *The Great Condé: A Life of Louis II de Bourbon, Prince of Condé*. London: John Murray, 1915.

Grever, John H. "The French Invasion of the Spanish Netherlands and the Provincial Assemblies in the Dutch Republic, 1667–1668." *Parliaments, Estates and Representation* 4 (June 1984): 25–35.

Haley, Kenneth. *William of Orange and the English Opposition, 1672–1674*. Oxford: Clarendon Press, 1953.

Hatton, Ragnhild M. "Nijmegen and the European Powers." In *The Peace of Nijmegen, 1676–1678/79*. Edited by J.A.H. Bots. Amsterdam: APA-Holland University Press, 1980.

Inglis-Jones, J.J. "The Grand Condé: Power Politics in France, Spain, and the Spanish Netherlands, 1652–1659." D.Phil. thesis, University of Oxford, 1994.

Israel, Jonathan I. "Spain and Europe from the Peace of Münster to the Peace of the Pyrenees, 1648–1659." In *Conflicts of Empires: Spain, the Low Countries and the Struggle for World Supremacy, 1585–1713*. London: Hambledon Press, 1997.

Kleinman, Ruth. *Anne of Austria, Queen of France*. Columbus: Ohio State University Press, 1985.

Leahigh, James F. "Diplomatic Relations between Charles II and Louis XIV (1668–1678)." Ph.D. diss., Georgetown University, 1934.

Livet, G. "International Relations and the Role of France, 1648–1660." In *The New Cambridge Modern History*, Volume IV. Edited by J.P. Cooper. Cambridge: Cambridge University Press, 1970.

Martin, Ronald. "The Marquis de Chamlay and the Dutch War." *Proceedings of the Annual Meeting of the Western Society for French History* 1 (1974): 61–72.

McIntosh, Claude T. "French Diplomacy during the War of Devolution, 1667–1668, The Triple Alliance, 1668, and the Treaty of Aix-la-Chapelle, 1668." Ph.D. diss., Ohio State University, 1973.

McKay, Derek. "Small-Power Diplomacy in the Age of Louis XIV: The Foreign Policy of the Great Elector during the 1660s and 1670s." In *Royal and Republican Sovereignty in Early Modern Europe: Essays in Memory of Ragnhild Hatton*. Edited by R. Oresko, G.C. Gibbs, and H.M. Scott. Cambridge: Cambridge University Press, 1997.

O'Connor, John T. "French Relations with the Papacy during the Dutch War." *Proceedings of the Annual Meeting of the Western Society for French History* 13 (1986): 51–60.

Pillorget, René. "Louis XIV and the Electorate of Trier, 1652–1676." In *Louis XIV and Europe*. London: Macmillan, 1976.

Prestage, Edgar. *The Diplomatic Relations of Portugal with France, England, and Holland from 1640 to 1668*. Watford: Voss and Michael, 1925.

Ranum, Orest. *The Fronde: A French Revolution*. New York: W.W. Norton and Company, 1993.

Rietbergen, P.J. "Papal Diplomacy and Mediation at the Peace of Nijmegen." In *The Peace of Nijmegen, 1676–1678/79*. Edited by J.A.H. Bots. Amsterdam: AHA-Holland Press, 1980.

Roelofsen, C.G. "The Negociations about Nijmegen's Juridical Status during the Peace Congress." In *The Peace of Nijmegen, 1676–1678/79*. Edited by J.A.H. Bots. Amsterdam: APA-Holland University Press, 1980.

Roorda, D.J. "The Peace of Nijmegen: The End of a Particular Period in Dutch History." In *The Peace of Nijmegen, 1676–1678/79.* Edited by J.A.H. Bots. Amsterdam: AHA-Holland Press, 1980.

Rowen, Herbert H. "Arnauld de Pomponne: Louis XIV's Moderate Minister." *The American Historical Review* 62 (April 1956): 531–49.

_____. "John de Witt and the Triple Alliance." *The Journal of Modern History* 26 (March 1954): 1–14.

_____. *John de Witt, Grand Pensionary of Holland, 1625–1672.* Princeton: Princeton University Press, 1978.

_____. *John de Witt: Statesman of the "True Freedom".* Cambridge: Cambridge University Press, 1986.

_____. "Pomponne and De Witt (1669–1671): A Study of French High Policy on the Eve of the Dutch War." Ph.D. diss., Columbia University, 1951.

_____. *The Ambassador Prepares for War: The Dutch Embassy of Arnauld de Pomponne, 1669–1671.* The Hague: Martinus Nijhoff, 1957.

_____. "The Origins of the *Guerre de Hollande*: France and the Netherlands, 1660–1672." *Proceedings of the Annual Meeting of the Western Society for French History* 2 (1975): 120–26.

_____. "The Peace of Nijmegen: De Witt's Revenge." In *The Peace of Nijmegen, 1676–1678/79.* Edited by J.A.H. Bots. Amsterdam: APA-Holland, 1980.

Satterfield, George D. *Princes, Posts and Partisans: The Army of Louis XIV and Partisan Warfare in the Netherlands, 1673–1678.* Leiden: Brill, 2003.

_____. "'Upon a Certain Science': The Army of Louis XIV and Partisan Warfare in the Netherlands, 1673–1678." Ph.D. diss., University of Illinois at Urbana-Champaign, 2002.

Scott, C.F. "The Peace of Nijmegen: Some Comments on Spanish Foreign Policy and the Activity of Don Pedro Ronquillo." In *The Peace of Nijmegen, 1676–1678/79.* Edited by J.A.H. Bots. Amsterdam: APA-Holland, 1980.

Sonnino, Paul. "Arnauld de Pomponne: Louis XIV's Minister for Foreign Affairs during the Dutch War." *Proceedings of the Annual Meeting of the Western Society for French History* 1 (1974): 49–60.

_____. "Hugues de Lionne and the Origins of the Dutch War." *Proceedings of the Annual Meeting of the Western Society for French History* 3 (1976): 68–78.

_____. "Jean-Baptiste Colbert and the Origins of the Dutch War." *European Studies Review* 13 (1983): 1–11.

_____. "Louis XIV and the Dutch War." In *Louis XIV and Europe*. Edited by R.M. Hatton. London: Macmillan, 1976.

_____. *Louis XIV and the Origins of the Dutch War*. Cambridge: Cambridge University Press, 1988.

_____. "Louis XIV's Correspondence, 'Memoirs,' and His View of the Papacy (1661–1667)." Ph.D. diss., University of California at Los Angeles, 1964.

_____. "Louis XIV's *Mémoires pour l'histoire de la guerre de Hollande*." *French Historical Studies* 8 (Spring 1973): 29–50.

_____. *Louis XIV's View of the Papacy, 1661–1667*. Berkeley: University of California Press, 1966.

_____. "The Marshal de Turenne and the Origins of the Dutch War." *Studies in History and Politics* 4 (1985): 125–36.

Stradling, Robert A. "A Spanish Statesman of Appeasement: Medina de las Torres and Spanish Policy, 1639–1670." *Historical Journal* 19 (1976): 1–31; reprinted in *Spain's Struggle for Europe, 1598–1668*. London: Hambledon Press, 1994.

_____. *Philip IV and the Government of Spain, 1621–1665*. Cambridge: Cambridge University Press, 1988.

Treasure, Geoffrey. *Louis XIV*. Harlow, London, and New York: Longman, 2001.

_____. *Mazarin: The Crisis of Absolutism in France*. London: Routledge, 1995.

_____. *Richelieu and Mazarin*. London: Routledge, 1998.

Trevelyan, Mary Caroline. *William the Third and the Defence of Holland, 1672–1674*. London: Longmans, Green and Company, 1930.

Trout, Andrew P. "The Proclamation of the Treaty of Nijmegen." *French Historical Studies* 5 (Fall 1968): 477–81.

Weyland, Max. *Turenne: Marshal of France*. London: George G. Harrap, 1930.

Wierema, A.C.L. "Denmark as an ally of the Dutch Republic during the '*Guerre d'Hollande*' (1674–1679). In *Baltic Affairs: Relations between the Netherlands and North-Eastern Europe, 1500–1800*. Edited by J.Ph.S Lemmink and J.S.A.M. van Koningsbrugge. Nijmegen: Institute for Northern and Eastern European Studies, 1990.

Wilkinson, Richard. *France and the Cardinals, 1610–1661*. London: Hodder and Stoughton, 1995.

ENGLISH FOREIGN POLICY UNDER CROMWELL AND CHARLES II, 1649–1685

Allen, D.F. "Charles II, Louis XIV and the Order of Malta." *European History Quarterly* 20 (1990): 323–40.

Anderson, R. "The Operations of the English Fleet, 1648–1652." *The English Historical Review* 31 (1916): 406–28.

_____. "The First Dutch War in the Mediterranean." *Mariner's Mirror* 49 (1963): 241–65.

Anon. *The Second Dutch War (De Tweede Engelse Oorlog) 1665–1667*. London: Her Majesty's Stationery Office, 1967.

Ashley, Maurice. *Charles II: The Man and the Statesman*. London: Weidenfeld and Nicolson, 1971.

_____. *Cromwell's Generals*. London: Jonathan Cape, 1954.

_____. *The Greatness of Oliver Cromwell*. London: Hodder and Stoughton, 1957.

Atkin, Malcolm. *Cromwell's Crowning Mercy: The Battle of Worcester, 1651*. Stroud: Sutton, 1998.

Atkinson, Christopher T. "Charles II's Regiments in France, 1672–1678." *Journal of the Society for Army Historical Research* 24 (1946): 53–65, 129–36, 161–72.

Aubrey, Philip. *Mr Secretary Thurloe: Cromwell's Secretary of State, 1652–1660*. London: Athlone Press,1990.

Battick, John F. "Cromwell's Navy and the Foreign Policy of the Protectorate, 1653–1658." Ph.D. diss., Boston University, 1967.

Belcher, Gerald L. "Anglo-Spanish Diplomatic Relations, 1660–1667." Ph.D. thesis, University of North Carolina at Chapel Hill, 1971.

_____. "Spain and the Anglo-Portuguese Alliance of 1661: A Reassessment of Charles II's Foreign Policy at the Restoration." *The Journal of British Studies* 15 (November 1975): 67–88.

Bliss, Robert M. *Restoration England: Politics and Government, 1660–1688*. London: Methuen, 1985.

Blok, Petrus J. *The Life of Admiral de Ruyter*. London: Ernest Benn, 1933; reprint, Westport: Greenwood Press, 1975.

Bowman, J. *The Protestant Interest in Cromwell's Foreign Relations*. Heidelberg: Winter, 1900.

Boxer, C.R. *The Anglo-Dutch Wars of the Seventeenth Century*. London: Her Majesty's Stationery Office, 1974.

_____. "Some Second Thoughts on the Third Anglo-Dutch War." *Transactions of the Royal Historical Society*, Fifth series, 19 (1969): 67–94.

Brinkmann, C. "Charles II and the Bishop of Münster in the Anglo-Dutch War of 1665–1666." *The English Historical Review* 21 (October 1906): 686–98.

Browning, A. *Thomas Osborne, Earl of Danby and Duke of Leeds, 1632–1712.* 3 volumes. Glasgow: Jackson, 1951.

Bruijn, J.R. "Dutch Privateering during the Second and Third Anglo-Dutch Wars." *Acta Historiae Neerlandicae* 9 (1977): 79–93.

Catterall, Ralph C.H. "Anglo-Dutch Relations, 1654–1660." In *Annual Report American Historical Assocation (1910)."* Washington, D.C.: U.S. Government Printing Office, 1912.

Childs, John "The British Brigade in France, 1672–1678." *History* 69 (October 1984): 384–97.

Coward, Barry. *Oliver Cromwell.* London: Addison, Wesley, Longman, 1991.

Crabtree, Roger. "The Idea of a Protestant Foreign Policy." In *Cromwell: A Profile.* Edited by I. Roots. New York: Hill and Wang, 1973.

Davies, Godfrey. *The Restoration of Charles II, 1658–1660.* San Marino: Huntington Library, 1955.

Davis, Ralph. *English Merchant Shipping and Anglo-Dutch Rivalry in the Seventeenth Century.* London: Her Majesty's Stationery Office, 1975.

DeVries, Harry. "The Anglo-Dutch War, 1672–1674." Ph.D. diss., University of Michigan, 1939.

Farnell, J.E. "The Navigation Act of 1651, the First Dutch War and the London Merchant Community." *The Economic History Review,* Second series 16 (1963): 439–54.

Feiling, Keith G. *British Foreign Policy, 1660–1672.* London: Macmillan, 1930.

Firth, Charles. *Cromwell's Army: A History of the English Soldier during the Civil Wars, the Commonwealth, and the Protectorate.* Third edition, London: Methuen, 1921; reprint, London: Greenhill Books, 1992.

_____. "Cromwell's Instructions to Colonel Lockhart in 1656." *The English Historical Review* 21 (1906): 742–46.

_____. "Royalist and Cromwellian Armies in Flanders, 1657–1661." *Transactions of the Royal Historical Society*, New series 17 (1903): 69–119.

_____. "Secretary Thurloe on the Relations of England and Holland." *The English Historical Review* 21 (1906): 319–27.

_____. *The Last Years of the Protectorate.* 2 volumes. London: Longmans, Green and Company, 1909.

Foley, Michael F., Jr. "John Thurloe and the Foreign Policy of the Protectorate, 1654–1658." Ph.D. thesis, University of Illinois, 1967.

Fox, Frank. *Great Ships: The Battlefleet of King Charles II.* Greenwich: Conway Maritime Press, 1980.

_____. "The English Naval Shipbuilding Programme of 1664." *Mariner's Mirror* 78 (1992): 277–92.

Francis, Samuel T. "Restoration Diplomacy: The Foreign Policy of Edward Hyde, First Earl of Clarendon, 1660–1667." Ph.D. diss., University of North Carolina at Chapel Hill, 1979.

Fraser, Antonia. *Cromwell: Our Chief of Men.* London: Weidenfeld and Nicolson, 1973.

_____. *Royal Charles: Charles II and the Restoration.* New York: Alfred A. Knopf, 1979.

Gardiner, Samuel Rawson. "Cromwell and Mazarin in 1652." *The English Historical Review* 11 (1896): 479–509.

_____. *History of the Commonwealth and Protectorate, 1649–1656.* 4 volumes. London: Longmans, Green and Company, 1903.

_____. *Oliver Cromwell.* London: Longmans, Green and Company, 1901.

Gaunt, Peter. *Oliver Cromwell.* Oxford: Basil Blackwell, 1996.

Geyl, Pieter. *Orange and Stuart, 1641–1672*. London: Weidenfeld and Nicolson, 1969.

Grainger, John D. *Cromwell Against the Scots: The Last Anglo-Scottish War, 1650–1652*. East Linton: Tuckwell Press, 1997.

Groenveld, Simon. "The English Civil War as a Cause of the First Anglo-Dutch War, 1640–1652." *The Historical Journal* 30 (1987): 541–66.

Grose, Clyde L. "England and Dunkirk." *The American Historical Review* 39 (1933–34): 1–27.

_____. "Louis XIV's Financial Relations with Charles II and the English Parliament." *The Journal of Modern History* 2 (June 1929): 177–204.

_____. "The Anglo-Dutch Alliance of 1678." *The English Historical Review* 39 (July and October 1924): 349–72, 526–51.

_____. "The Dunkirk Money, 1662." *The Journal of Modern History* 5 (March 1933): 1–18.

Hainesworth, Roger. *The Swordsmen in Power: War and Politics under the English Republic, 1649–1660*. Phoenix Mill: Sutton, 1997.

_____ and Christine Churches. *The Anglo-Dutch Naval Wars, 1652–1674*. Stroud: Sutton, 1998.

Haley, Kenneth. *An English Diplomat in the Low Countries: Sir William Temple and John de Witt, 1665–1672*. Oxford: Clarendon Press, 1986.

_____. *Charles II*. London: Historical Assocation, 1966.

_____. "English Policy at the Peace Congress of Nijmegen." In *The Peace of Nijmegen, 1676–1678/79*. Edited by J.A.H. Bots. Amsterdam: APA-Holland, 1980.

_____. "The Anglo-Dutch Rapprochement of 1677." *The English Historical Review* 73 (October 1958): 614–48.

_____. *The First Earl of Shaftesbury*. Oxford: Clarendon Press, 1968.

_____. *William of Orange and the English Opposition, 1672–1674*. Oxford: Clarendon Press, 1953.

Hansen, H. "The Opening Phase of the Third Dutch War Described by the Danish Envoy in London, March-June 1672." *The Journal of Modern History* 21 (1949): 97–108.

Hardacre, P.H. "The English Contingent in Portugal, 1662–1668." *Journal of the Society for Army Historical Research* 38 (1960): 112–25.

Hartmann, Cyril H. *Charles II and Madam*. London: W. Heinemann, 1934.

_____. *Clifford of the Cabal: A Life of Thomas, First Lord Clifford of Chudleigh, Lord High Treasurer of England (1630–1673)*. Kingswood: H. Heinemann, 1937.

Hill, Christopher. *God's Englishman: Oliver Cromwell and the English Revolution*. London: Weidenfeld and Nicolson, 1970.

Hornstein, Sari R. *The Restoration Navy and English Foreign Trade, 1674–1688: A Study in the Peacetime Use of Seapower*. Aldershot: Scolar Press, 1991.

Hutton, Ronald. *Charles the Second: King of England, Scotland, and Ireland*. Oxford: Clarendon Press, 1989.

Hutton, Ronald. *The British Republic, 1649–1660*. New York: St. Martin's Press, 1990.

_____. "The Making of the Secret Treaty of Dover, 1668–1670." *The Historical Journal* 29 (1986): 297–318.

_____. *The Restoration: A Political and Religious History of England and Wales, 1660–1667*. Oxford: Clarendon Press, 1985.

Israel, Jonathan I. "Competing Cousins: Anglo-Dutch Trade Rivalry." *History Today* 38 (July 1988): 17–22.

Jones, Guernsey. *The Diplomatic Relations between Cromwell and Charles Gustavus X of Sweden*. Lincoln: State Journal Company, 1897.

Jones, James R. *Charles II: Royal Politician*. London: Allen and Unwin, 1987.

_____. *The Anglo-Dutch Wars of the Seventeenth Century*. London: Longman, 1996.

Kenyon, John P. *Robert Spencer, Earl of Sunderland, 1641–1702*. London: Longmans, Green and Company, 1958.

Knachel, Philip A. *England and the Fronde: The Impact of the English Civil War and Revolution on France*. Ithaca: Cornell University Press, 1967.

Korr, Charles P. *Cromwell and the New Model Foreign Policy: England's Policy Toward France, 1649–1658*. Berkeley: University of California Press, 1975.

Kupperman, Karen Ordahl. "Errand to the Indies: Puritan Colonization from Providence Island through the Western Design." *William and Mary Quarterly*, Third series 45 (January 1988): 70–99.

Lee, Maurice, Jr. *The Cabal*. Urbana: University of Illinois Press, 1965.

MacLean, James N.M. "Montrose's Preparations for the Invasion of Scotland and Royalist Missions to Sweden, 1649–1651." In *Studies in Diplomatic History: Essays in Memory of David Bayne Horn*. Edited by R.M. Hatton and M.S. Anderson. London: Longman, 1970.

Miller, John. *Charles II*. London: Weidenfeld and Nicolson, 1991.

_____. *The Restoration and the England of Charles II*. Second edition. London: Addison, Wesley, Longman, 1997.

Murdoch, Steve. "The Search for Northern Allies: Stuart and Cromwellian Propagandists in Scandinavia, 1649–1660." In *Propaganda: Political Rhertoric and Identity, 1300–2000*. Edited by Bertrand Taithe and Tim Thornton. Stroud: Sutton, 1999.

Ogg, David. *England in the Reign of Charles II*. 2 volumes. Second edition. Oxford: Oxford University Press, 1956.

Ohlmeyer, Jane H. "Ireland Independent: Confederate Foreign Policy and International Relations during the mid-Seventeenth Century." In *Ireland form Independence to Occupation 1641–1660*. Edited by J.H. Olhmeyer. Cambridge: Cambridge University Press, 1984.

Ollard, Richard. *Man-of-War: Sir Robert Holmes and the Restoration Navy*. London: Hodder and Stoughton, 1969.

_____. *Cromwell's Earl: The Life of Edward Montagu, First Earl of Sandwich*. London: Harper Collins, 1994.

Payn, F.W. *Cromwell on Foreign Affairs: Together with Four Essays on Internal Matters*. London: C.J. Clay and Sons, 1901.

Pearsall, A.W.H., editor. *The Second Dutch War, 1665–1667*. London: Her Majesty's Stationery Office, 1967.

Pincus, Steven. "Popery, Trade and Universal Monarchy: The Ideological Context of the Outbreak of the Second Anglo-Dutch War." *The English Historical Review* 107 (January 1992): 1–29.

_____. *Protestantism and Patriotism: Ideologies and the Making of English Foreign Policy, 1650–1668*. Cambridge: Cambridge University Press, 1996.

Powell, J.R. *Robert Blake: General-at-Sea*. London: Collins, 1972.

Prestwich, Menna. "Diplomacy and Trade in the Protectorate." *The Journal of Modern History* 22 (1950): 103–21.

Price, J.L. "Restoration England and Europe." In *The Restored Monarchy, 1660–1688*. Edited by J.R. Jones. Totowa: Rowman and Littlefield, 1979.

Prior, W.R. "The Naval War with the Dutch, 1665–1667: The Diary of a Danish Sailor." *The United Service Magazine* 43 (1911): 355–61.

Quainton, C. Eden. "Colonel Lockhart and the Peace of the Pyrenees." *The Pacific Historical Review* 4 (September 1935): 267–80.

Roberts, Michael. "Cromwell and the Baltic." *The English Historical Review* 76 (July 1961): 402–46; reprinted in *Essays in Swedish History*. Minneapolis: University of Minnesota Press, 1967.

_____, editor. *Swedish Diplomats at Cromwell's Court, 1655–1656: The Missions of Peter Julius Coyet and Christer Bonde*. London: Royal Historical Society, 1988.

Rogers, P.G. *The Dutch in the Medway*. London: Oxford University Press, 1970.

Routledge, Frederick J. *England and the Treaty of the Pyrenees*. Liverpool: Liverpool University Press, 1953.

Rowen, Herbert H. *John de Witt, Grand Pensionary of Holland, 1625–1672*. Princeton: Princeton University Press, 1978.

_____. *John de Witt: Statesman of the "True Freedom"*. Cambridge: Cambridge University Press, 1986.

Schoolcraft, Henry L. "England and Denmark, 1660–1667." *The English Historical Review* 25 (July 1910): 457–79.

Seaward, Paul. "The House of Commons Committee of Trade and the Origins of the Second Anglo-Dutch War." *The Historical Journal* 30 (1987): 437–52.

_____. *The Restoration, 1660–1688*. London: Macmillan, 1991.

Shelley, R.J.A. "The Division of the English Fleet in 1666." *Mariner's Mirror* 25 (1939): 178–96.

Shomette, D.G and R.D. Haslach. *Raid on America: The Dutch Naval Campaign of 1672–1674*. Columbia: University of South Carolina Press, 1988.

Stradling, Robert A. "Anglo-Spanish Relations from the Restoration to the Peace of Aix-la-Chapelle, 1660–1668." Ph.D. diss., University of Wales, 1968.

_____. "Spanish Conspiracy in England, 1661–1663." *The English Historical Review* 87 (1972): 269–86; reprinted in *Spain's Struggle for Europe, 1598–1668*. London: Hambledon Press, 1994.

Strong, Frank. "The Causes of Cromwell's West Indian Expedition." *The American Historical Review* 4 (1898–99): 228–45.

Taylor, S.A.G. *The Western Design*. Kingston: Historical Society of Jamaica, 1965.

Venning, Timothy. *Cromwellian Foreign Policy*. New York: St. Martin's Press, 1995.

_____. "Cromwell's Foreign Policy and the Western Design." *Cromwelliana* (1994): 41–52.

Weber, R.E.J. "The Introduction of the Single line Ahead as a Battle Formation by the Dutch, 1665–1666." *Mariner's Mirror* 73 (1987): 5–19.

Wheeler, James Scott. *The Irish and British Wars, 1637–1654: Triumph, Tragedy, and Failure*. London and New York: Routledge, 2002.

Wilson, Charles. *Profit and Power: A Study of England and the Dutch Wars*. London: Longmans, Green, and Company, 1957; reprint, The Hague: Martinus Nijhoff, 1978.

Woolrych, Austin. *England without a King, 1649–1660*. London: Routledge, 1983.

_____. "The Cromwellian Protectorate: A Military Dictatorship?" *History* 75 (1990): 207–31.

FRENCH AGGRESSION, THE FORMATION OF THE GRAND ALLIANCE, AND THE NINE YEARS' WAR, 1679–1697

Ashley, Maurice. *James II*. Minneapolis: University of Minnesota Press, 1977.

_____. *The Glorious Revolution of 1688*. New York: Charles Scribner's Sons, 1966.

Aubrey, Philip. *The Defeat of James Stuart's Armada, 1692*. Leicester: Leicester University Press, 1979.

Barker, Thomas M. *Double Eagle and Crescent: Vienna's Second Turkish Siege and Its Historical Setting*. Albany: State University of New York Press, 1967.

Berresford-Ellis, Peter. *The Boyne Water: The Battle of the Boyne, 1690*. New York: St. Martin's Press, 1976.

Bingham, Richard B. "In Pursuit of Peace: The Rationale of French Diplomacy in Northern Europe, 1690–1691." M.A. thesis, University of Minnesota, 1967.

_____. "Louis XIV and the War for Peace: The Genesis of a Peace Offensive, 1686–1690." 3 volumes. Ph.D. thesis, University of Illinois at Chicago Circle, 1972.

Black, Jeremy. "The Revolution and the Development of English Foreign Policy." In *By Force or by Default?: The Revolution of 1688–1689*. Edited by Eveline Cruickshanks. Edinburgh: John Donald, 1989.

Carswell, John. *The Descent on England: A Study of the English Revolution of 1688 and Its European Background*. New York: John Day, 1969.

Chandler, David G. *Blenheim Preparation: Collected Essays on the Armies of William III and Marlborough*. Staplehurst: Spellmount, 2003.

_____. "Fluctuations in the Strength of Forces in English Pay Sent to Flanders during the Nine Years' War, 1688–1697." *War and Society* 1 (September 1988): 1–19.

_____. *Sedgemoor 1685: An Account and Anthology*. New York: St. Martin's Press, 1985.

Childs, John. "Secondary Operations of the British Army during the Nine Years' War, 1688–1697." *Journal of the Society for Army Historical Research* 73 (Summer 1995): 73–98.

_____. "1688." *History* 73 (1988): 398–424.

_____. "The Abortive Invasion of 1692." In *The Stuart Court in Exile and the Jacobites*. Edited by E. Cruickshanks and E. Corp. London: Hambledon Press, 1995.

_____. *The Army of James II and the Glorious Revolution*. Manchester: Manchester University Press, 1980.

_____. *The British Army of William III, 1689–1697*. Manchester: Manchester University Press, 1987.

_____. *The Nine Years War and the British Army, 1688–1697: The Operations in the Low Countries.* Manchester: Manchester University Press, 1991.

_____. "The Williamite War, 1689–1691." In *A Military History of Ireland.* Edited by T. Bartlett and K. Jeffrery. Cambridge: Cambridge University Press, 1996.

Clark, George N. "The Character of the Nine Years' War, 1688–1697." *Cambridge Historical Journal* 11 (1954): 168–82.

_____. *The Dutch Alliance and the War against French Trade, 1688–1697.* Manchester: Manchester University Press, 1923.

_____. "The Nine Years' War, 1688–1697." In *The New Cambridge Modern History*, Volume VI. Edited by J.S. Bromley. Cambridge: Cambridge University Press, 1970.

Clark, Ruth. *Sir William Trumbull in Paris, 1685–1686.* Cambridge: Cambridge University Press, 1938.

Danaher, Kevin and J.G. Simms. *The Danish Force in Ireland, 1690–1691.* Dublin: Stationery Office for the Irish Manuscripts Commission, 1962.

Davies, D. "James II, William of Orange, and the Admirals." In *By Force or By Default?: The Revolution of 1688–89.* Edited by E. Cruickshanks. Edinburgh: John Donald, 1989.

Davies, Godfrey. "The Control of British Foreign Policy by William III." In *Essays on the Later Stuarts.* San Marino: Huntington Library, 1958.

Doherty, Richard. *The Williamite War in Ireland, 1688–1691.* Dublin: Four Courts Press, 1998.

Earle, Peter. *Monmouth's Rebels: The Road to Sedgemoore, 1685.* New York: St. Martin's Press, 1977.

Ehrman, John. *The Navy in the War of William III, 1689–1697: Its State and Direction.* Cambridge: Cambridge University Press, 1953.

_____. "William III and the Emergence of a Mediterranean Naval Policy, 1692–1694." *The Cambridge Historical Journal* 9 (1949): 269–92.

Fayard, Janine. "Attempts to Build a 'Third Party' in Northern Germany, 1690–1694." In *Louis XIV and Europe*. Edited by R.M. Hatton. London: Macmillan, 1976.

Ferguson, Kenneth. "The Organisation of King William's Army in Ireland, 1689–1692." *Irish Sword* 18 (1990): 62–79.

George, Robert H. "The Financial Relations of Louis XIV and James II." *The Journal of Modern History* 3 (1931): 392–413.

Gibbs, G.C. "The Revolution in Foreign Policy." In *Britain after the Glorious Revolution, 1688–1714*. Edited by G. Holmes. London: Macmillan, 1969.

Gisselquist, Orloue N. "The French Ambassador, Jean Antoine de Mesmes, Comte d'Avaux, and French Diplomacy at The Hague, 1678–1684." Ph.D. thesis, University of Minnesota, 1968.

Gradish, Stephen F. "The Establishment of British Seapower in the Mediterranean, 1689–1713." *Canadian Journal of History* 10 (April 1975): 1–16.

Grew, Marion E. *William Bentinck and William III (Prince of Orange): The Life of Bentinck Earl of Portland from the Welbeck Correspondence*. London: John Murray, 1924; reprint, Port Washington: Kennikat Press, 1971.

Haley, Kenneth. "The Dutch, the Invasion of England, and the Alliance of 1689." In *The Revolution of 1688–1689: Changing Perspectives*. Edited by L.G. Schwoerer. Cambridge: Cambridge University Press, 1992.

Handen, Ralph D. "The End of an Era: Louis XIV and Victor Amadeus II." In *Louis XIV and Europe*. Edited by R.M. Hatton. London: Macmillan, 1976.

_____. "The Savoy Negotiations of the Comte de Tessé, 1693–1696." Ph.D. diss., Ohio State University, 1970.

Harding, Richard. "The Expeditions to Quebec, 1690–1711: The Evolution of British Trans-Atlantic Amphibious Power." *Guerres Maritimes, 1688–1713: IVes journées franco-britanniques d'historie de la marine, Portsmouth, 1er–4 avril 1992*. Vincennes: Service historique de la Marine, 1996.

Hatton, Ragnhild M. "Gratifications and Foreign Policy: Anglo-French Rivalry in Sweden during the Nine Years' War." In *William III and Louis XIV:*

Essays 1680–1720 by and for Mark A. Thomson. Edited by R.M. Hatton and J.S. Bromley. Liverpool: Liverpool University Press, 1968.

Israel, Jonathan I. "The Dutch Republic and the 'Glorious Revolution' of 1688/89 in England." In *1688: The Seaborne Alliance and Diplomatic Revolution*. Edited by C. Wilson and D. Proctor. London: Roundwood Press, 1989.

_____. "The Dutch Role in the Glorious Revolution." In *The Anglo-Dutch Moment: Essays on the Glorious Revolution and Its World Impact*. Edited by J. I. Israel. Cambridge: Cambridge University Press, 1991.

_____. "Propaganda in the Making of the Glorious Revolution." In *Across the Narrow Seas: Studies in the History and Bibliography of Britain and the Low Countries*. Edited by Susan Roach. London: British Library, 1991.

_____ and Geoffrey Parker. "Of Providence and Protestant Winds: The Spanish Armada of 1588 and the Dutch Armada of 1688." In *The Anglo-Dutch Moment: Essays on the Glorious Revolution and Its World Impact*. Edited by J. I. Israel. Cambridge: Cambridge University Press, 1991; reprint, In *Success is Never Final: Empire, War, and Faith in Early Modern Europe*. New York: Basic Books, 2002.

Jones, George Hilton. *Charles Middleton: The Life and Times of a Restoration Politician*. Chicago: University of Chicago Press, 1967.

_____. *Convergent Forces: Immediate Causes of the Revolution of 1688 in England*. Ames: Iowa State University Press, 1990.

_____. "William III's Diplomatic Preparations for His Expedition to England." *Durham University Journal* 79 (1987): 233–45.

Jones, James R. *Charles II: Royal Politician*. London: Allen and Unwin, 1987.

_____. "French Intervention in English and Dutch Politics, 1677–1688." In *Knights Errant and True Englishmen: British Foreign Policy, 1600–1800*. Edited by J. Black. Edinburgh: John Donald, 1989.

_____. *The Revolution of 1688 in England*. London: Weidenfeld and Nicolson, 1972.

_____. "William and the English." In *1688: The Seaborne Alliance and Diplomatic Revolution*. Edited by Charles Wilson and David Proctor. Greenwich: Roundwood Press, 1989.

Kenyon, John P. "William III." *History Today* 9 (September and October 1959): 581–88, 664–71.

Kurat, A.N. and John S. Bromley. "The Retreat of the Turks, 1683–1730." In *The New Cambridge Modern History*, Volume VI. Edited by J.S. Bromley. Cambridge: Cambridge University Press, 1970.

Lane, Margery. "The Diplomatic Service under William III." *Transactions of the Royal Historical Society*, Fourth Series 10 (1927): 87–110.

Leitsch, Walter. "1683, The Siege of Vienna." *History Today* 33 (July 1983): 37–40.

Livet, Georges. "Louis XIV and the Germanies." In *Louis XIV and Europe*. Edited by R.M. Hatton. London: Macmillan, 1976.

Lossky, Andrew. "Dutch Diplomacy and the Franco-Russian Trade Negotiations in 1681." In *Studies in Diplomatic History: Essays in Memory of David Bayne Horn*. Edited by R.M. Hatton and M.S. Anderson. London: Longman, 1970.

_____. "La Picquetière's Projected Mission to Moscow in 1682 and the Swedish Policy of Louis XIV." In *Essays in Russian History: A Collection Dedicated to George Vernadsky*. Edtied by A.D. Ferguson and A. Levin. Hamden: Archon Books, 1964.

_____. *Louis XIV, William III, and the Baltic Crisis of 1683*. Berkeley: University of California Press, 1954.

_____. "'Maxims of State' in Louis XIV's Foreign Policy in the 1680s." In *William III and Louis XIV: Essays 1680–1720 by and for Mark A. Thomson*. Edited by R.M. Hatton and J.S. Bromley. Liverpool: Liverpool University Press, 1968.

_____. "The General European Crisis of the 1680s." *European Studies Review* 10 (1986): 177–209.

MacCartney-Filgate, E. *The War of William III in Ireland*. London: Longmans, Green and Company, 1906.

McJimsey, Robert D. "The Englishman's Choice: English Opinion and the War of King William III, 1689–1697." Ph.D. thesis, University of Wisconsin, 1968.

Miller, John. *James II: A Study in Kingship*. Hove: Wayland, 1978.

_____. *The Glorious Revolution*. Second edition. London: Addison, Wesley, Longman, 1997.

Moore, Anthony. *Army of Brandenburg-Prussia 1680–1715*. London: Gosling Press, 1993.

Morgan, W.T. "The British West Indies during King William's War, 1689–97." *The Journal of Modern History* 2 (1930): 378–409.

Moses, N.H. "The British Navy and the Caribbean, 1689–1697." *Mariner's Mirror* 52 (1966): 13–40.

Mullett, Michael. *James II and English Politics, 1678–1688*. London: Routledge, 1994.

Mulloy, Sheila. "French Engineers with the Jacobite Army in Ireland, 1688–1691." *The Irish Sword* 15 (1983): 222–32.

_____. "The French Navy and the Jacobite War in Ireland. *Irish Sword* 18 (1990): 17–31.

Nordmann, Claude. "Louis XIV and the Jacobites." In *Louis XIV and Europe*. Edited by R.M. Hatton. London: Macmillan, 1976.

Oakley, Stewart P. *William III and the Northern Crowns during the Nine Years' War, 1689–1697*. New York: Garland, 1987.

O'Connor, John T. "Louis XIV's 'Cold War' with the Papacy: French Diplomats and Papal Nuncios." *Proceedings of the Annual Meeting of the Western Society for French History* 1 (1974): 127–36.

_____. "Louis XIV's Strategic Frontier in the Holy Roman Empire." *Proceedings of the Annual Meeting of the Western Society for French History* 2 (1975): 108–17.

_____. *Negotiator out of Season: The Career of Wilhelm Egon von Fürstenberg, 1629–1704.* Athens: University of Georgia Press, 1978.

_____. "William Egon von Fürstenberg and French Diplomacy in the Rhineland Prior to the Outbreak of the War of the League of Augsburg." Ph.D. thesis, University of Minnesota, 1965.

_____. "William Egon von Fürstenberg, German Agent in the Service of Louis XIV." *French Historical Studies* 5 (1967): 119–46.

O'Danachair, C. "The Danish Corps in Ireland, 1690–1691." *Irish Sword* 5 (1962): 2–9.

Ogg, David. *England in the Reigns of James II and William III.* Oxford: Oxford University Press, 1955.

Oresko, Robert. "The Diplomatic Background to the *Glorioso Rimpatrio:* The Rupture between Victorio Amedeo II and Louis XIV (1688–1690)." In *Dall'Europa Ale Valli Valdesi.* Edited by Albert de Lange. Torino: Claudiana Editrice, 1990.

_____. "The Glorious Revolution of 1688–1689 and the House of Savoy. In *The Anglo-Dutch Moment: Essays on the Glorious Revolution and Its World Impact.* Edited by J.I. Israel. Cambridge: Cambridge University Press, 1991.

Pilgrim, Donald G. "The Colbert-Seignelay Naval Reforms and the Beginnings of the War of the League of Augsburg." *French Historical Studies* 9 (1975): 235–62.

_____. "The Uses and Limitations of French Naval Power in the Reign of Louis XIV: The Administration of the Marquis de Seignelay, 1683–1690." Ph.D. thesis, Brown University, 1969.

Place, Richard. "Bavaria and the Collapse of Louis XIV's German Policy, 1687–1688." *The Journal of Modern History* 49 (September 1977): 369–93.

_____. "French Policy and the Turkish War, 1679–1688." Ph.D. thesis, University of Minnesota, 1963.

_____. "The Self-Deception of the Strong: France on the Eve of the War of the League of Augsburg." *French Historical Studies* 6 (1969–70): 459–73.

Powley, Edward B. *The Naval Side of King William's War: 16th/26th November 1688–14th June 1690*. London: Archon, 1972.

Price, J.L. "William III, England and the Balance of Power in Europe." *Groniek, Gronings Historisch Tijdschrift* 101 (1988): 67–78.

Rowlands, Guy. *An Army in Exile: Louis XIV and the Irish Forces of James II in France, 1691–1698*. London: Royal Stuart Society, 2001.

_____. "Louis XIV, Vittorio Amedeo II and French Military Failure in Italy, 1689–96." *The English Historical Review* 115 (June 2000): 534–69.

Rule, John C. "France caught between Two Balances: The Dilemma of 1688." In *The Revolution of 1688–1689: Changing Perspectives*. Edited by L.G. Schwoerer. Cambridge: Cambridge University Press, 1992.

Ryan, A.N. "William III and the Brest Fleet in the Nine Years' War." In *William III and Louis XIV: Essays 1680–1720 by and for Mark A. Thomson*. Edited by R.M. Hatton and J.S. Bromley. Liverpool: Liverpool University Press, 1968.

Sapherson, C.A. *William III at War, Scotland and Ireland: 1689–1691*. Leeds: Raider Books, 1987.

_____. *The British Army of William III*. Hopewell: OMM Publishing, 2002.

Shapiro, Sheldon. "The Relations between Louis XIV and Leopold of Austria from the Treaty of Nymegen to the Truce of Ratisbon." Ph.D. diss., University of California at Los Angeles, 1966.

Sheen, Charlie R. "The Fate of the Concept of Christendom in the Policy of Louis XIV: An Example from the King's Negotiations with the Empire, 1680–1684." *European Studies Review* 3 (1973): 283–89.

Simms, J.G. *Jacobite Ireland, 1685–1691*. London: Routledge and Kegan Paul, 1969.

_____. *The Siege of Derry*. Dublin: APCK, 1966.

_____. *War and Politics in Ireland, 1649–1730*. Edited by D.W. Hayton and G. O'Brien. London: Hambledon Press, 1986.

_____. "Williamite Peace Tactics, 1690–1691." *Irish Historical Studies* 8 (1953): 303–23; reprinted in *War and Politics in Ireland, 1649–1730*. Edited by D.W. Hayton and G. O'Brien. London: Hambledon Press, 1986.

Speck, William A. *Reluctant Revolutionaries: Englishmen and the Revolution of 1688*. Oxford: Oxford University Press, 1988.

_____. "The Orangist Conspiracy against James II." *The Historical Journal* 30 (1987): 453–62.

Storrs, Christopher. "Diplomatic Relations between William III and Victor Amadeus II (1690–1696)." Ph.D. thesis, University of London, 1990.

_____. "The Army of Lombardy and the Resilience of Spanish Power in the Reign of Carlos II (1665–1700)." *War in History* 4–5 (1997–98): 371–97, 1–22.

_____. "Machiavelli Dethroned: Victor Amadeus II and the Making of the Anglo-Savoyard Alliance of 1690." *European History Quarterly* 22 (1992): 347–82.

Stoye, John W. *The Siege of Vienna*. London: Collins, 1964.

Symcox, Geoffrey W. "Britain and Victor Amadeus II: Or The Use and Abuse of Allies." In *England's Rise to Greatness, 1660–1763*. Edited by S. Baxter. Berkeley: University of California Press, 1983.

_____. "Louis XIV and the Outbreak of the Nine Years' War." In *Louis XIV and Europe*. Edited by R.M. Hatton. London: Macmillan, 1976.

_____. "Louis XIV and the War in Ireland, 1689–1691: A Study in His Strategic Thinking and Decision-Making." Ph.D. diss., University of California at Los Angeles, 1967.

_____. *The Crisis of French Naval Power, 1688–1697: From the Guerre d'Escadre to the Guerre de Course*. The Hague: Martinus Nijhoff, 1974.

_____. *Victor Amadeus II: Absolutism in the Savoyard State, 1675–1730*. London: Thames and Hudson, 1983.

Thomson, Mark A. "Louis XIV and William III, 1689–1697." *The English Historical Review* 76 (1961): 37–58; reprinted in *William III and Louis XIV: Essays 1680–1720 by and for Mark A. Thomson*. Edited by R.M. Hatton and J.S. Bromley. Liverpool: Liverpool University Press, 1968.

Troost, Wouter. "William III, Brandenburg and the Construction of the anti-French Coalition, 1672–1688." In *The Anglo-Dutch Moment: Essays on the Glorious Revolution and Its World Impact*. Edited by J. I. Israel. Cambridge: Cambridge University Press, 1991.

Wilson, John. *Bavarian Army 1680–1715: The Uniform and Organization Guide*. London: Gosling Press, 1993.

Wilson, Lester N. "François de Callières (1645–1717): Diplomat and Man of Letters." Ph.D. thesis, University of Illinois, 1963.

THE PARTITION TREATIES AND THE WAR OF THE SPANISH SUCCESSION, 1697–1714

Arnade, Charles W. *The Siege of St. Augustine in 1702*. Gainesville: University of Florida Press, 1959.

Asher, Eugene L. "Louis XIV, William III, and the Holstein Question, 1697–1700." *University of Wichita Bulletin* 33 (February 1958): 3–15.

Atkinson, Christopher T., editor. *A Royal Dragoon in the Spanish War: A Contemporary Narrative*. London: Gale and Polden, 1938.

_____. "Brihuega, December 1710." *Journal of the Society for Army Historical Research* 21 (1943): 112–22.

_____. *Marlborough and the Rise of the British Army.* New York: G.P. Putnam's Sons, 1921.

_____. "Marlborough's Sieges." *Journal of the Society for Army Historical Research* 13 (1935): 195–205.

_____. "Marlborough's Sieges: Further Evidence." *Journal of the Society for Army Historical Research* 24 (1946): 83–87.

_____. "Queen Anne's War in the West Indies." *Journal of the Society for Army Historical Research* 24 (1946): 100–9, 183–97.

_____. "The Cost of Queen Anne's War." *Journal of the Society for Army Historical Research* 33 (1955): 174–83.

_____. "The Peninsular 'Second Front' in the Spanish Succession War." *Journal of the Society for Army Historical Research* 22 (1944): 223–33.

_____. "The War of the Spanish Succession: Campaigns and Negotiations." In *The Cambridge Modern History*, Volume V. Edited by A.W. Ward and others. Cambridge: Cambridge University Press, 1908.

_____. "Wynendael." *Journal of the Society for Army Historical Research* 34 (1956): 26–31.

_____ and J.W. Wijn. "The Ramillies Battlefield." *Journal of the Society for Army Historical Research* 32 (1954): 14–18.

Barnard, Jon. "From Bedburg to Blenheim: The Logistics of Marlborough's 1704 Campaign." M.A. thesis, University of Victoria, 2000.

Barnett, Correlli. *Marlborough.* London: Eyre Methuen, 1974.

Belfield, Eversley. *Oudenarde, 1708.* London: Charles Knight, 1972.

Belloc, Hilaire. *The Tactics and Strategy of the Great Duke of Marlborough.* Bristol: Arrowsmith, 1933.

Benda, Kálmán. "The Rákóczi War of Independence and the European Powers." In *From Hunyadi to Rákóczi: War and Society in Late Medieval and Early Modern Hungary*. Edited by J. Bak and B. Király. New York: Brooklyn College Press, 1982.

Bisson, Douglas R. "Public Opinion, Parliament and the Partition Treaties: England's Entry into the War of the Spanish Succession, 1698–1702." M.A. thesis, Ohio State University, 1981.

Boles, Laurence H., Jr. *The Huguenots, the Protestant Interest, and the War of the Spanish Succession, 1702–1714*. New York: Peter Lang, 1997.

Bourne, R. *Queen Anne's Navy in the West Indies*. New Haven: Yale University Press, 1934.

Bowen, H.G. "The Dutch at Malplaquet, 11 September 1709: Did the Prince of Orange Exceed His Orders?" *Journal of the Society for Army Historical Research* 40 (1962): 39–41.

Bromley, John S. "The French Privateering War, 1702–1713." In *Historical Essays, 1600–1750: Presented to David Ogg*. Edited by H.E. Bell and R.C. Ollard. London: Adam and Charles Black, 1963; reprinted in *Corsairs and Navies, 1660–1760*. London: Hambledon Press, 1987.

Burton, Ivor F. *The Captain-General: The Career of John Churchill, Duke of Marlborough, from 1702–1711*. London: Constable, 1968.

_____. "The Secretary of War and the Administration of the Army during the War of the Spanish Succession." Ph.D. thesis, University of London, 1960.

_____. "The Supply of Infantry for the War in the Peninsula, 1703–1707." *Bulletin of the Institute for Historical Research* 28 (1955): 35–62.

Carr Laughton, L.G. "The Battle of Vélez Málaga, 1704." *The Journal of the Royal United Service Institution* 68 (August 1923): 368–87.

Chandler, David G. *Blenheim Preparation: Collected Essays on the Armies of William III and Marlborough*. Staplehurst: Spellmount, 2003.

_____. *Marlborough as Military Commander*. London: B.T. Batsford, 1973.

_____. "The Campaign of 1704." *History Today* 12–13 (December 1962/ January 1963): 854–62, 33–43.

_____. "'The Old Corporal': Marlborough." *History Today* 22 (September 1972): 613–23.

_____. "The Siege of Alicante." *History Today* 19 (July 1969): 475–85.

Churchill, Winston S. *Marlborough: His Life and Times*. 4 volumes. London: George G. Harrap, 1933–38.

Clark, George N. "From the Nine Years' War to the War of the Spanish Succession." In *The New Cambridge Modern History*, Volume VI. Edited by J.S. Bromley. Cambridge: Cambridge University Press, 1970.

Coombs, Douglas S. "The Augmentation of 1709: A Study in the Workings of the Anglo-Dutch Alliance." *The English Historical Review* 72 (October 1972): 642–61.

_____. *The Conduct of the Dutch: British Opinion and the Dutch Alliance during the War of the Spanish Succession*. The Hague: Martinus Nijhoff, 1958.

Cruickshanks, Eveline. "Attempts to Restore the Stuarts, 1689–1696." In *The Stuart Court in Exile and the Jacobites*. Edited by E. Cruickshanks and E. Corp. London: Hambledon Press, 1995.

Davies, Godfrey. "The Reduction of the Army after the Peace of Ryswick, 1697." *The Journal of the Society for Army Historical Research* 28 (1950): 15–28.

Deane, John Marshall. *A Journal of Marlborough's Campaigns during the War of the Spanish Succession, 1704–1711*. Edited by D.G. Chandler. London: Society for Army Historical Research, 1984.

Denman, T.J. "The Debates over War Strategy, 1689–1714." Ph.D. diss., Cambridge University, 1984.

Dickinson, H.T. *Bolingbroke*. London: Constable, 1970.

_____. "The Capture of Minorca, 1708." *Mariner's Mirror* 51 (1965): 195–204.

_____. "Peterborough and the Capture of Barcelona, 1705." *History Today* 14 (1964): 705–15.

_____. "The Earl of Peterborough's Campaign in Valencia, 1706." *Journal of the Society for Army Historical Research* 45 (1967): 35–52.

_____. "The Recall of Lord Peterborough." *Journal of the Society for Army Historical Research* 47 (1969): 175–87.

Dickinson, William C. *Sidney Godolphin, Lord Treasurer, 1702–1710.* Lewiston: Edwin Mellen Press, 1990.

_____ and Eloise R. Hitchcock. *The War of the Spanish Succession, 1702–1713: A Selected Bibliography.* Westport: Greenwood Press, 1996.

Falkner, James. *Great and Glorious Days: The Duke of Marlborough's Battles, 1704–1709.* Staplehurst: Spellmount, 2002.

Fieldhouse, N.H. "A Note on the Negotiations for the Peace of Utrecht." *The American Historical Review* 40 (January 1935): 274–78.

_____. "St. John and Savoy in the War of the Spanish Succession." *The English Historical Review* 50 (1935): 278–91.

Fortescue, John. *Marlborough.* New York: D. Appleton and Company, 1932.

Francis, A. David. "John Methuen and the Anglo-Portuguese Treaties of 1703." *The Historical Journal* 3 (1960): 103–24.

_____. "Marlborough's March to the Danube, 1704." *Journal of the Society for Army Historical Research* 50 (Summer 1972): 78–100.

_____. "Portugal and the Grand Alliance." *Bulletin of the Institute of Historical Research* 38 (May 1965): 71–93.

_____. "Prince George of Hesse-Darmstadt and the Plans for the Expedition to Spain of 1702." *Bulletin of the Institute for Historical Research* 42 (May 1969): 58–75.

_____. *The First Peninsular War, 1702–1713*. London: Ernest Benn, 1975.

_____. "The Grand Alliance in 1698." *The Historical Journal* 10 (1967): 352–60.

_____. *The Methuens and Portugal, 1691–1708*. Cambridge: Cambridge University Press, 1966.

Frey, Linda. "Anglo-Prussian Relations, 1703–1708: Thomas Wentworth, Baron Raby's Mission to Berlin." Ph.D. diss., Ohio State University, 1971.

_____. "Franco-Prussian Relations, 1701–1706." *Proceedings of the Annual Meeting of the Western Society for French History* 3 (1976): 94–105.

_____. "Frederick I and His Court: A Fatal Indecision?" *Revue de l'Université d'Ottawa* 45 (1975): 478–90.

_____. "Thomas Wentworth's Mission at The Hague, 1711–1712." M.A. thesis, Ohio State University, 1968.

_____ and Marsha Frey. "A Question of Empire: Leopold I and the War of the Spanish Succession, 1701–1705." *Austrian History Yearbook* 14 (1978): 56–73.

_____. *A Question of Empire: Leopold I and the War of the Spanish Succession, 1701–1705*. New York: Columbia University Press, 1983.

_____. *Frederick I: The Man and His Times*. New York: Columbia University Press, 1984.

_____. "The Foreign Policy of Frederick I, King in Prussia, 1703–1711: A Fatal Vacillation?" *East European Quarterly* 9 (Fall 1975): 259–69.

_____. "The Latter Years of Leopold I and His Court, 1700–1705: A Pernicious Factionalism." *The Historian* 40 (May 1978): 479–91.

_____. "The Rákóczi Insurrection and the Disruption of the Grand Alliance." *Canadian-American Review of Hungarian Studies* 5 (Fall 1978): 17–29.

_____. *"Le Roi Soleil et Le Singe,* Louis XIV and Frederick I: Franco-Prussian Relations, 1707–1713." *Proceedings of the Annual Meeting of the Western Society for French History* 5 (1978): 14–21.

_____. "Rákóczi and the Maritime Powers: An Uncertain Friendship." In *Hunyadi to Rákóczi: War and Society in Late Medieval and Early Modern Hungary.* Edited by J.M. Bak and B.K. Király. New York: Brooklyn College Press, 1982.

_____. "The Anglo-Prussian Treaty of 1704." *Canadian Journal of History* 11 (December 1976): 283–94.

_____, editors. *The Treaties of the War of the Spanish Succession: An Historical and Critical Dictionary.* Westport: Greenwood Press, 1995.

Frey, Marsha. "A Boot of Contention: Franco-Austrian Conflict over Italy during the Early Years of the War of the Spanish Succession, 1701–1705." *Proceedings of the Annual Meeting of the Western Society for French History* 3 (1976): 118–26.

_____. "Austria's Role as an Ally of the Maritime Powers during the Early Years of the War of the Spanish Succession, 1701–1706." Ph.D. diss., Ohio State University, 1971.

_____. "Charles Townshend's Mission at The Hague, 1709–1711." M.A. thesis, Ohio State University, 1968.

Gaeddert, Dale A. "The Franco-Bavarian Alliance during the War of the Spanish Succession." Ph.D. diss., Ohio State University, 1969.

Garland, John. "Irish Officers in the Bavarian Service during the War of the Spanish Succession." *The Irish Sword* 14 (1981): 240–55.

Geike, Roderick and Isabel A Montgomery. *The Dutch Barrier, 1705–1719.* Cambridge: Cambridge University Press, 1930.

Gibson, John S. *Playing the Scottish Card: The Franco-Jacobite Invasion of 1708.* Edinburgh: Edinburgh University Press, 1988.

Gradish, Stephen F. "The Establishment of British Seapower in the Mediterranean, 1689–1713." *Canadian Journal of History* 10 (April 1975): 1–16.

Green, David. *Blenheim*. London: Collins, 1974.

Gregg, Edward. "'Power, Friends or Alliances': The Search for the Pretender's Bride." *Studies in History and Politics* 4 (1985): 35–54.

_____. *Queen Anne*. London: Routledge and Kegan Paul, 1980.

_____. *The Protestant Succession in International Politics, 1710–1716*. New York: Garland, 1986.

Harding, Richard. "The Expeditions to Quebec, 1690–1711: The Evolution of British Trans-Atlantic Amphibious Power." *Guerres Maritimes, 1688–1713: IVes journées franco-britanniques d'historie de la marine, Portsmouth, 1er–4 avril 1992*. Vincennes: Service Historique de la Marine, 1996.

Hartley, Janet M. *Charles Whitworth: Diplomat in the Age of Peter the Great*. Aldershot: Ashgate, 2002.

Hattendorf, John B. "Alliance, Encirclement, and Attrition: British Grand Strategy in the War of the Spanish Succession, 1702–1713." In *Grand Strategies in War and Peace*. Edited by Paul Kennedy. New Haven: Yale University Press, 1991.

_____. *England in the War of the Spanish Succession: A Study of the English View and Conduct of Grand Strategy, 1702–1712*. New York: Garland, 1987.

_____. "English Grand Strategy and the Blenheim Campaign of 1704." *The International History Review* 5 (February 1983): 3–19.

_____. "The Machinery for Planning and Execution of English Grand Strategy in the War of the Spanish Succession, 1702–1713." In *Changing Interpretations and New Sources in Naval History*. Edited by Robert W. Love, Jr. New York: Garland, 1980.

_____. "The Rákóczi Insurrection in English War Policy, 1703–1711." *Canadian-American Review of Hungarian Studies* 7 (Fall 1980): 91–102.

Hatton, Ragnhild M. *George I: Elector and King*. London: Thames and Hudson, 1978.

_____. "John Drummond in the War of the Spanish Succession: A Merchant Turned Diplomatic Agent." In *Studies in Diplomatic History: Essays in Memory of David Bayne Horn*. Edited by R.M. Hatton and M.S. Anderson. London: Longman, 1970.

Henderson, Nicholas. *Prince Eugen of Savoy: A Biography*. London: Weidenfeld and Nicolson, 1964.

Herman, Mark C. "Sir Thomas Wentworth, Third Earl of Strafford, and the Treaty of Utrecht, 1711–1713." Ph.D. diss., University of South Carolina, 1988.

Hill, Brian W. "Oxford, Bolingbroke, and the Peace of Utrecht." *The Historical Journal* 16 (1973): 241–63.

_____. *Robert Harley: Speaker, Secretary of State and Premier Minister*. New Haven: Yale University Press, 1988.

Hoff, B. van't, editor. *The Correspondence of John Churchill, First Duke of Marlborough, and Anthonie Heinsius, Grand Pensionary of Holland, 1701–1711*. The Hague: Martinus Nijhoff, 1951.

Hurgill, J.A.C. *No Peace without Spain*. Oxford: Kensal Press, 1991.

Ingrao, Charles W. "Guerilla Warfare in Early Modern Europe: The Kuruc War, 1703–1711." In *War and Society in East Central Europe*. Edited by B.K. Kiraly and G.E. Rothenberg. New York: Brooklyn College, 1979.

_____. *In Quest and Crisis: Emperor Joseph I and the Habsburg Monarchy*. West Lafayette: Purdue University Press, 1979.

Jones, James R. *Marlborough*. Cambridge: Cambridge University Press, 1993.

Kamen, Henry. *Philip V of Spain: The King Who Reigned Twice*. New Haven: Yale University Press, 2001.

_____. "The Destruction of the Spanish Silver Fleet at Vigo in 1702." *Bulletin of the Institute of Historical Research* 39 (1966): 165–73.

_____. *The War of the Succession in Spain, 1700–1715*. London: Weidenfeld and Nicolson, 1969.

Kearsey, A. *Marlborough and His Campaigns, 1702–1709*. Second edition. Aldershot: Gale and Polden, n.d.

Kemp, Anthony. *Weapons and Equipment of the Marlborough Wars*. Poole: Blandford Press, 1980.

Kenyon, John P. "William III." *History Today* 9 (September and October 1959): 581–88, 664–71.

Klaits, Joseph A. "Diplomacy and Public Opinion: Louis XIV, Colbert de Torcy and French War Propaganda, 1700–1713." 2 volumes. Ph.D. thesis, University of Minnesota, 1970.

Koningsbrugge, J.S.A.M. van. "A Time of War: Dutch-Baltic Relations in the Years 1709–1711." In *Baltic Affairs: Relations between the Netherlands and North-Eastern Europe, 1500–1800*. Edited by J.Ph.S Lemmink and J.S.A.M. van Koningsbrugge. Nijmegen: Institute for Northern and Eastern European Studies, 1990.

_____. "Of Diplomats, Merchants, and Regents: Dutch-Baltic Relations 1697–1709." In *Russians and Dutchmen. Proceedings of the Conference on the Relations between Russia and the Netherlands from the 16th to the 20th Century held at the Rijksmuseum Amsterdam, June 1989*. Edited by J. Braat, A.H. Huussen, Jr., B. Naarden, and C.A.L.M. Willemsen. Groningen: Institute for Northern and Eastern European Studies, 1993.

_____. "The Dutch Republic, Sweden and Russia, 1697–1708, and the Secret Activities of Cornelis Cruys and Johannes van den Burgh." In *Russia and the Low Countries in the Eighteenth Century*. Edited by Emmanuel Waegemans. Groningen: Institute for Northern and Eastern European Studies, 1998.

Lodge, Richard. "The Spanish Succession." *History*, New series 12 (1927–28): 333–38.

McKay, Derek. *Prince Eugene of Savoy*. London: Thames and Hudson, 1977.

MacLachlan, A.D. "The Great Peace: Negotiations for the Treaty of Utrecht, 1710–1713." Ph.D. diss., Cambridge University, 1965.

_____. "The Road to Peace, 1710–1713." In *Britain after the Glorious Revolution, 1689–1714*. Edited by G. Holmes. London: Macmillan, 1969.

Martin, M.A. "Diplomatic Relations between Great Britain and Spain, 1711–1714." Ph.D. diss., University of London, 1962.

Michael, Wolfgang. "The Treaties of Partition and the Spanish Succession." In *The Cambridge Modern History*, Volume V. Cambridge: Cambridge University Press, 1908.

Milne, June. "The Diplomacy of Dr. John Robinson at the Court of Charles XII of Sweden, 1697–1709." *Transactions of the Royal Historical Society*, Fourth series 30 (1948): 73–93.

Moore, Anthony. *Army of Brandenburg-Prussia 1680–1715*. London: Gosling Press, 1993.

Ostwald, Jamel. "The 'Decisive' Battle of Ramillies, 1706: Prerequisites for Decisiveness in Early Modern Warfare." *The Journal of Military History* 64 (July 2000): 649–78.

_____. "The Failure of the 'Strategy of Annihilation': Battle and Fortresses in the War of the Spanish Succession." M.A. thesis, Ohio State University, 1994.

_____. "Vauban's Siege Legacy in the War of the Spanish Succession, 1702–1712." Ph.D. diss., Ohio State University, 2002.

Owen, John H. *War at Sea under Queen Anne, 1702–1708*. Cambridge: Cambridge University Press, 1938.

Parnell, Arthur. *The War of Succession in Spain during the Reign of Queen Anne, 1702–1711*. Second edition. London: George Bell and Sons, 1905.

Pastor, Peter. "Hungarian-Russian Relations during the Rákóczi War of Independence." In *From Hunyadi to Rákóczi: War and Society in Late Medieval and Early Modern Hungary*. Edited by J. Bak and B. Király. New York: Brooklyn College Press, 1982.

Perjés, Géza. "Reflections on the Strategic Decisions of Ferenc II Rákóczi's War of Independence." In *From Hunyadi to Rákóczi: War and Society in Late*

Medieval and Early Modern Hungary. Edited by J. Bak and B. Király. New York: Brooklyn College Press, 1982.

Petrie, Charles. *The Marshal Duke of Berwick: The Picture of an Age.* London: Eyre and Spottiswoode, 1953.

Phelan, Ivan P. "Marlborough as Logistician." *Journal of the Society for Army Historical Research* 68–69 (1990–91): 253–57, 36–48, 103–119.

Pitt, H.G. "The Pacification of Utrecht." In *The New Cambridge Modern History,* Volume VI. Edited by J.S. Bromley. Cambridge: Cambridge University Press, 1970.

Prestage, Edgar. *Portugal and the War of the Spanish Succession: A Bibliography with Some Diplomatic Documents.* Cambridge: Cambridge University Press, 1938.

Roosen, William. "The Origins of the War of the Spanish Succession." In *The Origins of War in Early Modern Europe.* Edited by J. Black. Edinburgh: John Donald, 1987.

Rothstein, Andrew. *Peter the Great and Marlborough: Politics and Diplomacy in Converging Wars.* London: Macmillan, 1986.

Rule, John C. "Colbert de Torcy, an Emergent Bureaucracy, and the Formulation of French Foreign Policy, 1698–1715." In *Louis XIV and Europe.* Edited by R.M. Hatton. London: Macmillan Press, 1976.

_____. "France and the Preliminaries to the Gertruydenberg Conference, September 1709 to March 1710." In *Studies in Diplomatic History: Essays in Memory of David Bayne Horn.* Edited by R.M. Hatton and M.S. Anderson. London: Longman, 1970.

_____. "King and Minister: Louis XIV and Colbert de Torcy." In *William III and Louis XIV: Essays 1680–1720 by and for Mark A. Thomson.* Edited by R.M. Hatton and J.S. Bromley. Liverpool: Liverpool University Press, 1968.

_____. "The Preliminary Negotiations Leading to the Peace of Utrecht, 1702–1712." Ph.D. diss., Harvard University, 1958.

Schwoerer, Lois G. "The Role of William III in England in the Standing Army Controversy, 1697–1699." *Journal of British Studies* 5 (1966): 74–94.

Scouller, R.E. "Marlborough's Administration in the Field." *The Army Quarterly and Defence Journal* 95–95 (October 1967/January 1968): 197–208, 102–13.

_____. *The Armies of Queen Anne.* Oxford: Oxford University Press, 1966.

Slottman, William B. "Austro-Turkish Relations: Carlowitz and the Rákóczi Rebellion." Ph.D. diss., Harvard University, 1958.

_____. *Ferenc II Rákóczi and the Great Powers.* New York: Columbia University Press, 1997.

Snyder, Henry L. "The Formulation of Foreign and Domestic Policy in the Reign of Queen Anne: Memoranda by Lord Chancellor Cowper of Conversations with Lord Treasurer Godolphin." *The Historical Journal* 11 (1968): 144–60.

_____, editor. *The Marlborough-Godolphin Correspondence.* 3 volumes. Oxford: Oxford University Press, 1975.

Stamp, A.E. "The Meeting of the Duke of Marlborough and Charles XII at Altranstädt, April 1707." *Transactions of the Royal Historical Society*, New series 12 (1898): 103–16.

Stork-Penning, Johanna G. "The Ordeal of the States–Some Remarks on Dutch Politics during the War of the Spanish Succession." *Acta Historiae Neerlandica* 2 (1967): 107–41.

Storrs, Christopher. "Disaster at Darien (1698–1700)? The Persistence of Spanish Imperial Power on the Eve of the Demise of the Spanish Habsburgs." *European History Quarterly* 29 (1999): 5–38.

Sturgill, Claude C. *Claude Le Blanc: Civil Servant of the King.* Gainesville: University Presses of Florida, 1975.

_____. *Marshal Villars and the War of the Spanish Succession.* Lexington: University of Kentucky Press, 1965.

_____. "Marshal Villars in the War of the Spanish Succession." Ph.D. diss., University of Kentucky, 1963.

Sundstrom, Roy A. *Sidney Godolphin: Servant of the State*. Newark: University of Delaware Press, 1992.

Sweet, Paul R. "Prince Eugene of Savoy and Central Europe." *The American Historical Review* 57 (1951–52): 47–62.

Szarka, Andrew S. "Portugal, France, and the Coming of the War of the Spanish Succession, 1697–1703." Ph.D. diss., Ohio State University Press, 1976.

Taylor, Frank. *The Wars of Marlborough, 1702–1709*. 2 volumes. Oxford: Basil Blackwell, 1921.

Thomson, George Malcolm. *The First Churchill: The life of John, First Duke of Marlborough*. London: Martin Secker and Warburg, 1979.

Thomson, Mark A. "Louis XIV and the Grand Alliance, 1705–1710." *Bulletin of the Institute of Historical Research* 34 (1961): 16–35; reprinted in *William III and Louis XIV: Essays 1680–1720 by and for Mark A. Thomson*. Edited by R.M. Hatton and J.S. Bromley. Liverpool: Liverpool University Press, 1968.

_____. "Louis XIV and the Origins of the War of the Spanish Succession." *Transactions of the Royal Historical Society*, Fifth series 4 (1954): 111–34; reprinted in *William III and Louis XIV: Essays 1680–1720 by and for Mark A. Thomson*. Edited by R.M. Hatton and J.S. Bromley. Liverpool: Liverpool University Press, 1968.

_____. "Safeguarding the Protestant Succession, 1702–1718." *History* 39 (1954): 39–53; reprinted in *William III and Louis XIV: Essays 1680–1720 by and for Mark A. Thomson*. Edited by R.M. Hatton and J.S. Bromley. Liverpool: Liverpool University Press, 1968.

Thompson, Richard H. *Lothar Franz von Schönborn and the Diplomacy of the Electorate of Mainz: From the Treaty of Ryswick to the Outbreak of the War of the Spanish Succession*. The Hague: Martinus Nijhoff, 1973.

_____. "Lothar Franz von Schönborn and the Diplomacy of the Electorate of Mainz from the Treaty of Ryswick to the Outbreak of the War of the Spanish Succession." Ph.D. diss., Indiana University, 1970.

Torntoft, Preben. "William III and Denmark-Norway, 1697–1702." *The English Historical Review* 81 (January 1966): 1–25.

Trevelyan, George M. *England under Queen Anne.* 3 volumes. London: Longmans, Green and Company, 1930–34.

_____. "Peterborough and Barcelona, 1705." *Cambridge Historical Journal* 3 (1931): 253–59.

Trotter, Ben. S. "Vauban and the Question of the Spanish Succession." *Proceedings of the Annual Meeting of the Western Society for French History* 21 (1994): 61–70.

Turner, Mary. "Anglo-Portuguese Relations in the War of the Spanish Succession." Ph.D. diss., Oxford University, 1952.

Veenendaal, August J. "The Opening Phase of Marlborough's Campaign of 1708 in the Netherlands: A Version from Dutch Sources." *History* 35 (February/June 1950): 34–48.

_____. "The War of the Spanish Succession in Europe." In *The New Cambridge Modern History,* Volume VI. Edited by J.S. Bromley. Cambridge: Cambridge University Press, 1970.

Verney, Peter. *The Battle of Blenheim.* London: B.T. Batsford, 1976.

Welch, P.J. "The Maritime Powers and the Evolution of War Aims of the Grand Alliance." M.A. thesis, University of London, 1940.

Williams, Basil. *Stanhope: A Study in Eighteenth Century War and Diplomacy.* Oxford: Clarendon Press, 1932.

Wilson, John. *Bavarian Army 1680–1715: The Uniform and Organization Guide.* London: Gosling Press, 1993.

Wines, Roger. "The Franconian *Reichskreis* and the Holy Roman Empire in the War of the Spanish Succession." Ph.D. diss., Columbia University, 1961.

Wollman, David H. "Parliament and Foreign Affairs, 1697–1714." Ph.D. thesis, University of Wisconsin, 1970.

Wood, Curtis W., Jr. "A Study of Anglo-Dutch Relations in the Grand Alliance, 1701–1706." Ph.D. thesis, University of North Carolina at Chapel Hill, 1971.

THE STRUGGLE FOR SUPREMACY IN THE BALTIC AND THE TURKISH THREAT IN EASTERN EUROPE, 1648–1721

Aldridge, D. "Sir John Norris and the British Naval Expeditions in the Baltic Sea, 1715–1727." Ph.D. diss., University of London, 1972.

_____. "The Royal Navy in the Baltic, 1715–1717." In *Britain and the Northern Seas*. Edited by W. Minchinton. Pontefract: Lofthouse, 1988.

Altbauer, Dan. "The Diplomats of Peter the Great." *Jahrbücher für Geschichte Osteuropas* 28 (1980): 1–16.

_____. "The Diplomats of Peter the Great, 1689–1725." Ph.D. thesis, Harvard University, 1976.

Anderson, Matthew S. *Peter the Great*. London: Longman, 1978.

_____. *Peter the Great*. London: Historical Association, 1969.

_____. "Russia under Peter the Great and the Changed Relations of East and West." In *The New Cambridge Modern History*, Volume VI. Edited by J.S. Bromley. Cambridge: Cambridge University Press, 1970.

Anderson, R. "Denmark and the First Anglo-Dutch War." *Mariner's Mirror* 53 (1967): 55–61.

Arkayin, A. "The Second Siege of Vienna (1683) and Its Consequences." *Revue Internationale d'Histoire Militaire* 46 (1980): 107–17.

Barany, George. *The Anglo-Russian Entente Cordiale of 1697–1698: Peter I and William III at Utrecht*. New York: Columbia University Press, 1986.

Barker, Thomas M. *Double Eagle and Crescent: Vienna's Second Turkish Siege and Its Historical Setting.* Albany: State University of New York Press, 1967.

Bennigsen, A. "Peter the Great, the Ottoman Empire, and the Caucasus." *Canadian-American Slavonic Studies* 8 (1974): 311–18.

Black, Jeremy. "Anglo-Baltic Relations 1714–1748." In *Britain and the Northern Seas.* Edited by W. Minchinton. Pontefract: Lofthouse, 1988.

_____. "Russia's Rise as a European Power, 1650–1750." *History Today* 36 (August 1986): 21–28; reprinted in *Russia and Europe.* Edited by P. Dukes. London: Collins and Brown, 1991.

Bohlen, Avis. "Changes in Russian Diplomacy under Peter the Great." *Cahiers du monde russe et sovietique* 7 (1966): 341–58.

Bushkovich, P. *Peter the Great: The Struggle for Power, 1671–1725.* Cambridge: Cambridge University Press, 2001.

Cross, Anthony. *Peter the Great through British Eyes: Perceptions and Representations of the Tsar since 1698.* Cambridge: Cambridge University Press, 2000.

Eekman, Thomas. "Seven Years with Peter the Great: The Dutchman Jacob de Bie's Observations." In *Peter the Great and the West: New Perspectives.* Edited by Lindsey Hughes. New York: Palgrave, 2001.

Englund, Peter. *The Battle of Poltava: The Birth of the Russian Empire.* London: Victor Gollancz, 1992.

Frost, Robert I. *After the Deluge: Poland-Lithuania and the Second Northern War, 1655–1660.* Cambridge: Cambridge University Press, 1993.

_____. "*Initium Calamitatis Regni'?* John Casimir and Monarchical Power in Poland-Lithuania, 1648–1668." *European History Quarterly* 16 (1986): 181–207.

Grey, Ian. "Peter the Great and the Creation of the Russian Navy." *History Today* 11 (September 1961): 625–31.

Hansen, Harold A. "Opening Phase of the Third Dutch War Described by the Danish Envoy in London, March-June 1672." *The Journal of Modern History* 21 (June 1949): 97–108.

Hartley, Janet M. *Charles Whitworth: Diplomat in the Age of Peter the Great.* Aldershot: Ashgate, 2002.

Hatton, Ragnhild M. *Charles XII.* London: Historical Association, 1974.

_____. "Charles XII and the Great Northern War." In *The New Cambridge Modern History*, Volume VI. Edited by J.S. Bromley. Cambridge: Cambridge University Press, 1970.

_____. *Charles XII of Sweden.* London: Weidenfeld and Nicolson, 1968.

Herd, Graeme. "General Patrick Gordon of Auchleuchries: A Scot in Seventeenth-Century Russian Service." Ph.D. thesis, University of Aberdeen, 1994.

_____. "Peter the Great and the Conquest of Azov, 1695–1696." In *Peter the Great and the West: New Perspectives.* Edited by Lindsey Hughes. New York: Palgrave, 2001.

Hochedlinger, Michael. *Austria's Wars of Emergence, 1683–1797.* London: Longman, 2003.

Höglund, Lars-Eric. *Scanian War 1675–1679: Colours and Uniforms.* Karlstad: Acedia Press, n.d.

_____ and Åke Sallnäs. *Great Northern War 1700–1721: Colours and Uniforms.* Karlstad: Acedia Press, n.d.

Hughes, Lindsey. *Peter the Great: A Biography.* New Haven and London: Yale University Press, 2002.

_____. *Russia and the West: The Life of a Seventeenth-Century Westernizer, Prince Vasily Vasil'evich Golitsyn (1643–1714).* Newtonville, Mass.: Oriental Research Partners, 1984.

_____. *Russia in the Age of Peter the Great.* New Haven: Yale University Press, 1998.

_____. *Sophia: Regent of Russia, 1657–1704*. New Haven: Yale University Press, 1990.

_____, editor. *Peter the Great and the West: New Perspectives*. New York: Palgrave, 2001.

Jones, Robert E. "Why St. Petersburg?" In *Peter the Great and the West: New Perspectives*. Edited by Lindsey Hughes. New York: Palgrave, 2001.

Kamińska, Anna. *Brandenburg-Prussia and Poland: A Study in Diplomatic History (1669–1672)*. Marburg an der Lahn: Johann Gottfried Herder Institut, 1983.

Kaminski, A. *Republic vs. Autocracy: Poland, Lithuania and Russia 1686–1697*. Cambridge, Mass.: Harvard University Press, 1993.

Kirby, David. "Peter the Great and the Baltic." In *Peter the Great and the West: New Perspectives*. Edited by Lindsey Hughes. New York: Palgrave, 2001.

Klaits, Joseph A. "The Idea of a Diplomat in the Age of Louis XIV: The Danish Envoy Extraordinary to France, 1688." M.A. thesis, University of Minnesota, 1966.

Koht, Halvdan. "Scandinavian Preventive Wars in the 1650s." In *Studies in Diplomatic History and Historiography in Honour of George Peabody Gooch*. Edited by Arshag Ohannes Sarkissian. London: Longmans, Green and Company, 1961.

Koningsbrugge, J.S.A.M. van. "A Time of War: Dutch-Baltic Relations in the Years 1709–1711." In *Baltic Affairs: Relations between the Netherlands and North-Eastern Europe, 1500–1800*. Edited by J.Ph.S Lemmink and J.S.A.M. van Koningsbrugge. Nijmegen: Institute for Northern and Eastern European Studies, 1990.

_____. "Of Diplomats, Merchants, and Regents: Dutch-Baltic Relations 1697–1709." In *Russians and Dutchmen. Proceedings of the Conference on the Relations between Russia and the Netherlands from the 16th to the 20th Century held at the Rijksmuseum Amsterdam, June 1989*. Edited by J. Braat, A.H. Huussen, Jr., B. Naarden, and C.A.L.M. Willemsen. Groningen: Institute for Northern and Eastern European Studies, 1993.

_____. "The Dutch Republic, Sweden and Russia, 1697–1708, and the Secret Activities of Cornelis Cruys and Johannes van den Burgh." In *Russia and the Low Countries in the Eighteenth Century*. Edited by Emmanuel Waegemans. Groningen: Institute for Northern and Eastern European Studies, 1998.

Konstam, Angus. *Poltava, 1709: Russia Comes of Age*. London: Osprey, 1994.

Król, G. "The Northern Threat: Anglo-Russian Diplomatic Relations, 1716–1727." Ph.D. Diss., University of London, 1992.

Kurat, A.N. "The Ottoman Empire under Mehmed IV." In *The New Cambridge Modern History*, Volume V. Cambridge: Cambridge University Press, 1961.

_____. "The Retreat of the Turks, 1683–1730." In *The New Cambridge Modern History*, Volume VI. Edited by J.S. Bromley. Cambridge: Cambridge University Press, 1970.

Laskowski, Otton. *Sobieski, King of Poland*. Glasgow: Polish Library, 1944.

Lee, Stephen J. *Peter the Great*. London: Routledge, 1993.

Lewitter, L.R. "Peter the Great, Poland and the Westernization of Russia." *Journal of the History of Ideas* 14 (1958): 493–506.

_____. "Poland, Russia and the Treaty of Vienna of 5 January 1719." *The Historical Journal* 13 (1970): 3–30.

_____. "Russia, Poland and the Baltic, 1697–1721." *The Historical Journal* 11 (1968): 3–34.

_____. "The Russo-Polish Treaty of 1686 and Its Antecdents." *The Polish Review* 9 (1964): No. 3, 5–29; No. 4, 21–37.

Lindenov, Christopher. *The First Triple Alliance: The Letters of Christopher Lindenov, Danish Envoy to London, 1668–1672*. Edited by W. Westergaard. New Haven: Yale University Press, 1947.

Longworth, Philip. *Alexis: Tsar of all the Russias*. London: Secker and Warburg, 1984.

_____. "Tsar Alexis Goes to War." In *Russia and Europe*. Edited by P. Dukes, London: Collins and Brown, 1991.

Lossky, Andrew. "The Baltic Question, 1679–1689." Ph.D. diss., Yale University, 1948.

Luh, Jürgen. "The Using of Peter the Great's Visit to Prussia by Frederick III of Brandenburg." In *Around Peter the Great: Three Centuries of Dutch-Russian Relations*. Edited by Carel Horstmeier, Hans van Koningsbrugge, Ilja Nieuwland, and Emmanuel Waegemans. Groningen: Institute for Northern and Eastern European Studies, 1997.

Lundkvist, Sven. "The Experience of Empire: Sweden as a Great Power." In *Sweden's Age of Greatness, 1632–1718*. Edited by M. Roberts. London: Macmillan, 1973.

Marcincowski, Karol. *The Crisis of the Polish-Swedish War, 1655–1660*. Privately printed, 1950.

Marshall, William. *Peter the Great*. London: Longman, 1996.

Massie, Robert K. *Peter the Great: His Life and World*. New York: Alfred Knopf, 1980.

Moulton, James R. "Peter the Great and the Russian Military Campaigns during the Final Years of the Great Northern War, 1719–1721." Ph.D. thesis, University of Denver, 2000.

O'Brien, C. Bickford. *Muscovy and the Ukraine: From the Pereiaslavl Agreement to the Truce of Andrusovo, 1654–1667*. Berkeley: University of California Press, 1963.

_____. "Russia and Turkey, 1677–1681: The Treaty of Bakhchisarai." *The Russian Review* 12 (1953): 259–68.

_____. *Russia under Two Tsars, 1682–1689: The Regency of Sophia Alekseevna*. Berkeley: University of California Press, 1952.

Pernal, Andrew B. "The Polish Commonwealth and the Ukraine: Diplomatic Relations, 1648–1659." Ph.D. thesis, University of Ottawa, 1977.

Roberts, Michael. "Charles X and the Great Parenthesis: A Reconsideration." In *From Oxenstierna to Charles XII: Four Studies*. Cambridge: Cambridge University Press, 1991.

_____. "Charles XI." *History* 50 (June 1965): 160–92; reprinted in *Essays in Swedish History*. Minneapolis: University of Minnesota Press, 1967.

Rothenberg, Gunther E. *The Austrian Military Border in Croatia, 1522–1747*. Urbana: University of Illinois Press, 1960.

Rothstein, Andrew. *Peter the Great and Marlborough: Politics and Diplomacy in Converging Wars*. London: Macmillan, 1986.

Rystad, Göran. "Magnus Gabriel de la Gardie." In *Sweden's Age of Greatness, 1631–1718*. Edited by M. Roberts. London: Macmillan, 1973.

_____. "Sweden and the Nijmegen Congress." In *The Peace of Nijmegen, 1676–1678/79*. Edited by J.A.H. Bots. Amsterdam: APA-Holland University Press, 1980.

Sass, Charles. "The Election Campaign in Poland in the Years 1696–1697." *The Journal of Central European Affairs* 12 (July 1952): 111–27.

Stein, Mark Lewis. "Seventeenth-Century Ottoman Forts and Garrisons on the Habsburg Frontier." Ph.D. diss., University of Chicago, 2001.

Stevens, Carol B. "Why Seventeenth-Century Muscovite Campaigns against Crimea Fell Short of What Counted." *Russian History* 19 (1992): 487–504.

Stoye, John W. *The Siege of Vienna*. London: Collins, 1964.

Subtelny, O. "Mazepa, Peter I, and the Question of Treason." *Harvard Ukrainian Studies* 2 (1978): 158–84.

Sumner, Bernard H. *Peter the Great and the Emergence of Russia*. London: Hodder and Stoughton, 1950.

_____. *Peter the Great and the Ottoman Empire*. Oxford: Basil Blackwell, 1949; reprint, Hamden: Archon Books, 1965.

Upton, Anthony F. *Charles XI and Swedish Absolutism*. Cambridge: Cambridge University Press, 1998.

Warner, Richard H. "The Kožuchovo Campaign of 1694 or The Conquest of Moscow by Preobraženskoe." *Jahrbücher für Geschichte Osteuropas* 13 (1965): 487–96.

Wierema, A.C.L. "Denmark as an ally of the Dutch Republic during the '*Guerre d'Hollande*' (1674–1679). In *Baltic Affairs: Relations between the Netherlands and North-Eastern Europe, 1500–1800*. Edited by J.Ph.S Lemmink and J.S.A.M. van Koningsbrugge. Nijmegen: Institute for Northern and Eastern European Studies, 1990.

Wójcik, Zbigniew. "From the Peace of Oliwa to the Truce of Bakhchisarai: International Relations in Eastern Europe, 1660–1681." *Acta Poloniae Historica* 34 (1976): 255–80.

_____. "King John III of Poland and the Turkish Aspects of His Foreign Policy." *Turk Tarih Kurumu: Belleten* 44 (1980): 659–73.

_____. "Some Problems of Polish-Tartar Relations in the Seventeenth Century: The Financial Aspects of the Polish-Tartar Alliance in the Years 1654–1666." *Acta Poloniae Historica* 13 (1966): 87–102.

PART XIII
EUROPE IN THE
EIGHTEENTH CENTURY,
1715–1789

EUROPE, 1715–1789

Anderson, Matthew S. *Europe in the Eighteenth Century, 1713–1783*. Second edition. London: Longman, 1976.

_____. "Great Britain and the Barbary States in the Eighteenth Century." *Bulletin of the Institute of Historical Research* 29 (1956): 87–107.

_____. "Great Britain and the Growth of the Russian Navy in the Eighteenth Century." *Mariner's Mirror* (1956): 132–46.

Aksan, Virginia H. *An Ottoman Statesman in War and Peace: Ahmed Resmi Efendi, 1700–1783*. Leiden: E.J. Brill, 1995.

Bagger, Hans. "The Role of the Baltic in Russian Foreign Policy, 1721–1773." In *Imperial Russian Foreign Policy*. Edited by H. Ragsdale. Cambridge: Cambridge University Press, 1993.

Barton, H.A. "Russia and the Problem of Sweden-Finland, 1721–1809." *East European Quarterly* 5 (1972): 431–55.

Baugh, Daniel A. "Withdrawing from Europe: Anglo-French Maritime Geopolitics, 1750–1800." *The International History Review* 20 (March 1998): 1–32.

Black, Jeremy. "Anglo-Spanish Naval Relations in the Eighteenth Century." *Mariner's Mirror* 77 (1991): 235–58.

_____. "Britain's Foreign Alliances in the Eighteenth Century." *Albion* 20 (Winter 1988): 573–602.

_____. "British Foreign Policy in the Eighteenth Century: A Survey." *Journal of British Studies* 26 (January 1987): 26–53.

_____. "British Naval Power and International Commitments: Political and Strategic Problems, 1688–1770." In *Parameters of British Naval Power, 1650–1850*. Edited by M. Duffy. Exeter: Exeter University Press, 1992.

_____. *Europe in the Eighteenth Century, 1700–1789*. New York: St. Martin's, 1990.

_____. *Jacobitism and British Foreign Policy under the First Two Georges, 1714–1760*. Huntingdon: Royal Stuart Society, 1988.

_____. "Mid-Eighteenth Century Conflict with Particular Reference to the Wars of the Polish and Austrian Successions." In *The Origins of War in Early Modern Europe*. Edited by J. Black. Edinburgh: John Donald, 1987.

_____. *Natural and Necessary Enemies: Anglo-French Relations in the Eighteenth Century*. London: Duckworth, 1986.

_____. "On the 'Old System' and the 'Diplomatic Revolution' of the Eighteenth Century." *The International History Review* 12 (May 1990): 301–23.

_____. "The British Navy and British Foreign Policy in the First Half of the Eighteenth Century." *Studies in History and Politics* 4 (1985): 135–54.

_____. "The British State and Foreign Policy in the Eighteenth Century." *Trivium* 23 (1988): 127–48.

_____. "The Development of Anglo-Sardinian Relations in the First Half of the Eighteenth Century." *Studi Piemontese* 12 (1983): 48–59.

_____. "The House of Lords and British Foreign Policy, 1720–1748." In *A Pillar of the Constitution: The House of Lords in British Politics, 1640–1784*. Edited by Clyve Jones. London: Hambledon Press, 1989.

_____. *The Rise of the European Powers, 1679–1793*. London: Edward Arnold, 1990.

Blanning, Timothy C.W. "Louis XV and the Decline of the French Monarchy." *History Review* 22 (1995): 20–24.

Bromley, John S. "The Second Hundred Years' War (1689–1815)." In *Britain and France: Ten Centuries*. Edited by Douglas Johnson and others. Folkestone: Dawson, 1980; reprinted in *Corsairs and Navies, 1660–1760*. London: Hambledon Press, 1987.

Carter, Alice Clare. "The Dutch Barrier Fortresses in the Eighteenth Century, As Shown in the De Ferraris Map." In *La Cartographie au XVIIIe Siècle et l'oeuvre du comte de Ferraris (1726–1814)*. Brussels: Crédit Communal de Belgique, 1978.

Christie, Ian R. *Crisis of Empire: Great Britain and the American Colonies, 1754–1783*. London: Edward Arnold, 1966.

_____. *Wars and Revolutions: Britain, 1760–1815*. London: Edward Arnold, 1982.

Conn, Stetson. *Gibraltar in British Diplomacy in the Eighteenth Century*. New Haven: Yale University Press, 1942.

Dorn, W.L. *Competition for Empire, 1740–1763*. New York: Harper and Brothers, 1940.

Dunthorne, Hugh. "Prince and Republic: The House of Orange in Dutch and Anglo-Dutch Politics during the First Half of the Eighteenth Century." *Studies in History and Politics* 4 (1985): 19–34.

Eccles, William J. "The Role of the American Colonies in Eighteenth-Century French Foreign Policy." In *Essays on New France*. Oxford: Oxford University Press, 1987.

Ellis, K.L. "British Communications and Diplomacy in the Eighteenth Century." *Bulletin of Historical Research* 31 (1958): 159–67.

Feldbæk, Ole. "Denmark and the Baltic, 1720–1864." In *In Quest of Trade and Security: The Baltic in Power Politics, 1500–1900*, Volume I. Edited by G. Rystad, K.-R. Böhme, and W.M. Carlsgen. Lund: Lund University Press, 1994.

Ferling, John. *Struggle for a Continent: The Wars of Early America*. Arlington Heights: Harlan Davidson, 1993.

Gershoy, Leo. *From Despotism to Revolution, 1763–1789*. New York: Harper and Brothers, 1944.

Gibbs, Graham C. "English Attitudes Towards Hanover and the Hanoverian Succession in the First Half of the Eighteenth Century." In *England und Hannover*. Edited by Adolf M. Birke and Kurt Kluxen. Munich: Saur, 1986.

_____. "Laying Treaties before Parliament in the Eighteenth Century." In *Studies in Diplomatic History: Essays in Memory of David Bayne Horn*. Edited by R.M. Hatton and M.S. Anderson. London: Longman, 1970.

Gooch, George Peabody. *Louis XIV: The Monarchy in Decline*. London: Longmans, Green and Company, 1956.

Goodwin, A., editor. *The American and French Revolutions, 1763–1793*. Volume VIII in *The New Cambridge Modern History*. Cambridge: Cambridge University Press, 1965.

Greene, Jack P., John J. Tepaske, Edward L. Cox, Kenneth R. Maxwell, and Anne Perotin-Dumon. "The Atlantic Empires in the Eighteenth Century." *The International History Review* 6 (November 1984): 507–69.

Gwyn, Julian. "The Royal Navy in North America, 1712–1776." In *The British Navy and the Use of Naval Power in the Eighteenth Century*. Edited by J. Black and P. Woodfine. Atlantic Highlands: Humanities Press International, 1989.

Hargreaves-Mawdsley, W.N. *Eighteenth-Century Spain, 1700–1788: A Political, Diplomatic and Institutional History*. London: Macmillan, 1979.

Hatton, Ragnild M. "England and Hanover 1714–1837." In *England und Hannover*. Edited by Adolf M. Birke and Kurt Kluxen. Munich: Saur, 1986.

_____. *The Anglo-Hanoverian Connection, 1714–1760*. London: University of London, 1982.

Hayes, James. "The Royal House of Hanover and the British Army, 1714–1760." *Bulletin of the John Rylands Library* 40 (1957–58): 328–57.

Hochedlinger, Michael. *Austria's Wars of Emergence, 1683–1797*. London: Longman, 2003.

Horn, David Bayne. *Great Britain and Europe in the Eighteenth Century*. Oxford: Clarendon Press, 1967.

_____. *The British Diplomatic Service, 1689–1789*. Oxford: Clarendon Press, 1961.

_____. "The Machinery for the Conduct of British Foreign Policy in the Eighteenth Century." *Journal of the Society of Archivists* 3 (1965–69): 229–40.

Houlding, J.A. *Fit for Service: The Training of the British Army, 1715–1795*. Oxford: Clarendon Press, 1981.

Ingrao, Charles W. "Conflict or Consensus? Habsburg Absolutism and Foreign Policy 1700–1748." *Austrian History Yearbook* 19–20 (1983–84): 33–41.

_____. "Habsburg Strategy and Geopolitics during the Eighteenth Century." In *East Central European Society and War in the Pre-Revolutionary Eighteenth Century*. Edited by G.E. Rothenberg, B.K. Kiraly, and P.F. Sugar. Boulder: Greenwood, 1982.

Jones, George H. *The Mainstream of Jacobitism*. Cambridge, Mass.: Harvard University Press, 1954.

Kaplan, Lawrence S. *Colonies into Nation: American Diplomacy, 1763–1801*. New York: Macmillan, 1972.

Kurat, A.N. "The Retreat of the Turks, 1683–1730." In *The New Cambridge Modern History*, Volume VI. Edited by J.S. Bromley. Cambridge: Cambridge University Press, 1970.

Langford, Paul. *The Eighteenth Century, 1688–1815*. London: Adam and Charles Black, 1976.

Lenman, Bruce. *Britain's Colonial Wars, 1688–1783*. London: Pearson Education, 2001.

_____. *The Jacobite Risings in Britain, 1689–1746*. London: Eyre Methuen, 1980.

Langley, Lester D. *The Americas in the Age of Revolution, 1750–1850*. New Haven: Yale University Press, 1996.

Lindsay, J.O. "International Relations." In *The New Cambridge Modern History*, Volume VII. Edited by J.O. Lindsay. Cambridge: Cambridge University Press, 1957.

_____, editor. *The Old Regime, 1713–1763*. Volume VII in *The New Cambridge Modern History*. Cambridge: Cambridge University Press, 1957.

Lodge, Richard. *Great Britain and Prussia in the Eighteenth Century*. Oxford: Oxford University Press, 1923; reprint, New York: Octagon, 1972.

_____. "The Maritime Powers in the Eighteenth Century." *History* 15 (1930–31): 246–52.

Lukowski, Jerzy T. *Liberty's Folly: The Polish-Lithuanian Commonwealth in the Eighteenth Century, 1697–1795*. London: Routledge, 1991.

McNeill, J.R. *Atlantic Empires of France and Spain: Havana and Louisbourg, 1700–1763*. Chapel Hill: University of North Carolina Press, 1985.

Misiunas, R.J. "The Baltic Question after Nystad." *Baltic History* 3 (1974): 71–90.

Ogg, David. *Europe of the Ancien Régime, 1715–1783*. New York: Harper and Row, 1964.

Quazza, Guido. "Italy's Role in the European Problems of the First Half of the Eighteenth Century." In *Studies in Diplomatic History: Essays in Memory of David Bayne Horn*. Edited by R.M. Hatton and M.S. Anderson. London: Longman, 1970.

Parry, J.H. *Trade and Dominion: The European Overseas Empire in the Eighteenth Century*. London: Weidenfeld and Nicolson, 1971.

Peckham, Howard H. *The Colonial Wars, 1689–1762*. Chicago: University of Chicago Press, 1964.

Pintner, Walter M. *Russia as a Great Power, 1709–1856: Reflections on the Problem of Relative Backwardness with Special Reference to the Russian Army and Russian Society*. Washington, D.C.: Kennan Institute for Advanced Russian Studies, 1978.

_____. "Russia's Military Style, Russian Society and Russian Power in the Eighteenth Century." In *Russia and the West in the Eighteenth Century*. Edited by A.G. Cross. Newtonville, Mass.: Oriental Research Partners, 1983.

Ragsdale, Hugh. "Russian Projects of Conquest in the Eighteenth Century." In *Imperial Russian Foreign Policy*. Edited by H. Ragsdale. Cambridge: Cambridge University Press, 1993.

Ranum, Orest. "Louis XV and the Price of Pacific Inclination." *The International History Review* 13 (May 1991): 331–38.

Roberts, Michael. *The Age of Liberty: Sweden, 1719–1772*. Cambridge: Cambridge University Press, 1986.

Roberts, Penfield. *The Quest for Security, 1715–1740*. New York: Harper and Brothers, 1947.

Robson, Eric. "The Armed Forces and the Art of War." In *The New Cambridge Modern History*, Volume VII. Edited by J.O. Lindsay. Cambridge: Cambridge University Press, 1957.

Roider, Karl A. *Austria's Eastern Question, 1700–1790*. Princeton: Princeton University Press, 1982.

_____. "Origins of Wars in the Balkans, 1660–1792." In *The Origins of Wars in Early Modern Europe*. Edited by J. Black. Edinburgh: John Donald, 1987.

_____. "Reform and Diplomacy in the Eighteenth-Century Habsburg Monarchy." In *State and Society in Early Modern Austria*. Edited by Charles W. Ingrao. West Lafayette: Purdue University Press, 1994.

Schweizer, Karl W. "Scotsmen and the British Diplomatic Service, 1714–1789." *Scottish Tradition* 7–8 (1977–78): 115–36.

Shennan, J.H. *International Relations in Europe, 1689–1789*. London: Routledge, 1995.

Sorel, Albert. *Europe and the French Revolution: The Political Traditions of the Old Regime*. London: Collins, 1969.

Speck, William A. *Stability and Strife: England, 1714–1760*. London: Edward Arnold, 1977.

Thomson, Mark A. *The Secretaries of State, 1681–1782*. Oxford: Clarendon Press, 1932; reprint, London: Frank Cass and Company, 1968.

Ward, Adolphus. *Great Britain and Hanover: Some Aspects of the Personal Union*. Oxford: Clarendon Press, 1899; reprint, New York: Haskell House, 1971.

Western, J.R. "Armed Forces and the Art of War: Armies." In *The New Cambridge Modern History, Volume VIII*. Edited by A. Goodwin. Cambridge: Cambridge University Press, 1965.

_____. "War on a New Scale: Professionalism in Armies, Navies and Diplomacy." In *The Eighteenth Century*. Edited by A. Cobban. London: Thames and Hudson, 1969.

Williams, Glyndwr. *The Expansion of Europe in the Eighteenth Century: Overseas Rivalry, Discovery, and Exploitation*. New York: Walker and Company, 1966.

EUROPE IN THE AGE OF THE QUADRUPLE ALLIANCE, 1715–1739

Aldridge, D. "Sir John Norris and the British Naval Expeditions in the Baltic Sea, 1715–1727." Ph.D. diss., University of London, 1972.

_____. "The Royal Navy in the Baltic, 1715–1717." In *Britain and the Northern Seas*. Edited by W. Minchinton. Pontefract: Lofthouse, 1988.

Armstrong, Edward. *Elisabeth Farnese: "The Termagant of Spain."* London: Longmans, Green and Company, 1892.

Anisimove, E.V. "The Imperial Heritage of Peter the Great in the Foreign Policy of His Early Successors." In *Imperial Russian Foreign Policy*. Edited by H. Ragsdale. Cambridge: Cambridge University Press, 1993.

Baxter, Stephen B. "The Myth of the Grand Alliance in the Eighteenth Century." In *Anglo-Dutch Cross Currents in the Seventeenth and Eighteenth Centuries*. Edited by S. Baxter and P. Sellin. Los Angeles: William Andrews Clark Memorial Library, University of California, 1976.

Black, Jeremy. "An 'Ignoramus' in European Affairs?" *British Journal for Eighteenth-Century Studies* 6 (1983): 55–65.

_____. "Anglo-Austrian Relations, 1725–1740: A Study in Failure." *British Journal for Eighteenth-Century Studies* 12 (1989): 24–45.

_____. "Anglo-Baltic Relations, 1715–1748." In *Britain and the Northern Seas*. Edited by W. Minchinton. Pontefract: Lofthouse, 1988.

_____. "British Foreign Policy, 1727–1731." Ph.D. thesis, Durham University, 1983.

_____. "British Neutrality in the War of the Polish Succession, 1733–1735." *The International History Review* 8 (August 1986): 345–66.

_____. *British Foreign Policy in the Age of Walpole*. Edinburgh: John Donald, 1985.

_____. "Foreign Policy in the Age of Walpole." In *Britain the Age of Walpole*. Edited by J. Black. New York: St. Martin's Press, 1984.

_____. "French Foreign Policy in the Age of Fleury Reassessed." *The English Historical Review* 103 (1988): 359–84.

_____. "Fresh Light on the Fall of Townshend." *The Historical Journal* 29 (1986): 41–64.

_____. "From Alliance to Confrontation: Anglo-French Relations, 1731–1740." *Francia* 19 (1992); 23–45.

_____. "George II Reconsidered: A Consideration of George's Influence in the Conduct of Foreign Policy in the First Years of his Reign." *Mitteilungen des Österreichischen Staatsarchivs* 35 (1982): 35–56.

_____. "Jacobitism and British Foreign Policy, 1731–1735." In *The Jacobite Challenge*. Edited by J. Black and E. Cruikshanks. Edinburgh: John Donald, 1989.

_____. "Parliament and Foreign Policy in the Age of Walpole: The Case of the Hessians." In *Knights Errant and True Englishmen: British Foreign Policy, 1600–1800*. Edited by J. Black. Edinburgh: John Donald, 1989.

_____. "Parliament and the Political and Diplomatic Crisis of 1717–1718." *Parliamentary History* 3 (1984): 77–101.

_____. "1733: The Failure of British Diplomacy?" *Durham University Journal* 74 (1982): 199–209.

_____. "The Anglo-French Alliance, 1716–1731: A Study in Eighteenth-Century International Relations." *Francia* 13 (1986): 295–310.

_____. *The Collapse of the Anglo-French Alliance, 1727–1731*. Gloucester: Alan Sutton, 1987.

_____. "The Problems of the Small State: Bavaria and Britain in the Second Quarter of the Eighteenth Century." *European History Quarterly* 19 (1989): 5–36.

_____. "When 'Natural Allies' Fall Out: Anglo-Austrian Relations, 1725– 1740." *Mitteilungen des Österreichischen Staatsarchivs* 36 (1983): 120–49.

Cady, P.S. "Horatio Walpole and the Making of the Treaty of Seville, 1728– 1730." Ph.D. thesis, Ohio State University, 1976.

Carsten, F.L. "British Diplomacy and the Giant Grenadiers of Frederick William I." *History Today* 1 (November 1951): 55–60; reprinted in *Essays in Germany History*. London: Hambledon Press, 1985.

Cassels, Lavender. *The Struggle for the Ottoman Empire, 1717–1740*. London: John Murray, 1966.

Chance, James F. *George I and the Northern War: A Study of British-Hanoverian Policy in the North of Europe in the Years 1709 to 1721*. London: Smith, Elder and Company, 1909.

_____. "George I and Peter the Great after the Peace of Nystad." *The English Historical Review* 26 (April 1911): 278–309.

_____. *The Alliance of Hanover: A Study of British Foreign Policy in the Last Years of George I*. London: J. Murray, 1923.

_____. "The Antecedents of the Treaty of Hanover." *The English Historical Review* 28 (1913): 691–718.

_____. "The Baltic Expedition and Northern Treaties of 1715." *The English Historical Review* 17 (July 1902).

_____. "The Northern Affairs in 1724." *The English Historical Review* 27 (1912): 483–511.

_____. "The Northern Question in 1716." *The English Historical Review* 18–19 (1903–4).

_____. "The Northern Question in 1717." *The English Historical Review* 20 (1905).

_____. "The Northern Question in 1718." *The English Historical Review* 21 (July 1906).

_____. "The Northern Pacification of 1719–1720." *The English Historical Review* 22–23 (1907–8).

_____. "The Northern Policy of George I, to 1718." *Transactions of the Royal Historical Society*, New Series 20 (1906): 79–107.

_____. "The Northern Treaties of 1719–1720." *Transactions of the Royal Historical Society*, Third series 1 (1907): 99–137.

_____. "The Treaty of Charlottenberg." *The English Historical Review* 27 (1912): 52–77.

Dickinson, H.T. *Walpole and the Whig Supremacy*. London: English Universities Press, 1973.

Dunthorne, Hugh. *The Maritime Powers, 1721–1740: A Study of Anglo-Dutch Relations in the Age of Walpole*. New York: Garland, 1986.

Ergang, Robert. *The Potsdam Führer: Frederick William I, Father of Prussian Militarism*. New York: Columbia University Press, 1941.

Fann, Willerd R. "Foreigners in the Prussian Army, 1713–1756: Some Statistical and Interpretive Problems." *Central European History* 23 (March 1990): 76–84.

_____. "Peacetime Attrition in the Army of Frederick William I, 1713–1740." *Central European History* 11 (1978): 323–34.

Florovsky, A.V. "Russo-Austrian Conflicts in the Early Eighteenth Century." *Slavonic and East European Review* 47 (1969): 94–114.

Geike, Roderick and Isabel A Montgomery. *The Dutch Barrier, 1705–1719*. Cambridge: Cambridge University Press, 1930.

Gibbs, Graham C. "Britain and the Alliance of Hanover, April 1725-February 1726." *The English Historian Review* 73 (1958): 404–30.

_____. "Newspapers, Parliament and Foreign Policy in the Age of Stanhope and Walpole." *Mélanges offerts à G. Jacquemyns*. Edited by G. Jacquemyns. Brussels: Université libre de Bruxelles, 1968.

_____. "Parliament and Foreign Policy in the Age of Stanhope and Walpole." *The English Historical Review* 77 (1962): 18–37.

_____. "Parliament and Foreign Policy, 1715–1731." M.A. thesis, University of Liverpool, 1953.

_____. "Parliament and the Treaty of the Quadruple Alliance." In *William III and Louis XIV*. Edited by R.M. Hatton and J.S. Bromley. Liverpool: Liverpool University Press, 1968.

Hartley, Janet M. *Charles Whitworth: Diplomat in the Age of Peter the Great*. Aldershot: Ashgate, 2002.

Hatton, Ragnhild M. *Diplomatic Relations Between Great Britain and the Dutch Republic, 1714–1721*. London: East and West, 1950.

_____. *George I: Elector and King*. London: Thames and Hudson, 1978.

_____. "New Light on George I of Great Britain." In *England's Rise to Greatness, 1660–1763*. Edited by S. Baxter. Berkeley: University of California Press, 1983.

Henderson, Nicholas. *Prince Eugen of Savoy: A Biography*. London: Weidenfeld and Nicolson, 1964.

Hildner, E.G. "The Role of the South Sea Company in the Diplomacy Leading to the War of Jenkins' Ear." *Hispanic American Historical Review* 18 (1938): 322–41.

Hughes, Michael. *Law and Politics in the Eighteenth Century: The Imperial Aulic Council in the Reign of Charles VI*. Woodbridge: Boydell Press, 1988.

Ingrao, Charles W. "The Pragmatic Sanction and the Theresian Succession: A Reevaluation." In *The Habsburg Dominions under Maria Theresa*. Edited by W.J. McGill. Washington, Pa.: Washington and Jefferson College, 1980.

Jones, George Hilton. *Great Britain and the Tuscan Question, 1710–1737*. New York: Vantage, 1998.

Kamen, Henry. *Philip V of Spain: The King Who Reigned Twice*. New Haven: Yale University Press, 2001.

Król, G. "The Northern Threat: Anglo-Russian Diplomatic Relations, 1716–1727." Ph.D. Diss., University of London, 1992.

Lewitter, L.R. "Poland, Russia and the Treaty of Vienna of 5 January 1719." *The Historical Journal* 13 (1970): 3–30.

_____. "Russia, Poland and the Baltic, 1697–1721." *The Historical Journal* 11 (1968): 3–34.

Lindgren, Raymond E. "A Projected Invasion of Sweden, 1716." *Huntington Library Quarterly* 7 (May 1944): 223–46.

Lodge, Richard. "English Neutrality in the War of the Polish Succession." *Transactions of the Royal Historical Society*, Fourth series, 14 (1931): 141–74.

_____. "The Anglo-French Alliance, 1716–1731." In *Studies in Anglo-French History during the Eighteenth, Nineteenth, and Twentieth Centuries.* Edited by Alfred Coville and Harold Temperley. Cambridge: Cambridge University Press, 1935; reprint, Freeport, NY: Books for Librarians Press, 1967.

_____. "The Treaty of Seville, 1729." *Transactions of the Royal Historical Society*, Fourth series 16 (1933): 1–45.

Longworth, Philip. *The Three Empresses: Catherine I, Anne and Elizabeth of Russia.* New York: Holt, Rinehart and Winston, 1972.

Martin, M. "The Secret Clause: Britain and Spanish Ambitions in Spain, 1712–1731." *European Studies Review* 6 (1976): 407–25.

McKay, Derek. *Allies of Convenience: Diplomatic Relations Between Great Britain and Austria, 1714–1719.* New York: Garland, 1986.

_____. "Bolingbroke, Oxford and the Defence of the Utrecht Settlement in Southern Europe." *The English Historical Review* 86 (1971): 264–84.

_____. *Prince Eugene of Savoy.* London: Thames and Hudson, 1977.

_____. "The Struggle for Control of George I's Northern Policy, 1718–1719." *The Journal of Modern History* 45 (September 1973): 367–86.

McLachlan, Jean O. *Trade and Peace with Old Spain, 1667–1750: A Study on the Influence of Commerce on Anglo-Spanish Diplomacy in the First Half of the Eighteenth Century.* Cambridge: Cambridge University Press, 1940; reprint, New York: Octagon, 1974.

Michael, Wolfgang. *England under George I: The Beginnings of the Hanoverian Dynasty.* London: Macmillan, 1936; reprint, Westport: Greenwood Press, 1981.

_____. *England under George I: The Quadruple Alliance.* London: Macmillan, 1939.

Moulton, James R. "Peter the Great and the Russian Military Campaigns during the Final Years of the Great Northern War, 1719–1721." Ph.D. diss., University of Denver, 2000.

Murray, John J. *George I, the Baltic and the Whig Split of 1717: A Study in Diplomacy and Propaganda.* London: Routledge and Kegan Paul, 1969.

_____. "Scania and the End of the Northern Alliance (1716)." *The Journal of Modern History* 16 (June 1944): 81–92.

_____. "The Görtz-Gyllenborg Arrests: A Problem in Diplomatic Immunity." *The Journal of Modern History* 28 (December 1956): 325–37.

_____. "The United Provinces and the Anglo-Dutch Squadron of 1715." *Bijdragen voor de Geschiedenis der Nederlanden* 8 (1953): 20–45.

Pǎrvev, Ivan. *Habsburgs and Ottomans between Vienna and Belgrade (1683–1739).* New York: Columbia University Press, 1995.

Plumb, J.H. *Sir Robert Walpole.* 2 volumes. London: Cresset Press, 1956–60.

Reading, Douglas K. *The Anglo-Russian Commercial Treaty of 1734.* New Haven: Yale University Press, 1938.

Roberts, Penfield. *The Quest for Security, 1715–1740.* New York: Harper and Brothers, 1947.

Roider, Karl A., Jr. "Futile Peacemaking: Austria and the Congress of Nemirov (1737)." *Austrian History Yearbook* 12–13 (1976–77): 95–115.

_____. "The Perils of Eighteenth-Century Peacemaking: Austria and the Treaty of Belgrade, 1739." *Central European History* 5 (1972): 195–207.

_____. "The Pragmatic Sanction." *Austrian History Yearbook* 8 (1972): 153–58.

_____. *The Reluctant Ally: Austria's Policy in the Austro-Turkish War, 1737–1739.* Baton Rouge: Louisiana State University Press, 1972.

Rothenberg, Gunther E. *The Austrian Military Border in Croatia, 1522–1747.* Urbana: University of Illinois Press, 1960.

Shennan, J.H. *Philippe Duke of Orleans: Regent of France, 1715–1723.* London: Thames and Hudson, 1979.

Stoye, John W. "Emperor Charles VI: The Early Years of the Reign." *Transactions of the Royal Historical Society*, Fifth series, 12 (1962): 63–84.

Storrs, Christopher. *War, Diplomacy and the Rise of Savoy, 1690–1720.* Cambridge: Cambridge University Press, 1999.

Sturgill, Claude. "From Utrecht to the Little War with Spain: Peace at Almost Any Price Had to Be the Case." In *The Origins of War in Early Modern Europe.* Edited by J. Black. Edinburgh: John Donald, 1987.

Sutton, John L. *The King's Honor and the King's Cardinal: The War of the Polish Succession.* Lexington: University Press of Kentucky, 1980.

Symcox, Geoffrey W. *Victor Amadeus II of Savoy: Absolutism in the Savoyard State, 1675–1730.* London: Thames and Hudson, 1983.

Taylor, David J. "Russian Foreign Policy, 1725–1739." Ph.D. diss., University of East Anglia, 1983.

Temperley, H.W.V. "The Causes of the War of Jenkin's Ear (1739)." *Transactions of the Royal Historical Society*, Third Series 3 (1909): 197–236.

Williams, Basil. *Carteret and Newcastle: A Contrast in Contemporaries.* Cambridge: Cambridge University Press, 1943; reprint, London: Frank Cass and Company, 1966.

_____. *Stanhope: A Study in Eighteenth Century War and Diplomacy.* Oxford: Clarendon Press, 1932.

_____. "The Foreign Policy of England under Walpole." *The English Historical Review* 15 (1900): 251–76, 479–94, 665–98.

_____. "The Foreign Policy of England under Walpole." *The English Historical Review* 16 (1901): 67–83, 308–27. 439–51.

Wilson, Arthur McCandless. *French Foreign Policy during the Administration of Cardinal Fleury, 1726–1743: A Study in Diplomacy and Commercial Development.* Cambridge, Mass.: Harvard University Press, 1936; reprint, Wesport: Greenwood Press, 1972.

Woodfine, Philip. *Britannia's Glories: The Walpole Ministry and the 1739 War with Spain.* Woodbridge: Boydell Press, 1998.

_____. "Horace Walpole and British Relations with Spain, 1738." *Camden Miscellany*, Fifth series 32 (1994): 277–311.

_____. "Ideas of Naval Power and the Conflict with Spain, 1737–1742." In *The British Navy and the Use of Naval Power in the Eighteenth Century.* Edited by J. Black and P.L. Woodfine. Leicester: Leicester University Press, 1988.

_____. "The Anglo-Spanish War of 1739." In *The Origins of War in Early Modern Europe.* Edited by J. Black. Edinburgh: John Donald, 1987.

_____. "The War of Jenkin's Ear: A New Voice in the Wentworth-Vernon Debate." *Journal of the Society for Army Historical Research* 65 (1987): 67–91.

FROM THE WAR OF THE AUSTRIAN SUCCESSION TO THE SEVEN YEARS' WAR, 1739–1763

Anderson, Fred. *Crucible of War: The Seven Years' War and the Fate of Empire in British North America, 1754–1766.* New York: Alfred A. Knopf, 2000.

Anderson, Matthew S. *The War of the Austrian Succession, 1740–1748*. London: Longman, 1995.

Aksan, Virginia H. "Ottoman-French Relations, 1739–1768." In *Studies on Ottoman Diplomatic History*. Edited by Sinan Kuneralp. Istanbuhl: Isis Press, 1987.

Anisimov, Evgeny V. *Empress Elizabeth: Her Reign and Her Russia, 1741–1761*. Gulf Breeze: Academic International Press, 1995.

Asprey, Robert B. *Frederick the Great: The Magnificent Enigma*. New York: Ticknor and Fields, 1986.

Atkinson, Christopher T. "British Strategy and Battles in the Westphalian Campaign, 1758–62." *Journal of the Royal United Services Institute* 79 (1934): 733–40.

Ayling, Stanley. *The Elder Pitt, Earl of Chatham*. London: Collins, 1976.

Batzel, John Charles. "Austria and the First Three Treaties of Versailles, 1755–1758." Ph.D. thesis, Brown University, 1974.

Baxter, Stephen B. "The Conduct of the Seven Years' War." In *England's Rise to Greatness, 1660–1763*. Edited by S. Baxter. Berkeley: University of California Press, 1983.

Black, Jeremy. *America or Europe?: British Foreign Policy, 1739–1763*. London: University College London Press, 1998.

_____. "Anglo-Baltic Relations 1714–1748." In *Britain and the Northern Seas*. Edited by W. Minchinton. Pontefract: Lofthouse, 1988.

_____. "Anglo-French Relations in the Mid-Eighteenth Century, 1740–1756. *Francia* 17 (1990): 45–79.

_____. "Anglo-Wittelsbach Relations, 1730–1742." *Zeitschrift für Bayerische Landesgeschicte* 55 (1992): 307–45.

_____. "British Foreign Policy and the War of the Austrian Succession, 1740–1748: A Research Priority." *Canadian Journal of History* 21 (1986): 313–31.

_____. *Culloden and the '45*. New York: St. Martin's Press, 1990.

_____. "Naval Power and British Foreign Policy in the Age of Pitt the Elder." In *The British Navy and the Use of Naval Power in the Eighteenth Century*. Edited by J. Black and P. Woodfine. Atlantic Highlands: Humanities Press International, 1989.

_____. *Pitt the Elder*. Cambridge: Cambridge University Press, 1992.

_____. "Territorial Gain on the Continent: An Overlooked Aspect of Mid-Eighteenth Century British Foreign Policy." *Durham University Journal* 86 (1994): 43–50.

_____. "The British Attempt to Preserve the Peace in Europe, 1748– 1755." In *Zwischenstaatliche Friedenswahrung in Mittelalter und Früher Neuzeit*. Edited by Heinz Duchhardt. Cologne and Vienna: Broschiert, 1991.

Brennan, James F. *Enlightened Despotism in Russia: The Reign of Elisabeth, 1741– 1762*. New York: Peter Lang, 1987.

Browning, Reed. "The British Orientation of Austrian Foreign Policy, 1749– 1754." *Central European History* 1 (December 1968): 299–323.

_____. *The Duke of Newcastle*. New Haven: Yale University Press, 1975.

_____. "The Duke of Newcastle and the Financial Management of the Seven Years' War in Germany." *Journal of the Society for Army Historical Research* 49 (1971): 20–35.

_____. "The Duke of Newcastle and the Financing of the Seven Years' War in Germany." *Journal of Economic History* 31 (1971): 344–77.

_____. "The Duke of Newcastle and the Imperial Election Plan, 1749– 1754." *Journal of British Studies* 7 (1967–68): 28–47.

_____. *The War of the Austrian Succession*. New York: St. Martin's Press, 1993.

Brumwell, Stephen. *Redcoats: The British Soldier and War in the Americas, 1755– 1763*. Cambridge: Cambridge University Press, 2001.

Butler, Rohan. *Choiseul: Father and Son, 1719–1754*. Oxford: Oxford University Press, 1980.

_____. "The Secret Compact of 1753 between the Kings of France and of Naples." In *Royal and Republican Sovereignty in Early Modern Europe: Essays in Memory of Ragnhild Hatton*. Edited by R. Oresko, G.C. Gibbs, and H.M. Scott. Cambridge: Cambridge University Press, 1997.

Butterfield, Herbert. "The Reconstruction of an Historical Episode: The History of the Enquiry into the Origins of the Seven Years' War." In *Man on His Past*. Cambridge: Cambridge University Press, 1955.

Carter, Alice Clare. "How to Revise Treaties without Negotiating: Commonsense, Mutual Fears and the Anglo-Dutch Trade Disputes of 1759." In *Studies in Diplomatic History: Essays in Memory of David Bayne Horn*. Edited by R.M. Hatton and M.S. Anderson. London: Longman, 1970.

_____. *The Dutch Republic in Europe in the Seven Years' War*. London: Macmillan, 1971.

Charteris, Sir Evan E. *William Augustus, Duke of Cumberland: His Early Life and Times (1721–1748)*. London: Edward Arnold, 1913.

_____. *William Augustus, Duke of Cumberland and the Seven Years' War*. London, Hutchinson, n.d. [1925].

Chartrand, Rene. *Louis XV's Army*. 5 volumes. Botley: Osprey, 1996–98.

_____. *Louisbourg 1758: Wolfe's First Siege*. Botley: Osprey, 2001.

_____. *Quebec 1759: The Heights of Abraham: The Armies of Wolfe and Montcalm*. Botley: Osprey, 1999.

_____. *Ticonderoga 1758: Montcalm's Victory against All Odds*. Botley: Osprey, 2000.

Christelow, Alan. "Economic Background of the Anglo-Spanish War of 1762." *The Journal of Modern History* 18 (March 1946): 22–36.

Clayton, T.R. "The Duke of Newcastle, the Earl of Halifax, and the American Origins of the Seven Years' War." *The Historical Journal* 24 (1981): 571–603.

Corbett, Julian S. *England in the Seven Years' War: A Study in Combined Strategy.* 2 volumes. Second edition. London: Longmans, Green and Company, 1918; reprint, New York: AMS Press, 1973.

Cudmore, Wendy. "Sir Robert Walpole and the Treaty of Vienna, 16 March 1731." M.A. thesis, University of London, 1978.

Dalton, Charles. *George the First's Army, 1714–1727.* 2 volumes. London: Eyre and Spottiswoode, 1910–12.

Dann, Uriel. *Hanover and Great Britain, 1740–1760: Diplomacy and Survival.* Leicester: Leicester University Press, 1991.

Daiches, David. *Charles Edward Stuart: The Life and Times of Bonnie Prince Charlie.* London: Thames and Hudson, 1973.

Dickson, P.G.M. "English Negotiations with Austria, 1737–1752." In *Statesmen, Scholars and Merchants: Essays in Eighteenth Century History Presented to Dame Lucy Sutherland.* Edited by A. Whiteman and others. Oxford: Clarendon Press, 1973.

Doran, Patrick F. *Andrew Mitchell and Anglo-Prussian Diplomatic Relations during the Seven Years' War.* New York: Garland, 1986.

Dorn, W.L. *Competition for Empire, 1740–1763.* New York: Harper and Brothers, 1940.

Duffy, Christopher. *Frederick the Great: A Military Life.* London: Routledge and Kegan Paul, 1985.

_____. *Instrument of War: Volume I of the Austrian Army in the Seven Years' War.* Rossmont, Illinois: Emperor's Press, 2000.

_____. *The Army of Frederick the Great.* Newton Abbot: David and Charles, 1974.

_____. *The Army of Maria Theresa: The Armed Forces of Imperial Austria, 1740–1780*. New York: Hippocrene, 1977.

_____. *The '45: Bonnie Prince Charlie and the Untold Story of the Jacobite Rising*. London: Cassell, 2003.

_____. "The Seven Years' War as Limited War." In *East-Central European Society and War in the Pre-Revolutionary Eighteenth Century Euorpe*. Edited by G.E. Rothenberg, B.K. Kiraly, and P.F. Sugar. Boulder: Social Science Monographs, 1982.

_____. *The Wild Goose and the Eagle: A Life of Marshal von Browne, 1705– 1757*. London: Chatto and Windus, 1964.

Duffy, Michael. "The Establishment of the Western Squadron as the Linchpin of British Naval Strategy." In *Parameters of British Naval Power, 1650–1850*. Exeter: University of Exeter Press, 1992.

Dyck, Harvey L. "Pondering the Russian Fact: Kaunitz and the Catherinian Empire in the 1770s." *Canadian Slavonic Papers* 22 (1981): 451–69.

Edwardes, Michael. *The Battle of Plassey and the Conquest of Bengal*. London: B.T. Batsford, 1963.

Eldon, C.W. *England's Subsidy Policy Towards the Continent during the Seven Years' War*. Philadelphia: Times and News, 1938.

Fann, Willerd R. "Foreigners in the Prussian Army, 1713–1756: Some Statistical and Interpretive Problems." *Central European History* 23 (March 1990): 76–84.

Fraser, E.J.S. "The Pitt-Newcastle Coalition and the Conduct of the Seven Years' War, 1757–1760." Ph.D. thesis, Oxford University, 1976.

Furneaux, Rupert. *The Seven Years' War*. London: Granada, 1973.

Geyl, Pieter. "Holland and England during the War of the Austrian Succession." *History*, New series 10 (1925–26): 47–51.

Gipson, L.H. "British Diplomacy in the Light of Anglo-Spanish New World Issues, 1750–1757." *The American Historical Review* 51 (July 1946): 627–48.

Gradish, S. *The Manning of the Navy in the Seven Years' War.* London: Royal Historical Society, 1980.

Graham, Gerald S. *Empire of the North Atlantic: The Maritime Struggle for North America.* Toronto: University of Toronto Press, 1950.

_____. "The Naval Defence of British North America, 1739–1763." *Transactions of the Royal Historical Society,* Fourth series 30 (1948): 95–110.

_____. "The Planning of the Beauséjour Operation and the Approaches to War in 1755." *New England Quarterly* 41 (1968): 551–66.

Grant, Charles. *The Battle of Fontenoy.* London: William Luscombe, 1975.

Grant, W.L. "Canada versus Guadaloupe: An Episode in the Seven Year's War." *The American Historical Review* 17 (1912): 735–43.

Gwyn, Julian. "French and British Naval Power at the Two Sieges of Louisbourg, 1745 and 1758." *Nova Scotia Historical Review* 10 (1990): 63–93.

Hackman, W.K. "English Military Expeditions to the Coast of France, 1757–1761." Ph.D. diss., University of Michigan, 1969.

_____. "The British Raid on Rochefort, 1757." *Mariner's Mirror* 64 (1978): 263–75.

Harding, Richard H. "'A Golden Adventure': Combined Operations in the Caribbean, 1740–1742: A Re-Examination of the Walpole Ministry's Response to War with Spain." Ph.D. diss., University of London, 1985.

_____. *Amphibious Warfare in the Eighteenth Century: The British Expedition to the West Indies, 1740–1742.* Woodbridge: Boydell Press, 1991.

_____. "Sir Robert Walpole's Ministry and the Conduct of the War with Spain, 1739–1741." *Bulletin of the Institute for Historical Research* 60 (1987): 299–320.

Harfield, A. "The British Expedition to Manila, 1762–1763." *Journal of the Society for Army Historical Research* 66 (1988): 101–11.

Harrington, Peter. *Culloden 1746: The Highland Clan's Last Charge.* Botley: Osprey, 1999.

_____. *Plassey 1757.* London: Osprey, 1994.

Haythornthwaite, Philip. *Austrian Army 1740–1780.* 2 volumes. London: Osprey, 1994.

_____. *Frederick the Great's Army.* 3 volumes. London: Osprey, 1991–92.

Hebbert, F.J. "Belle-Ile and the Secret Expedition." *Transactions of the Hunterian Society* (1980): 193–210.

_____. "The Belle-Ile Expedition of 1761." *Journal of Army Historical Reearch* 64 (1986): 81–93.

Higonnet, Patrice Louis-René. "The Origins of the Seven Years' War." *The Journal of Modern History* 40 (1968): 57–90.

Hitsman, J. and C. Bond. "The Assault Landing at Louisburg, 1758." *Canadian Historical Review* 35 (1954): 314–30.

Holbroke, B. "The Siege and Capture of Belle-Isle, 1761." *Journal of the Royal United Services Institution* 43 (1899): 160–83, 520–34.

Horn, David Bayne. *Frederick the Great and the Rise of Prussia.* London: English Universities Press, 1964.

_____. "Saxony in the War of the Austrian Succession." *The English Historical Review* 44 (1929): 33–47.

_____. *Sir Charles Hanbury Williams and European Diplomacy (1747–1758).* London: George G. Harrap and Company, 1930.

_____. "The Cabinet Controversy on Subsidy Treaties in Time of Peace, 1749–1750." *The English Historical Review* 45 (1930): 463–66.

_____. "The Diplomatic Revolution." In *The New Cambridge Modern History*, Volume VII. Edited by J.O. Lindsay. Cambridge: Cambridge University Press, 1957.

_____. "The Duke of Newcastle and the Origins of the Diplomatic Revolution." In *The Diversity of History: Essays in Honour of Sir Herbert Butterfield*. Edited by J.H. Elliott and H.G. Koenigsberger. Ithaca: Cornell University Press, 1970.

_____. "The Origins of a Proposed Election of a King of the Romans, 1748–1750." *The English Historical Review* 42 (1927): 361–70.

Horowitz, Sidney. "Franco-Russian Relations, 1740–1746." Ph.D. thesis, New York University, 1951.

Hubatsch, Walther. *Frederick the Great: Absolutism and Administration*. London: Thames and Hudson, 1973.

Kaplan, Herbert H. *Russia and the Outbreak of the Seven Years' War*. Berkeley: University of California Press, 1968.

Keep, John L.H. "Feeding the Troops: Russian Army Supply Policies during the Seven Years' War." *Canadian Slavonic Papers* 29 (1987): 24–44.

Kennett, Lee. *The French Armies in the Seven Years' War: A Study in Military Organization and Administration*. Durham: Duke University Press, 1967.

Kistler, Charles E. "British Diplomacy and Russia during the Seven Years' War." Ph.D. diss., University of Michigan, 1946.

Knowles, Sir Lees. *Minden and the Seven Years' War*. London: Simpkin, 1914.

Konstam, Angus. *Russian Army of the Seven Years' War*. London: Osprey, 1996.

Lemmink, J.Ph.S. "Dutch Convoys in the Baltic during the Russo-Swedish War 1741–1743." In *Baltic Affairs: Relations between the Netherlands and North-Eastern Europe, 1500–1800*. Edited by J.Ph.S Lemmink and J.S.A.M. van Koningsbrugge. Nijmegen: Institute for Northern and Eastern European Studies, 1990.

Leonard, Carol S. *Reform and Regicide: The Reign of Peter III of Russia*. Blooming-ton: Indiana University Press, 1993.

Lodge, Richard. "An Episode in Anglo-Russian Relations during the War of the Austrian Succession." *Transactions of the Royal Historical Society*, Fourth series, 9 (1926): 63–83.

_____. "Lord Hynford's Embassy to Russia, 1744–1749." *The English Historical Review* 46 (1931): 48–76, 389–422.

_____. "Russia, Prussia, and Great Britain, 1742–1744." *The English Historical Review* 45 (1930): 579–611.

_____. "Sir Benjamin Keene: A Study in Anglo-Spanish Relations." *Transactions of the Royal Historical Society*, Fourth series 15 (1932): 1–43.

_____. "The Continental Policy of Great Britain, 1740–1760." *History*, New series 16 (1930–31): 246–51.

_____. "The First Anglo-Russian Treaty, 1739–1742." *The English Historical Review* 43 (1928): 354–75.

_____. "The Hanau Controversy in 1744 and the Fall of Carteret." *The English Historical Review* 38 (1923): 509–31.

_____. "The Maritime Powers in the Eighteenth Century." *History*, New series 15 (1930–31): 246–51.

_____. "The Mission of Henry Legge to Berlin, 1748." *Transactions of the Royal Historical Society*, Fourth series, 14 (1931): 1–38.

_____. "The So-Called Treaty of Hanau." *The English Historical Review* 38 (1923): 384–407.

_____. "The Treaty of Abo and the Swedish Succession." *The English Historical Review* 43 (1928): 540–71.

_____. "The Treaty of Worms." *The English Historical Review* 44 (1929): 220–55.

_____. *Studies in Eighteenth-Century Diplomacy, 1740–1748*. London: John Murray, 1930; reprint, Westport: Greenwood Press,1970.

Longworth, Philip. *The Three Empresses: Catherine I, Anne and Elizabeth of Russia*. New York: Holt, Rinehart and Winston, 1972.

Macartney, C.A. *Maria Theresa and the House of Austria*. London: English Universities Press, 1969.

MacDonogh, Giles. *Frederick the Great: A Life in Deed and Letters*. London: Weidenfeld and Nicolson, 1999.

Mackesy, Piers. *The Coward of Minden: The Affair of Lord George Sackville*. London: Allen Lane, 1979.

Marcus, G. *Quiberon Bay: The Campaign in the Homes Waters, 1959*. London: Hollis and Carter, 1960.

Marston, Daniel. *The French-Indian War 1754–1760*. Botley: Osprey, 2002.

_____. *The Seven Years' War*. Botley: Osprey, 2001.

Massie, A.W. "Great Britain and the Defence of the Low Countries, 1744–1748." Ph.D. thesis, Oxford University, 1988.

McCrory-Pargellis, Stanley. *Lord Loudoun in America*. Princeton: Princeton University Press, 1933.

McGill, William J. "Kaunitz: The Personality of Political Algebra." In *The Habsburg Dominions under Maria Theresa*. Edited by W.J. McGill. Washington, Pa.: Washington and Jefferson College, 1980.

_____. *Maria Theresa*. New York: Twayne, 1972.

_____. "The Roots of Policy: Kaunitz in Italy and the Netherlands, 1742–1746." *Central European History* 1 (June 1968): 131–49.

_____. "The Roots of Policy: Kaunitz in Vienna and Versailles, 1749–1753." *The Journal of Modern History* 43 (1971): 228–44.

_____. "Wenzel Anton von Kaunitz-Rittberg and the Congress of Aix-la-Chapelle, 1748." *Duquesne Review* 14 (1969): 154–67.

McLynn, Frank J. *Charles Edward Stuart: A Tragedy in Many Acts*. London: Routledge, 1988.

_____. *France and the Jacobite Rising of 1745*. Edinburgh: Edinburgh University Press, 1981.

_____. "Issues and Motives in the Jacobite Rising of 1745." *The Eighteenth Century: Theory and Interpretation* 23 (1982): 97–133.

_____. "Sea Power and the Jacobite Rising of 1745." *Mariner's Mirror* 67 (1981): 163–72.

_____. *The Jacobite Army in England, 1745: The Final Campaign*. Edinburgh: John Donald, 1983.

Mediger, Walther. "Great Britain, Hanover and the Rise of Prussia." In *Studies in Diplomatic History: Essays in Memory of David Bayne Horn*. Edited by R.M. Hatton and M.S. Anderson. London: Longman, 1970.

Middleton, R.N. "French Policy and Russia after the Peace of Aix-la-Chapelle, 1749–1753: A Study of the Pre-History of the Diplomatic Revolution of 1756." Ph.D. diss., Columbia University, 1968.

Middleton, Richard. "British Naval Strategy, 1755–1762: The Western Squadron." *Mariner's Mirror* 75 (1989): 349–67.

_____. "Naval Administration in the Age of Pitt and Anson, 1755–1763." In *The British Navy and the Use of Naval Power in the Eighteenth Century*. Edited by J. Black and P. Woodfine. Atlantic Highlands: Humanities Press International, 1989.

_____. "Pitt, Anson and the Admiralty, 1756–1761." *History* 55 (June 1970): 189–98.

_____. "The Administration of Newcastle and Pitt: The Departments of State and the Conduct of the War, 1754–1760, with Particular Reference to the Campaigns in North America." Ph.D. thesis, Exeter University, 1969.

_____. *The Bells of Victory: The Pitt-Newcastle Ministry and the Conduct of the Seven Years' War, 1757–1762*. Cambridge: Cambridge University Press, 1985.

_____. "The Duke of Newcastle and the Conduct of Patronage during the Seven Years' War, 1757–1762." *British Journal of Eighteenth-Century Studies* 12 (1989): 175–85.

_____. "The Reinforcement for America, Summer 1757." *Bulletin of the Institute of Historical Research* 41 (1968): 58–72.

Millar, Simon. *Kolin 1757: Frederick the Great's First Defeat*. Botley: Osprey, 2001.

_____. *Rossbach and Leuthen 1757: Prussia's Eagle Resurgent*. Botley: Osprey, 2002.

_____. *Zorndorf 1758*. Botley: Osprey, 2003.

Nathan, J.S. "The Heyday of the Balance of Power: Frederick the Great and the Decline of the Old Regime." *United States Naval War College Review* 33 (1980): 53–67.

Oglesby, J.C.M. "British Attacks on the Caracas Coast, 1743." *Mariner's Mirror* 58 (1972): 71–79.

Oliva, L.J. *Misalliance: A Study of French Policy in Russia during the Seven Years' War*. New York: New York University Press, 1964.

Orr, Michael. *Dettingen, 1743*. London: Charles Knight, 1972.

Pares, Richard. "American versus Continental Warfare, 1739–1763." *The English Historical Review* 51 (1936): 429–65.

_____. *Colonial Blockade and Neutral Rights, 1739–1763*. Oxford: Clarendon Press, 1938.

_____. *War and Trade in the West Indies, 1739–1763*. Oxford: Clarendon Press, 1936.

Peters, Marie. *The Elder Pitt*. London: Addison, Wesley, Longman, 1998.

Pick, Robert. *Empress Maria Theresa: The Earlier Years, 1717–1757*. London: Weidenfeld and Nicolson, 1966.

Plumb, J.H. *Chatham*. London: Collins, 1953.

Pritchard, James. *Anatomy of a Disaster: The 1746 French Expedition to North America*. Montreal: McGill-Queens University Press, 1995.

_____. *Louis XV's Navy, 1748–1762: A Study of Organization and Administration*. Kingston: McGill-Queen's University Press, 1987.

Rashed, Zenab Esmat. *The Peace of Paris, 1763*. Liverpool: Liverpool University Press, 1951.

Reid, Stuart. *1745: A Military History of the Last Jacobite Rising*. New York: Sarpedon, 1996.

_____. *Culloden Moor 1746: The Death of the Jacobite Cause*. Botley: Osprey, 2002.

_____. *King George's Army 1740–1793*. 3 volumes. London: Osprey, 1995–96.

_____. *Quebec 1759: The Battle that Won Canada*. Botley: Osprey, 2003.

Rice, Geoffrey W. "British Consuls and Diplomats in the Mid-Eighteenth Century: An Italian Example." *The English Historical Review* 92 (1977): 834–46.

_____. "Lord Rochford at Turin, 1749–1755: A Pivotal Phase in Anglo-Italian Relations in the Eighteenth Century." In *Knights Errant and True Englishmen: British Foreign Policy, 1600–1800*. Edited by J. Black. Edinburgh: John Donald, 1989.

_____. "The Diplomatic Career of the Fourth Earl of Rochford at Turin, Madrid and Paris, 1749–1769." Ph.D. thesis, University of Canterbury, New Zealand, 1973.

Richmond, Herbert W. *The Navy in the War of 1739–1748*. 3 volumes. Cambridge: Cambridge University Press, 1920.

Riley, J.C. *The Seven Years' War and the Old Regime in France: The Economic and Financial Toll.* Princeton: Princeton University Press, 1986.

Ritter, Gerhard. *Frederick the Great: A Historical Profile.* Berkeley: University of California Press, 1968.

_____. "Frederician Warfare." In *Frederick the Great: A Profile.* Edited by Peter Paret. New York: Macmillan, 1972.

Robson, Eric. "The Seven Years' War." In *The New Cambridge Modern History*, Volume VII. Edited by J.O. Lindsay. Cambridge: Cambridge University Press, 1957.

Roider, Karl A., Jr. "The Oriental Academy in the *Theresienzeit.*" In *The Habsburg Dominions under Maria Theresa.* Edited by W.J. McGill. Washington, Pa.: Washington and Jefferson College, 1980.

Rose, J. Holland. "Frederick the Great and England, 1756–1763." *The English Historical Review* 29 (1914): 79–93.

Rothenberg, Gunther E. *The Austrian Military Border in Croatia, 1522–1747.* Urbana: University of Illinois Press, 1960.

Savory, Reginald. *His Britannic Majesty's Army in Germany during the Seven Years' War.* Oxford: Clarendon Press, 1966.

Schieder, Theodor. *Frederick the Great.* Edited by S. Berkeley and H.M. Scott. London: Longman, 2000.

Schweizer, Karl W. "Britain and Prussia, 1758–1761." In *England, Prussia and the Seven Years' War: Studies in Alliance Politics and Diplomacy.* Lewiston: Edwin Mellen Press, 1989.

_____. "Britain, Prussia and the Accession of Peter III." In *England, Prussia and the Seven Years' War: Studies in Alliance Politics and Diplomacy.* Lewiston: Edwin Mellen Press, 1989.

_____. "Britain, Prussia and the Prussian Territories on the Rhine, 1762–1763." *Studies in History and Politics* 4 (1985): 101–12; reprinted in *England, Prussia and the Seven Years' War: Studies in Alliance Politics and Diplomacy.* Lewiston: Edwin Mellen Press, 1989.

_____. *England, Prussia and the Seven Years' War: Studies in Alliance Politics and Diplomacy.* Lewiston: Edwin Mellen Press, 1989.

_____. *Frederick the Great, William Pitt, and Lord Bute: The Anglo-Prussian Alliance, 1756–1763.* New York: Garland, 1991.

_____. "Lord Bute and the Prussian Subsidy, 1762: An Unnoticed Document." *Notes and Queries* (1989): 58–61.

_____. "Lord Bute, Newcastle, Prussia and the Hague Overtures." *Albion* 8 (1977): 72–97; reprinted in *England, Prussia and the Seven Years' War: Studies in Alliance Politics and Diplomacy.* Lewiston: Edwin Mellen Press, 1989.

_____. "The Alliance Takes Shape, 1756–1758." In *England, Prussia and the Seven Years' War: Studies in Alliance Politics and Diplomacy.* Lewiston: Edwin Mellen Press, 1989.

_____. "The Non-Renewal of the Anglo-Prussian Subsidy Treaty, 1761–1762: An Historical Revision." *Canadian Journal of History* 13 (1978): 382–98; reprinted in *England, Prussia and the Seven Years' War: Studies in Alliance Politics and Diplomacy.* Lewiston: Edwin Mellen Press, 1989.

_____. "The Outbreak of War: A System Perspective." In *England, Prussia and the Seven Years' War: Studies in Alliance Politics and Diplomacy.* Lewiston: Edwin Mellen Press, 1989.

_____. "The Seven Years' War: A System Perspective." In *The Origins of War in Early Modern Europe.* Edited by J. Black. Edinburgh: John Donald, 1987.

_____. "The Termination of the Prussian Subsidy." In *England, Prussia and the Seven Years' War: Studies in Alliance Politics and Diplomacy.* Lewiston: Edwin Mellen Press, 1989.

_____. "William Pitt, Lord Bute, and the Peace Negotiations with France, May-September 1761." *Albion* 13 (1981): 262–75.

_____ and C.S.Leonard. "Britain, Prussia, Russia and the Galitzin Letter: A Reassessment." *Historical Journal* 26 (1983): 531–56; reprinted in

England, Prussia and the Seven Years' War: Studies in Alliance Politics and Diplomacy. Lewiston: Edwin Mellen Press, 1989.

Scott, Hamish M. *The Emergence of the Eastern Powers, 1756–1775*. Cambridge: Cambridge University Press, 2001.

_____. "The 'True Principles of the Revolution': The Duke of Newcastle and the Idea of the Old System." In *Knights Errant and True Englishmen: British Foreign Policy, 1660–1800*. Edinburgh: John Donald, 1989.

Sherrard, O.A. *Lord Chatham*. 3 volumes. London: Bodley Head, 1952–58.

Showalter, Dennis. *The Wars of Frederick the Great*. London: Longman, 1996.

Shy, John. *Toward Lexington: The Role of the British Army in the Coming of the American Revolution*. Princeton: Princeton University Press, 1965.

Skrine, F.H. *Fontenoy and Great Britain's Share in the War of the Austrian Succession*. Edinburgh: W. Blackwood and Sons, 1906.

Sosin, Jack. "Louisbourg and the Peace of Aix-la-Chapelle, 1748." *William and Mary Quarterly*, Third series 14 (1957): 516–35.

Speck, William A. *The Butcher: The Duke of Cumberland and the Suppression of the 45*. Oxford: Basil Blackwell, 1982; reprint, Caernarfon: Welsh Academic Press, 1995.

Spencer, Frank. "The Anglo-Prussian Breach of 1762: An Historical Revision." *History* 41 (1956): 100–12.

Swanson, Carl E. "American Privateering and Imperial Warfare, 1739–1748." *William and Mary Quarterly*, Third series 42 (1985): 357–82.

Syrett, David. "The Methodology of British Amphibious Operations during the Seven Years' and American Wars." *Mariner's Mirror* 58 (August 1972): 269–80.

_____. "The Navy Board and Transports for Cartagena, 1740." *War in History* 9 (April 2002): 127–42.

_____. *The Siege and Capture of Havana 1762*. London: Navy Records Society, 1970.

Szabo, Franz A.J. *Kaunitz and Enlightened Absolutism, 1753–1780*. Cambridge: Cambridge University Press, 1994.

Talbot Rice, Tamara. *Elizabeth: Empress of Russia*. New York: Praeger, 1970.

Thomson, Mark A. "The War of the Austrian Succession." In *The New Cambridge Modern History*, Volume VII. Edited by J.O. Lindsay. Cambridge: Cambridge University Press, 1957.

Tracy, Nicholas. *Manila Ransomed: The British Assault on Manila in the Seven Years' War*. Exeter: University of Exeter Press, 1995.

_____. "The Capture of Manila, 1762." *Mariner's Mirror* 55 (1969): 311–23.

Tunstall, Brian. *Admiral Byng and the Loss of Minorca*. London: P. Allan and Company, 1928.

_____. *William Pitt, Earl of Chatham*. London: Hodder and Stoughton, 1938.

Ward, Matthew C. "'The European Method of Warring is Not Practiced Here': The Failure of British Military Policy in the Ohio Valley, 1755–1759." *War in History* 4 (July 1997): 247–63.

Warner, Oliver. *With Wolfe to Quebec: The Path to Glory*. London: Collins, 1972.

West, Jenny. *Gunpowder, Government and War in the Mid-Eighteenth Century*. Woodbridge: Boydell Press, 1991.

White, Jon Manchip. *Marshal of France: The Life and Times of Maurice, Comte de Saxe (1696–1750)*. Chicago: Rand McNally and Company, 1962.

Wilkinson, Spenser. *The Defence of Piedmont, 1742–1748: A Prelude to the Study of Napoleon*. Oxford: Clarendon Press, 1927.

Williams, Basil. *Carteret and Newcastle: A Contrast in Contemporaries.* Cambridge: Cambridge University Press, 1943; reprint, London: Frank Cass and Company, 1966.

_____. "Carteret and the So-Called Treaty of Hanau." *The English Historical Review* 49 (1934): 684–87.

_____. *The Life of William Pitt, Earl of Chatham.* 2 volumes. London: Longmans, Green and Company, 1913–14.

Woodbridge, John D. *Revolt in Prerevolutionary France: The Prince de Conti's Conspiracy against Louis XV, 1755–1757.* Baltimore: The Johns Hopkins University Press, 1995.

Woodfine, Philip. "Ideas of Naval Power and the Conflict with Spain, 1737–1742." In *The British Navy and the Use of Naval Power in the Eighteenth Century.* Edited by J. Black and P. Woodfine. Atlantic Highlands: Humanities Press International, 1989.

EUROPE AND THE RISE OF THE EASTERN POWERS, 1763–1789

Abarca, Ramón Eugenio. "Bourbon 'Revanche' against England: The Balance of Power, 1763–1770." Ph.D. diss., University of Notre Dame, 1964.

_____. "Classical Diplomacy and Bourbon 'Revanche' Strategy, 1763–1770." *Review of Politics* 32 (1970): 313–37.

Aiton, A.S. "Spain and the Family Compact, 1770–1773." In *Hispanic American Essays.* Edited by A. Curtis Wilgus. Chapel Hill: University of North Carolina, 1942.

Aksan, Virginia H. "Feeding the Ottoman Troops on the Danube, 1768–1774." *War and Society* 13 (1995): 1–14.

_____. "Ottoman-French Relations, 1739–1768." In *Studies on Ottoman Diplomatic History.* Edited by Sinan Kuneralp. Istanbuhl: Isis Press, 1987.

_____. "The One-Eyed Fighting the Blind: Mobilization, Supply, and Command in the Russo-Turkish War of 1768–1774." *The International History Review* 15 (May 1993): 221–38.

Alexander, John T. *Catherine the Great: Life and Legend.* New York: Oxford University Press, 1989.

Alstyne, R.W. Van. *Empire and Independence: The International History of the American Revolution.* New York: Wiley, 1965.

Anderson, Matthew S. "British Diplomatic Relations with the Mediterranean, 1763–1778." Ph.D. thesis, University of Edinburgh, 1952.

_____. "European Diplomatic Relations, 1763–1790." In *The New Cambridge Modern History,* Volume VIII. Edited by A. Goodwin. Cambridge: Cambridge University Press, 1965.

_____. "Great Britain and the Russian Fleet, 1769–1770." *Slavonic and East European Review* 31 (1952–53): 148–63.

_____. "Great Britain and the Russo-Turkish War of 1768–1774." *The English Historical Review* 69 (January 1954): 39–58.

_____. "Great Britain and the Growth of the Russian Navy in the Eighteenth Century." *Mariner's Mirror* 42 (1956): 132–46.

_____. "Russia in the Mediterranean, 1788–1791: A Little-Known Chapter in the History of Naval Warfare and Privateering." *Mariner's Mirror* 45 (February 1959): 25–35.

_____. "The Great Powers and the Russian Annexation of the Crimea." *Slavonic and East European Review* 37 (1958–59): 17–42.

Aretin, Karl Otmar Freiherr von. "Russia as a Guarantor Power of the Imperial Constitution under Catherine II." *The Journal of Modern History* 78 (December 1986): S141-S160.

Asprey, Robert B. *Frederick the Great: The Magnificent Enigma.* London: Costello, 1986.

Atwood, Rodney. *The Hessians: Mercenaries from Hessen-Kassel in the American Revolution*. Cambridge: Cambridge University Press, 1980.

Bakhrushin, Sergei V. and Sergei D. Skazkin. "Diplomacy." Translated by M. Raeff. In *Catherine the Great: A Profile*. New York: Hill and Wang, 1972.

Barton, H. Arnold. "Gustav III of Sweden and the East Baltic, 1771–1792." *Journal of Baltic Studies* 7 (1976): 13–30.

_____. "Sweden and the War of American Independence." *William and Mary Quarterly* 23 (1966): 408–30.

Baugh, Daniel A. "Why did Britain Lose Command of the Sea during the War for America?" In *The British Navy and the Use of Naval Power in the Eighteenth Century*. Edited by J. Black and P. Woodfine. Atlantic Highlands: Humanities Press International, 1989.

Beales, Derek. *Joseph II: In the Shadow of Maria Theresa, 1741–1780*. Cambridge: Cambridge University Press, 1987.

_____ and Timothy C.W. Blanning. "Prince Kaunitz and 'The Primacy of Domestic Policy.'" *The International History Review* 2 (October 1980): 619–24.

Bemis, Samuel Flagg. "British Secret Service and the French-American Alliance." *The American Historical Review* 29 (1923–24): 474–95.

_____. *The Diplomacy of the American Revolution*. New Haven: Yale University Press, 1935; reprint, Edinburgh: Oliver and Boyd, 1957.

Bernard, Paul. *Joseph II*. New York: Twayne, 1968.

_____. *Joseph II and Bavaria: Two Eighteenth-Century Attempts at German Unification*. The Hague: Martinus Nijhoff, 1965.

_____. "Kaunitz and the Cost of Diplomacy." *East European Quarterly* 17 (1983): 1–14.

Black, Jeremy. "Anglo-French Relations in the Age of the French Revolution, 1787–1793." *Francia* 14 (1987): 407–33.

_____. "Anglo-Russian Relations after the Seven Years' War." *Scottish Slavonic Review* 9 (1987): 27–37.

_____. *British Foreign Policy in an Age of Revolutions, 1783–1793.* Cambridge: Cambridge University Press, 1994.

_____. "British Policy Towards Austria, 1780–1793." *Mitteilungen des Österreichischen Staatsarchivs* 42 (1992): 188–228.

_____. "Naval Power, Strategy and Foreign Policy, 1775–1791." In *Parameters of British Naval Power, 1650–1850.* Edited by M. Duffy. Exeter: Exeter University Press, 1992.

_____. "Sir Robert Ainslie: His Majesty's Agent-Provocateur?: British Foreign Policy and the International Crisis of 1787." *European History Quarterly* 14 (1984): 253–83.

_____. "The Crown, Hanover and the Shift in British Foreign Policy in the 1760s." In *Knights Errant and True Englishmen: British Foreign Policy, 1600–1800.* Edited by J. Black. Edinburgh: John Donald, 1989.

_____. "The Marquis of Carmarthen and Relations with France, 1784–1787." *Francia* 12 (1984): 283–303.

_____. *War for America: The Fight for Independence, 1775–1783.* New York: St. Martin's Press, 1991.

Blanning, Timothy C.W. *Joseph II.* London: Longman, 1994.

_____. "'That Horrid Electorate' or 'Ma Patrie Germanique'? George III, Hanover, and the *Fürstenbund* of 1785." *The Historical Journal* 20 (1977): 311–44.

_____ and Carl Haase. "George III, Hanover and the Regency Crisis." In *Knights Errant and True Englishmen: British Foreign Policy, 1600–1800.* Edited by J. Black. Edinburgh: John Donald, 1989.

Breen, Kenneth. "Divided Command: The West Indies and North America, 1780–1781." In *The British Navy and the Use of Naval Power in the Eighteenth Century.* Edited by J. Black and P. Woodfine. Atlantic Highlands: Humanities Press International, 1989.

Brooke, John. *King George III*. New York: McGraw Hill, 1972.

Brown, Alan S. "The Impossible Dream: The North Ministry, the Structure of Politics, and Conciliation." In *The American Revolution and "A Candid World"*. Edited by L. Kaplan. Kent: Kent State University Press, 1977.

Brown, G.S. "The Anglo-French Naval Crisis, 1778: A Study of Conflict in the North Cabinet." *William and Mary Quarterly*, Third Series 13 (1956): 3–25.

Butterfield, Herbert. "British Foreign Policy, 1762–1765." *The Historical Journal* 6 (1963): 131–40.

Chartrand, Rene. *The French Army in the American War of Independence*. London: Osprey, 1992.

Clendenning, P. "The Anglo-Russian Treaty of 1766." Ph.D. thesis, Cambridge University, 1976.

Cobban, A. *Ambassadors and Secret Agents: The Diplomacy of the First Earl of Malmesbury at The Hague*. London: Jonathan Cape, 1954.

Conway, Stephen. *The War of American Independence, 1775–1783*. London: Edward Arnold, 1995.

Corwin, E.S. *French Policy and the American Alliance of 1778*. Princeton: Princeton University Press, 1916; reprint, Gloucester, Mass.: Peter Smith, 1969.

_____. "The French Objective in the American Revolution." *American Historical Review* 21 (1915–16): 33–62.

Crout, Robert Rhodes. "In Search of a 'Just and Lasting Peace': The Treaty of 1783, Louis XVI, Vergennes, and the Regeneration of the Realm." *The International History Review* 5 (August 1983): 364–98.

Davidson, Roderic H. "The Treaty of Kuchuk Kaynardja: A Note on Its Italian Text." *The International History Review* 10 (November 1988): 611–20.

DeConde, Alexander. "The French Alliance in Historical Speculation." In *Diplomacy and Revolution: The Franco-American Alliance of 1778*. Edtied by R. Hoffman and P. Albert. Charlottesville: University Press of Virginia, 1981.

Dippel, H. "Prussia's English Policy after the Seven Years' War." *Central European History* 4 (1971): 195–214.

Dixon, Simon. *Catherine the Great.* London: Longman, 2001.

Donaghay, Marie. "The Anglo-French Negotiations of 1786–1787." Ph.D. diss., University of Virginia, 1970.

Duffy, Christopher. *Frederick the Great: A Military Life.* London: Routledge and Kegan Paul, 1985.

_____. *The Army of Frederick the Great.* Newton Abbot: David and Charles, 1974.

_____. *The Army of Maria Theresa: The Armed Forces of Imperial Austria, 1740–1780.* New York: Hippocrene, 1977.

Dull, Jonathan R. *A Diplomatic History of the American Revolution.* New Haven: Yale University Press, 1985.

_____. "Benjamin Franklin and the Nature of American Diplomacy." *The International History Review* 5 (August 1983): 346–63.

_____. *Franklin the Diplomat: The French Mission.* Philadelphia: American Philosophical Society, 1982.

_____. *The French Navy and American Independence: A Study in Arms and Diplomacy, 1774–1787.* Princeton: Princeton University Press, 1975.

_____. "Vergennes, Rayneval, and the Diplomacy of Trust." In *Peace and Peacemakers: The Treaty of 1783.* Edited by R. Hoffman and P.J. Albert. Charlottesville: University Press of Virginia, 1986.

Dyck, Harvey L. "Pondering the Russian Fact: Kaunitz and the Catherinian Empire in the 1770s." *Canadian Slavonic Papers* 22 (1981): 451–69.

Ehrman, John. *The British Government and Commercial Negotiations with Euorpe, 1783–1793.* Cambridge: Cambridge University Press, 1962.

_____. *The Younger Pitt.* 3 volumes. London: Constable, 1969–96.

Escott, M.M. "Britain's Relations with France and Spain, 1763–1771." Ph.D. thesis, University of Wales, 1988.

Evans, Howard V. "The Nootka Sound Controversy in Anglo-French Diplomacy (1790)." *The Journal of Modern History* 46 (December 1974): 609–40.

Fisher, A.W. *The Russian Annexation of the Crimea, 1772–1783*. Cambridge: Cambridge University Press, 1970.

Fox, Frank. "Negotiating with the Russians: Ambassador Ségur's Mission to St. Petersburg, 1784–1789." *French Historical Studies* 7 (1971): 47–71.

Gershoy, Leo. *From Despotism to Revolution, 1763–1789*. New York: Harper and Brothers, 1944.

Goebel, Julius. *The Struggle for the Falkland Islands: A Study in Legal and Diplomatic History*. New Haven: Yale University Press, 1927.

Graham, Gerald S. *The Royal Navy in the War of American Independence*. London: Her Majesty's Stationery Office, 1976.

Greenbaum, Louis S. "Talleyrand and Vergennes: The Debut of a Diplomat." *Catholic Historical Review* 56 (1970): 543–50.

Griffiths, David M. "American Commercial Diplomacy in Russia, 1780 to 1783." *William and Mary Quarterly*, Third series 27 (1970): 379–410.

_____. "Catherine the Great, the British Opposition, and the American Revolution." In *The American Revolution and "A Candid World"*. Edited by L. Kaplan. Kent: Kent State University Press, 1977.

_____. "Nikita Panin, Russian Diplomacy and the American Revolution." *Slavic Review* 28 (1969): 1–24.

_____. "Russian Court Politics and the Question of an Expansionist Foreign Policy under Catherine II, 1762–1783." Ph.D. thesis., Cornell University, 1967.

_____. "The Rise and Fall of the Northern System: Court Politics and Foreign Policy in the First Half of Catherine II's Reign." *Canadian-American Slavic Studies* 4 (1970): 547–69.

Hagen, William W. "The Partitions of Poland and the Crisis of the Old Regime in Prussia, 1772–1806." *Central European History* 9 (June 1976): 115–28.

Hall, Thadd E. *France and the Eighteenth-Century Corsican Question.* New York: New York University Press, 1971.

Hardman, John. *French Politics, 1774–1789: From the Accession of Louis XVI to the Fall of the Bastille.* London: Longman, 1995.

_____. *Louis XVI.* New Haven: Yale University Press, 1993.

_____ and M. Price, editors. *Louis XVI and the Comte de Vergenes: Correspondence, 1774–1787.* Oxford: Clarendon Press, 1998.

Harlow, V.T. *The Founding of the Second British Empire, 1763–1793.* 2 volumes. London: Longmans, Green and Company, 1952–64.

Henderson, W.O. "The Anglo-French Commercial Treaty of 1786." *Economic History Review*, Second series 10 (1957–58): 104–12.

Higginbotham, Donald. *The War of American Independence: Military Attitudes, Policies, and Practice, 1763–1789.* New York: Macmillan, 1971.

Hoffman, Ronald and Peter J. Albert, editors. *Diplomacy and Revolution: The Franco-American Alliance of 1778.* Charlottesville: University Press of Virginia, 1981.

_____, editors. *Peace and Peacemakers: The Treaty of 1783.* Charlottesville: University Press of Virginia, 1986.

Horn, David Bayne. *British Public Opinion and the First Partition of Poland.* London: Oliver and Boyd, 1945.

_____. *Frederick the Great and the Rise of Prussia.* London: English Universities Press, 1964.

Horsman, Reginald. *The Diplomacy of the New Republic, 1776–1815.* Arlington Heights: Harlan Davidson, 1985.

Hubatsch, Walther. *Frederick the Great: Absolutism and Administration.* London: Thames and Hudson, 1973.

Hutson, James H. *John Adams and the Diplomacy of the American Revolution.* Lexington: University of Kentucky Press, 1980.

_____. "The American Negotiations: The Diplomacy of Jealousy." In *Peace and Peacemakers: The Treaty of 1783.* Edited by R. Hoffman and P.J. Albert. Charlottesville: University Press of Virginia, 1986.

_____. "The Partition Treaty and the Declaration of American Independence." *Journal of American History* 58 (1971–72): 877–96.

Ingrao, Charles W. "The Hessian Mercenary State and the American Revolution." *Studies in History and Politics* 4 (1985): 113–22.

_____. *The Hessian Mercenary State: Ideas, Institutions, and Reform under Frederick II, 1760–1785.* Cambridge and New York: Cambridge University Press, 1987.

Jarrett, Derek. *The Begetters of Revolution: England's Involvement with France, 1759–1789.* Totowa: Rowman and Littlefield, 1973.

Jewsbury, George. "Chaos and Corruption: The Comte de Langeron's Critique of the 1787–1792 Russo-Turkish War." *Studies in History and Politics* 3 (1983/84): 73–83.

Jones, M.A. "American Independence in Its Imperial, Strategic, and Diplomatic Aspects." In *The New Cambridge Modern History*, Volume VIII. Edited by A. Goodwin. Cambridge: Cambridge University Press, 1965.

Kaiser, Thomas E. "Who's Afraid of Marie Antoinette?: Diplomacy, Austrophobia and the Queen." *French History* 14 (2000): 241–71.

Kaplan, Herbert H. *The First Partition of Poland.* New York: Columbia University Press, 1962.

Kaplan, Lawrence S. *Colonies into Nation: American Diplomacy, 1763–1801.* New York: Macmillan, 1972.

_____, editor. *The American Revolution and "A Candid World".* Kent: Kent State University Press, 1977.

_____. "Toward Isolationism: The Rise and Fall of the Franco-American Alliance, 1775–1801." In *The American Revolution and "A Candid World".* Edited by L. Kaplan. Kent: Kent State University Press, 1977.

Kennett, Lee. *French Forces in America, 1780–1783.* Westport: Greenwood Press, 1977.

Konopczynski, W. "England and the First Partition of Poland." *Journal of Central European Affairs* 8 (1948–49): 1–23.

Konstam, Angus. *Guilford Courthouse 1781.* Botley: Osprey, 2002.

Kulak, Zbigniew. "The Plans and Aims of Frederick II's Policy Towards Poland." *Polish Western Affairs* 22 (1981): 70–101.

Lalaguna Lasala, J.A. "England, Spain and the Family Compact, 1763–1783." Ph.D. thesis, University of London, 1968.

Lambert, Francis X. "The Foreign Policy of the Duc de Choiseul, 1763–1770." Ph.D. diss., Harvard University, 1952.

Lang, Daniel G. *Foreign Policy in the Early Republic: The Law of Ntaions and the Balance of Power.* Baton Rouge: Louisiana State University Press, 1985.

LeDonne, John P. "Outlines of Russian Military Administration, 1762–1796. Part I: Troop Strength and Deployment." *Jahrbücher für Geschichte Osteuropas Neue Folge* 31 (1983): 321–47.

_____. *Ruling Russia: Politics and Administration in the Age of Absolutism, 1762–1796.* Princeton: Princeton University Press, 1984.

Lentin, T. "*La Hollande—'une puissance endormie*': M.M. Shcherbatov's Observations on the Outbreak of the Anglo-Dutch War, 1780." In *Russia and the Low Countries in the Eighteenth Century.* Edited by Emmanuel Waegemans. Groningen: Institute for Northern and Eastern European Studies, 1998.

Lewitter, L.R. "The Partitions of Poland." In *The New Cambridge Modern History*, Volume VIII. Edited by A. Goodwin. Cambridge: Cambridge University Press, 1965.

_____. "The Partitions of Poland." *History Today* 8–9 (1958–59): 813–20, 30–39.

Lint, Gregg L. "Preparing for Peace: The Objectives of the United States, France, and Spain in the War of the American Revolution." In *Peace and Peacemakers: The Treaty of 1783*. Edited by R. Hoffman and P.J. Albert. Charlottesville: University Press of Virginia, 1986.

_____."The Law of Nations and the American Revolution." In *The American Revolution and "A Candid World"*. Edited by L. Kaplan. Kent: Kent State University Press, 1977.

Longworth, Philip. *The Art of Victory: The Life and Achievements of Field-Marshal Suvorov, 1729–1800*. New York: Holt, Rinehart and Winston, 1965.

Lukowski, Jerzy T. "Guarantee or Annexation: A Note on Russian Plans to Acquire Polish Territory Prior to the First Partition of Poland." *Bulletin of the Institute of Historical Research* 56 (1983): 60–65.

_____. *The Partitions of Poland, 1772, 1793, 1795*. London: Addison, Wesley, Longman, 1999.

_____. "Towards Partition: Polish Magnates and Russian Intervention in Poland during the Early Reign of Stanisław August Poniatowski." *Historical Journal* 28 (1985): 557–74.

Macartney, C.A. *Maria Theresa and the House of Austria*. London: English Universities Press, 1969.

MacDonogh, Giles. *Frederick the Great: A Life in Deed and Letters*. London: Weidenfeld and Nicolson, 1999.

Mackesy, Piers. "British Strategy in the War of American Independence." *Yale University Review* 52 (1963): 539–57.

_____. *The War for America, 1775–1783*. Cambridge, Mass.: Harvard University Press, 1964.

Madariaga, Isabel de. *Britain, Russia and the Armed Neutrality of 1780: Sir James Harris's Mission to St. Petersburg during the American Revolution.* London: Hollis and Carter, 1962.

_____. *Catherine the Great: A Short History.* New Haven: Yale University Press, 1990.

_____. *Russia in the Age of Catherine the Great.* London: Weidenfeld and Nicolson, 1981.

_____. "The Secret Austro-Russian Treaty of 1781." *Slavonic and East European Review* 38 (1959–60): 114–45.

_____. "The Use of British Secret Funds at St. Petersburg, 1777–1782." *Slavonic and East European Review* 32 (1953–54): 464–74.

Marks, Frederick W., III. *Independence on Trial: Foreign Affairs and the Making of the Constitution.* Baton Rouge: Louisiana State University Press, 1973; reprint, Delaware: Scholarly Press, 1986.

Marston, Daniel. *The American War of Independence.* Botley: Osprey, 2002.

Mayer, Matthew Z. "Joseph II and the Austro-Ottoman War, 1788–1791." Ph.D. diss., Cambridge University, 2002.

_____. "Joseph II and the Campaign of 1788 against the Ottoman Turks." M.A. thesis, McGill University, 1997.

McGill, William J., Jr. *Maria Theresa.* New York: Twayne, 1972.

Metcalf, Michael F. *Russia, England and Swedish Party Politics, 1762–1766: The Interplay between Great Power Diplomacy and Domestic Politics during Sweden's Age of Liberty.* Totowa: Rowman and Littlefield, 1977.

Miller, Daniel A. *Sir Joseph Yorke and Anglo-Dutch Relations, 1774–1780.* The Hague: Mouton, 1970.

Misiunas, R.J. "Russia and Sweden, 1772–1778." Ph.D. diss., Yale University, 1971.

Morris, Richard B. *The Peacemakers: The Great Powers and American Independence.* New York: Harper and Row, 1965; reprint, Boston: Northeastern University Press, 1983.

Morrissen, Brendan. *Boston 1775: The Shot Heard Around the World.* Botley: Osprey, 2000.

_____. *Saratoga 1777.* Botley: Osprey, 2000.

_____. *Yorktown 1781: The World Turned Upside Down.* London: Osprey, 1997.

Murphy, Orville T. *Charles Gravier, Comte de Vergennes: French Diplomacy in the Age of Revolution, 1719–1787.* Albany: State University of New York Press, 1982.

_____. "Charles Gravier de Vergennes: Profile of an Old Regime Diplomat." *Political Science Quarterly* 83 (1968): 400–18.

_____. "Dupont de Nemours and the Anglo-French Commercial Treaty of 1786." *The Economic History Review* 19 (1966): 569–80.

_____. "Louis XVI and the Pattern and Costs of a Policy Dilemma: Russia and the Eastern Question, 1787–1788." *Proceedings of the Consortium on Revolutionary Europe* 16 (1986): 264–74.

_____. "The Battle of Germantown and the Franco-American Alliance of 1778." *Pennsylvania Magazine of History and Bioraphy* 82 (1958): 55–64.

_____. "The Comte de Vergennes, the Newfoundland Fisheries and the Peace Negotiations of 1783." *Canadian Historical Review* 46 (1965): 32–46.

_____. *The Diplomatic Retreat of France and Public Opinion on the Eve of the French Revolution, 1783–1789.* Washington, D.C.: Catholic University of America Press, 1998.

_____. "The View from Versailles: Charles Gravier Comte de Vergennes's Perceptions of the American Revolution." In *Diplomacy and Revolution: The Franco-American Alliance of 1778.* Edited by R. Hoffman and P.J. Albert. Charlottesville: University Press of Virginia, 1981.

Oakley, Stewart P. "Gustavus III of Sweden." *Studies in History and Politics* 4 (1985): 69–86.

_____. "Gustavus III's Plans for War with Denmark in 1783–1784." In *Studies in Diplomatic History: Essays in Memory of David Bayne Horn.* Edited by R.M. Hatton and M.S. Anderson. London: Longman, 1970.

Padover, Saul K. "Prince Kaunitz and the First Partition of Poland." Ph.D. diss., University of Chicago, 1932.

_____. "Prince Kaunitz's Résumé of His Eastern Policy, 1763–1771." *The Journal of Modern History* 5 (September 1933): 352–65.

Palmer, Robert R. *The Age of the Democratic Revolution: A Political History of Europe and America, 1760–1800.* 2 volumes. Princeton: Princeton University Press, 1959–64.

Patterson, A. Temple. *The Other Armada: The Franco-Spanish Attempt to Invade Britain in 1779.* Manchester: Manchester University Press, 1960.

Peckham, Howard H. *The War for Independence: A Military History.* Chicago: University of Chicago Press, 1958.

Perkins, Bradford. "The Peace of Paris: Patterns and Legacies." In *Peace and Peacemakers: The Treaty of 1783.* Edited by R. Hoffman and P.J. Albert. Charlottesville: University Press of Virginia, 1986.

Petrie, Charles. *King Charles III of Spain: An Enlightened Despot.* New York: John Day, 1971.

Price, Munro. "The Dutch Affair and the Fall of the *Ancien Régime,* 1784–1787." *The Historical Journal* 38 (1995): 875–905.

Raeff, Marc. "In the Imperial Manner." In *Catherine the Great: A Profile.* Edited by Marc. Raeff. New York: Hill and Wang, 1972.

Ragsdale, Hugh. "Evaluating the Traditions of Russian Aggression: Catherine II and the Greek Project." *Slavonic and East European Review* 66 (1988): 91–117.

_____. "Montmorin and Catherine's Greek Project: Revolution in French Foreign Policy." *Cahiers du monde russe et soviétique* 27 (1986): 27–44.

_____. "New Light on the Greek Project: A Preliminary Report." In *Russia and the World of the Eighteenth Century*. Edited by R.P. Bartlett, A.G. Cross, and K. Rasmussen. Columbus, Ohio: Slavica, 1988.

Ramsey, John Fraser. *Anglo-French Relations, 1763–1770: A Study of Choiseul's Foreign Policy*. Berkeley: University of California Press, 1939.

Reddaway, W.F. "Great Britain and Poland, 1762–1772." *The Cambridge Historical Journal* 4 (1932–34): 233–62.

_____. "Macartney in Russia, 1765–1767." *The Cambridge Historical Journal* 3 (1929–31): 260–94.

Rice, Geoffrey W. "Great Britain, the Manila Ransom, and the First Falkland Islands Dispute with Spain, 1766." *The International History Review* 2 (July 1980): 386–409.

Reid, Stuart. *King George's Army 1740–1793*. 3 volumes. London: Osprey, 1995–96.

Ritcheson, Charles R. *Aftermath of Revolution: British Policy Toward the United States, 1783–1795*. Dallas: Southern Methodist University Press, 1969.

_____. "Britain's Peacemakers, 1782–1783: 'To an Astonishing Degree Unfit for the Task'?" In *Peace and Peacemakers: The Treaty of 1783*. Edited by R. Hoffman and P.J. Albert. Charlottesville: University Press of Virginia, 1986.

_____. "The Earl of Shelburne and Peace with America, 1782–1783: Vision and Reality." *The International History Review* 5 (August 1983): 322–45.

Ritter, Gerhard. *Frederick the Great: A Historical Profile*. Berkeley: University of California Press, 1968.

Roberts, Michael. *British Diplomacy and Swedish Politics, 1758–1773*. London: Macmillan, 1980.

_____. "Great Britain and the Swedish Revolution, 1772–1773." *Historical Journal* 7 (1964): 1–46; reprinted in *Essays in Swedish History.* Minneapolis: University of Minnesota Press, 1967.

_____. "Great Britain, Denmark and Russia, 1763–1770." In *Studies in Diplomatic History: Essays in Memory of David Bayne Horn.* Edited by R.M. Hatton and M.S. Anderson. London: Longman, 1970.

_____. "Macartney in Russia." *The English Historical Review* Supplement 7 (1974).

_____. *Splendid Isolation 1763–1780.* Reading: University of Reading, 1970.

Roider, Karl A. "Kaunitz, Joseph II and the Turkish War." *Slavonic and East European Review* 54 (October 1976): 538–56.

Rose, J. Holland. "Great Britain and the Dutch Question in 1787–1788." *The American Historical Review* 14 (1908–9): 262–83.

_____. "The Franco-British Commercial Treaty of 1786." *The English Historical Review* 23 (1908): 709–24.

Roslund-Mercurio, C.L. "The American Colonial Rebellion and Swedish British Diplomacy, 1775–1778." *Historisk Tidskrift* 94 (1974): 475–89.

_____. "The Problem of Neutral Rights in Swedish Relations with Great Britain, 1775–1780." Ph.D. diss., Syracuse University, 1972.

Schama, Simon. *Patriots and Liberators: Revolution in the Netherlands, 1780–1813.* London: Collins, 1977.

Schieder, Theodor. *Frederick the Great.* Edited by S. Berkeley and H.M. Scott. London: Longman, 2000.

Schmidt, K.R. "Problems Connected with the Last Polish Royal Election: A Study in the Development of Count Panin's Northern System." *Scando-Slavica* 2 (1956): 134–48.

_____. "The Treaty of Commerce between Great Britain and Russia in 1766: A Study in the Development of Count Panin's Northern System." *Scando-Slavica* 1 (1954): 115–34.

Schulte Nordholt, Jan Willem. *The Dutch Republic and American Independence*. Chapel Hill: University of North Carolina Press, 1982.

Scott, Hamish M. "Anglo-Austrian Relations after the Seven Years' War: Lord Stormont in Vienna, 1763–1772." Ph.D. thesis, University of London, 1977.

_____. "Aping the Great Powers: Frederick the Great and the Defence of Prussia's International Position, 1763–1786." *German History* 12 (1994): 286–307.

_____. "British Foreign Policy in the Age of the American Revolution." *The International History Review* 6 (February 1984): 113–25.

_____. *British Foreign Policy in the Age of the American Revolution*. Oxford: Clarendon Press, 1990.

_____. "Choiseul: The Making of a Diplomat." *The International History Review* 3 (August 1982): 414–20.

_____. "France and the Polish Throne, 1763–1764." *Slavonic and East European Review* 53 (1975): 370–88.

_____. "Frederick II, the Ottoman Empire and the origins of the Russo-Prussian Alliance of April 1764." *European Studies Review* 7 (1977): 153–75.

_____. "Great Britain, Poland and the Russian Alliance, 1763–1767." *The Historical Journal* 19 (1976): 53–74.

_____. "Kaunitz and the Western Powers after the Seven Years' War." *Staatskanzler Wenzel Anton von Kaunitz-Rietberg, 1711–1794*. Edited by Grete Klingenstein and Franz A.J. Szabo. Graz: Verlag Schnider, 1996.

_____. "Louis XVI and Vergennes." *The International History Review* 21 (December 1999): 941–44.

_____. "Prussia's Royal Foreign Minister: Frederick the Great and the Administration of Prussian Diplomacy." In *Royal and Republican Sovereignty in Early Modern Europe: Essays in Memory of Ragnhild Hatton*. Edited by R. Oresko, G.C. Gibbs, and H.M. Scott. Cambridge: Cambridge University Press, 1997.

_____. "Sir Joseph Yorke, Dutch Politics and the Origins of the Fourth Anglo-Dutch War." *Historical Journal* 31 (1988): 571–89.

_____. *The Emergence of the Eastern Powers, 1756–1775*. Cambridge: Cambridge University Press, 2001.

_____. "The Importance of Bourbon Naval Reconstruction to the Strategy of Choiseul after the Seven Years' War." *The International History Review* 1 (January 1979): 17–35.

Showalter, Dennis E. "Hubertusberg to Auerstädt: The Prussian Army in Decline?" *German History* 12 (1994): 308–33.

Sorel, Albert. *The Eastern Question in the Eighteenth Century: The Partition of Poland and the Treaty of Kainardji*. London: Methuen, 1898; reprint, New York: Howard Fertig, 1969.

Spencer, Frank. "The Diplomatic Correspondence of John, Fourth Earl of Sandwich, during his Secretaryship of State in the Northern Department, September 9, 1763-July 10, 1765." Ph.D. thesis, University of Manchester, 1953.

_____, editor. *The Fourth Earl of Sandwich: Diplomatic Correspondence, 1763–1765*. Manchester: Manchester University Press, 1961.

Stinchcombe, William C. "John Adams and the Model Treaty." In *The American Revolution and "A Candid World"*. Edited by L. Kaplan. Kent: Kent State University Press, 1977.

_____. *The American Revolution and the French Alliance*. Syracuse: Syracuse University Press, 1969.

Stine, John E. "King Frederick William II and the Decline of the Prussian Army, 1786–1797." Ph.D. diss., University of Southern Carolina, 1980.

Stockley, A.P. "Britain, France and the Peace Negotiations of 1782–1783." Ph.D. diss., Cambridge University, 1994.

Stourzh, Gerald. *Benjamin Franklin and American Foreign Policy*. Second edition. Chicago: University of Chicago Press, 1969.

Syrett, David. "Defeat at Sea: The Impact of American Naval Operations upon the British, 1775–1778." In *Maritime Dimensions of the American Revolution*. Washington, D.C.: Department of the Navy, 1977.

_____. *Neutral Rights and the War in the Narrow Seas, 1778–1782*. Fort Leavenworth: Combat Studies Institute, 1985.

_____. "The Failure of the British Effort in America, 1777." In *The British Navy and the Use of Naval Power in the Eighteenth Century*. Edited by J. Black and P. Woodfine. Atlantic Highlands: Humanities Press International, 1989.

_____. "The Methodology of British Amphibious Operations during the Seven Years' and American Wars." *Mariner's Mirror* 58 (August 1972): 269–80.

_____. *The Royal Navy in American Waters, 1775–1783*. Aldershot: Scolar Press, 1989.

Szabo, Franz A.J. *Kaunitz and Enlightened Absolutism, 1753–1780*. Cambridge: Cambridge University Press, 1994.

_____. "Prince Kaunitz and the Balance of Power." *The International History Review* 1 (July 1979): 399–407.

_____. "Prince Kaunitz and the Primacy of Domestic Policy: A Response." *The International History Review* 2 (October 1980): 625–35.

_____. "Unwanted Navy: Habsburg Naval Armaments under Maria Theresa." *Austrian History Yearbook* 17–18 (1981–82): 29–53.

Temperley, Harold. *Frederic the Great and Kaiser Joseph: An Episode of War and Diplomacy in the Eighteenth Century*. London: Duckworth and Company, 1915; reprint, Second edition. London: Frank Cass and Company, 1968.

Toborg, A. "Frederick II of Prussia and His Relations with Great Britain during the American Revolution." Ph.D. diss., Columbia University, 1965.

Topolski, J. "Reflections on the First Partition of Poland (1772)." *Acta Poloniae Historica* 27 (1973): 89–104.

_____. "The Polish-Prussian Frontier during the Period of the First Partition (1772–1777)." *Polish Western Affairs* 10 (1969): 81–110.

Thomson, Gladys Scott. *Catherine the Great and the Expansion of Russia*. London: English Universities Press, 1947.

Tracy, Nicholas. "British Assessments of French and Spanish Naval Reconstruction, 1763–1768." *Mariner's Mirror* 61 (1975): 73–85.

_____. *Navies, Deterrence and American Independence: Britain and Seapower in the 1760s and 1770s*. Vancouver: University of British Columbia Press, 1988.

_____. "Parry of a Threat to India, 1768–1774." *Mariner's Mirror* 59 (1973): 35–48.

_____. "The Administration of the Duke of Grafton and the French Invasion of Corsica." *Eighteenth Century Studies* 8 (1974–75): 169–82.

_____. "The Falkland Islands Crisis of 1770: Use of Naval Force." *The English Historical Review* 90 (1975): 40–75.

_____. "The Gunboat Diplomacy of the Government of George Grenville, 1764–1765: The Honduras, Turks' Island, and Gambian Incidents. *The Historical Journal* 18 (1974): 711–31.

Tucker, Robert W. and David C. Hendrickson. *The Fall of the First British Empire: Origins of the War of American Independence*. Baltimore: Johns Hopkins University Press, 1982.

Van Alstyne, Richard W. *Empire and Independence: The International History of the American Revolution*. New York: John Wiley and Sons, 1965.

_____. "Great Britain, the War for Independence, and the "Gathering Storm" in Europe, 1775–1778." *The Huntington Library Quarterly* 27 (August 1964): 311–46.

Wright, Esmond. "The British Objectives, 1780–1783: 'If Not Dominion Then Trade.'" In *Peace and Peacemakers: The Treaty of 1783*. Edited by R. Hoffman and P.J. Albert. Charlottesville: University Press of Virginia, 1986.

Zamoyski, Adam. *The Last King of Poland*. London: Weidenfeld and Nicolson, 1992.

PART XIV
EUROPE IN THE AGE OF
THE FRENCH REVOLUTION
AND NAPOLEONIC WARS,
1789–1815

EUROPE, 1789–1815

Anderson, Matthew S. *The Eastern Question, 1774–1923*. London: Macmillan, 1966.

Barton, H. Arnold. *Scandinavia in the Revolutionary Era, 1760–1815*. Minneapolis: University of Minnesota Press, 1986.

Brunn, Geoffrey. *Europe and the French Imperium, 1799–1814*. New York: Harper and Brothers, 1938.

_____. "The Balance of Power during the Wars, 1793–1814." In *The New Cambridge Modern History*, Volume IX. Edited by C.W. Crawley. Cambridge: Cambridge University Press, 1965.

Chartrand, Rene. *Napoleon's Guns* 1792–1815. 2 volumes. Botley: Osprey, 2003.

Christie, Ian R. *Wars and Revolutions: Britain, 1760–1815*. London: Edward Arnold, 1982.

Connelly, Owen. *The French Revolution and Napoleonic Era*. Third Edition. Fort Worth: Harcourt, 2000.

Crawley, C.W. *War and Peace in an Age of Upheaval, 1793–1830*. Volume IX in *The New Cambridge Modern History*. Cambridge: Cambridge University Press, 1965.

Crouzet, F. "Wars, Blockade and Economic Change in Europe, 1792–1815." *The Journal of Economic History* 24 (1964): 567–88.

Dickinson, H.T. "The Impact of the French Revolution and the French Wars, 1789–1815." In *Britain and the French Revolution, 1789–1815*. Edited by H.T. Dickinson. New York: St. Martin's Press, 1989.

Duffy, Michael. "British Diplomacy and the French Wars, 1789–1815." In *Britain and the French Revolution, 1789–1815*. Edited by H.T. Dickinson. New York: St. Martin's Press, 1989.

Fedorak, Charles John. "The Royal Navy and British Amphibious Operations during the Revolutionary and Napoleonic Wars." *Military Affairs* 52 (July 1988): 141–46.

Glover, Michael. *The Napoleonic Wars: An Illustrated History 1792–1815*. London: B.T. Batsford, 1979.

Guy, A.J., editor. *The Road to Waterloo: The British Army and the Struggle against Revolutionary and Napoleonic France, 1793–1815*. Stroud: Sutton, 1990.

Henry, Chris. *British Napoleonic Artillery 1793–1815, Volume II—Siege and Coastal Artillery*. Botley: Osprey, 2003.

Hofschroer, Peter. *Prussian Light Infantry, 1792–1815*. London: Osprey, 1984.

_____. *Prussian Line Infantry, 1792–1815*. London: Osprey, 1984.

_____. *Prussian Staff and Specialist Troops 1791–1815*. Botley: Osprey, 2003.

Hollins, David. *Austrian Napoleonic Artillery 1792–1815*. Botley: Osprey, 2003.

Horward, Donald D. "The Proud Adversaries: Masséna and the Archduke Charles." In *Austria in the Age of the French Revolution, 1789–1815*. Edited by K. Brauer and W.E. Wright. Minneapolis: Center for Austrian Studies, University of Minnesota, 1990.

Iiams, Thomas M. *Peacemaking from Vergennes to Napoleon: French Foreign Relations in the Revolutionary Era, 1774–1814*. Huntington, N.Y.: Krieger, 1979.

Langley, Lester D. *The Americas in the Age of Revolution, 1750–1850*. New Haven: Yale University Press, 1996.

Lobanov-Rostovsky, A.A. *Russia and Europe, 1789–1825*. Durham: Duke University Press, 1947.

Mackesy, Piers. "Problems of an Amphibious Power: Britain against France, 1793–1815." *Naval War College Review* 30 (1978): 16–25.

_____. "Strategic Problems of the British War Effort." In *Britain and the French Revolution, 1789–1815*. Edited by H.T. Dickinson. New York: St. Martin's Press, 1989.

Ross, Steven T. *European Diplomatic History, 1789–1815: France against Europe*. New York: Anchor Books, 1969; reprint, Malabar, Florida: Robert E. Krieger, 1981.

Rothenberg, Gunther E. *Napoleon's Great Adversaries: The Archduke Charles and the Austrian Army, 1792–1814*. Bloomington: Indiana University Press, 1983.

_____. *The Art of Warfare in the Age of Napoleon*. Bloomington: Indiana University Press, 1978.

_____. "The Origins, Causes, and Extension of the Wars of the French Revolution and Napoleon." *Journal of Interdisciplinary History* 18 (Spring 1988): 771–93.

Rudé, George. *Revolutionary Europe, 1783–1815*. New York: Harper and Row, 1964.

Schama, Simon. *Patriots and Liberators: Revolution in the Netherlands, 1780–1813*. London: Collins, 1977.

Schroeder, Paul W. *The Transformation of European Politics, 1763–1848*. Oxford: Clarendon Press, 1994.

Shanahan, William O. *Prussian Military Reforms, 1786–1813*. New York: Columbia University Press, 1945.

Shaw, S.J. *Between Old and New: The Ottoman Empire under Sultan Selim III, 1789–1807*. Cambridge, Mass.: Harvard University Press, 1971.

Sherwig, J.M. *Guineas and Gunpowder: British Foreign Aid in the Wars with France, 1793–1815*. Cambridge, Mass.: Harvard University Press, 1969.

Sutherland, D.M.G. *France 1789–1815: Revolution and Counter-Revolution*. London: Fontanta, 1985.

Webb, Paul. "Construction, Repair and Maintenance in the Battle Fleet of the Royal Navy, 1793–1815." In *The British Navy and the Use of Naval Power in the Eighteenth Century*. Edited by J. Black and P. Woodfine. Atlantic Highlands: Humanities Press International, 1989.

FRENCH REVOLUTIONARY WARS, 1789–1801

Ammon, Harry. *The Genet Mission*. New York: W.W. Norton and Sons, 1973.

Anderson, Matthew S. "Russia in the Mediterranean, 1788–1791: A Little-Known Chapter in the History of Naval Warfare and Privateering." *Mariner's Mirror* 45 (February 1959): 25–35.

Atkin, Muriel. "The Pragmatic Diplomacy of Paul I: Russia's Relations with Asia, 1796–1801." *Slavic Review* 38 (1979): 60–74.

Barnby, H.G. *The Prisoners of Algiers: An Account of the Forgotten American-Algerian War, 1785–1797*. London: Oxford University Press, 1966.

Bemis, Samuel Flagg. *Jay's Treaty: A Study in Commerce and Diplomacy*. Revised edition. New Haven: Yale University Press, 1962.

_____. *Pinckney's Treaty: America's Advantage from Europe's Distress, 1783–1800*. Revised edition. New Haven: Yale University Press, 1960.

Bernard, J.F. *Talleyrand: A Biography*. New York: G.P. Putnam's Sons, 1973.

Biro, Sydney S. *The German Policy of Revolutionary France: A Study in French Diplomacy during the War of the First Coalition, 1792–1797.* 2 volumes. Cambridge, Mass.: Harvard University Press, 1957.

Black, Jeremy. "Anglo-French Relations in the Age of the French Revolution, 1787–1793." *Francia* 14 (1987): 407–33.

_____. "British Policy Towards Austria, 1780–1793." *Mitteilungen des Österreichischen Staatsarchivs* 42 (1992): 188–228.

_____. *British Foreign Policy in an Age of Revolutions, 1783–1793.* Cambridge: Cambridge University Press, 1994.

_____. "The Coming of War between Britain and France, 1792–93." *Francia* 20 (1993): 69–108.

Blanning, Timothy C.W. *Reform and Revolution in Mainz, 1743–1803.* Cambridge: Cambridge University Press, 1974.

_____. "The French Revolution and Europe." In *Rewriting the French Revolution.* Edited by C. Lucas. Oxford: Clarendon Press, 1991.

_____. *The French Revolution in Germany: Occupation and Resistance in the Rhineland, 1792–1802.* Oxford: Clarendon Press, 1983.

_____. *The French Revolutionary Wars, 1787–1802.* London: Edward Arnold, 1996.

_____. *The Origins of the French Revolutionary Wars.* London: Longman, 1986.

Bowman, Albert H. *The Struggle for Neutrality: Franco-American Diplomacy during the Federalist Era.* Knoxville: University of Tennessee Press, 1974.

Boycott-Brown, Martin. *The Road to Rivoli: Napoleon's First Campaign.* London: Cassell, 2001.

Boyd, Julian P. *Number 7: Alexander Hamilton's Secret Attempts to Control American Foreign Policy.* Princeton: Princeton University Press, 1964.

Brinton, Crane. *A Decade of Revolution, 1789–1799*. New York: Harper and Brothers, 1934.

Broersma, Henk. "The Dutch Image of the Russians around the Anglo-Russian Invasion of 1799." In *Around Peter the Great: Three Centuries of Dutch-Russian Relations*. Edited by Carel Horstmeier, Hans van Koningsbrugge, Ilja Nieuwland, and Emmanuel Waegemans. Groningen: Institute for Northern and Eastern European Studies, 1997.

Chandler, David G. *The Campaigns of Napoleon*. New York: Macmillan, 1967.

Clapham, John Harold. *The Causes of the War of 1792*. Cambridge: Cambridge University Press, 1899.

Coombs, Jerald A. *The Jay Treaty: Political Battleground of the Founding Fathers*. Berkeley: University of California Press, 1970.

Cormack, William S. "Legitimate Authority in Revolution and War: The French Navy in the West Indies, 1789–1793." *The International History Review* 18 (February 1996): 1–27.

Crimmin, Patricia. "The Royal Navy and the Levant Trade, c.1795-c.1805." In *The British Navy and the Use of Naval Power in the Eighteenth Century*. Edited by J. Black and P. Woodfine. Atlantic Highlands: Humanities Press International, 1989.

Dakin, Douglas. "The Congress of Vienna, 1814–1815 and Its Antecedents." In *Europe's Balance of Power, 1815–1848*. Edited by Alan Sked. London: Macmillan, 1979.

Dean, Martin C. *Austrian Policy During the French Revolutionary Wars, 1796–1799*. Vienna: MHD Sonderreihe, 1993.

DeConde, Alexander. *Entangling Alliance: Politics and Diplomacy under George Washington*. Durham: Duke University Press, 1958; reprint, Westport: Greenwood Press, 1974.

_____. *The Quasi-War: The Politics and Diplomacy of the Undeclared War with France, 1797–1801*. New York: Charles Scribner's Sons, 1966.

Deutsch, Harold C. *The Genesis of Napoleonic Imperialism.* Cambridge, Mass. Harvard University Press, 1938.

Dixon, Simon. *Catherine the Great.* London: Longman, 2001.

Doyle, William. *The Oxford History of the French Revolution.* Oxford: Clarendon Press, 1989.

Duffy, Christopher. *Eagles over the Alps: Suvorov in Italy and Switzerland, 1799.* Chicago: Emperor's Press, 1999.

Duffy, Michael. "'A Particular Service': The British Government and the Dunkirk Expedition of 1793." *The English Historical Review* 91 (1976): 529–54.

_____. "British Policy in the War against Revolutionary France," In *Britain and Revolutionary France: Conflict, Subversion and Propaganda.* Edited by Colin Jones. Exeter: Exeter University Press, 1983.

_____. "British War Policy: The Austrian Alliance, 1793–1801." Ph.D. diss., Oxford University, 1971.

_____. "Pitt, Grenville and the Control of British Foreign Policy in the 1790s." In *Knights Errant and True Englishmen: British Foreign Policy, 1600–1800.* Edited by J. Black. Edinburgh: John Donald, 1989.

_____. *Soldiers, Sugar and Seapower: The British Expeditions to the West Indies and the War against Revolutionary France.* Oxford: Clarendon Press, 1987.

_____. *The Younger Pitt.* London: Longman, 2000.

Dwyer, Philip G. "Prussia and the Armed Neutrality: The Invasion of Hanover in 1801." *The International History Review* 15 (November 1993): 661–87.

_____. *Talleyrand.* London: Longman, 2002.

_____. "The Politics of Prussian Neutrality, 1795–1805." *German History* 12 (1994): 351–73.

Ehrman, John. *The Younger Pitt.* 3 volumes. London: Constable, 1969–96.

Ellis, Geoffrey. *Napoleon.* London: Longman, 1997.

Evans, Howard V. "The Nootka Sound Controversy in Anglo-French Diplomacy (1790)." *The Journal of Modern History* 46 (December 1974): 609–40.

Fedorak, Charles John. "The French Capitulation in Egypt and the Preliminary Anglo-French Treaty of Peace in October 1801: A Note." *The International History Review* 15 (August 1993): 525–34.

Feldbæk, Ole. *Denmark and the Armed Neutrality, 1800–1801: Small Power Policy in a World War.* Copenhagen: Akademisk Forlag, Universitetsforlaget i København, 1980.

_____. "The Anglo-Danish Convoy Conflict of 1800." *Scandinavian Journal of History* 2 (1977): 161–82.

_____. "The Anglo-Russian Rapprochement of 1801: A Prelude to the Peace of Amiens." *Scandinavian Journal of History* 3 (1978): 208–27.

_____. "The Foreign Policy of Tsar Paul I, 1800–1801: An Interpretation." *Jahrbücher für Geschichte Osteuropas* 30 (1982): 16–35.

Ferrero, Guglielmo. *The Gamble: Bonaparte in Italy, 1796–1797.* London: G. Bell and Sons, 1961.

Ford, Guy Stanton. *Hanover and Prussia, 1795–1803: A Study in Neutrality.* New York: Columbia University Press, 1903; reprint, New York, AMS Press, 1967.

Fremont-Barnes, Gregory. *The French Revolutionary Wars.* Botley: Osprey, 2001.

Frey, Linda and Marsha Frey. "'The Reign of the Charlatans is Over': The French Revolutionary Attack on Diplomatic Practice." *The Journal of Modern History* 65 (December 1993): 706–44.

Fryer, W.R. *Republic or Restoration in France? 1794–1797: The Politics of French Royalism, with Particular Reference to the Activities of A.B.J. d'André.* Manchester: Manchester University Press, 1965.

Glover, Richard. "Arms and the British Diplomat in the French Revolutionary Era." *The Journal of Modern History* 29 (September 1957): 199–212.

Godechot, Jacques. *The Counter-Revolution: Doctrine and Action, 1789–1804.* Translated by S. Attanasio. London: Routledge and Kegan Paul, 1972.

Griffith, Paddy. *The Art of War of Revolutionary France, 1789–1802.* London: Greenhill Books, 1998.

Harbron, John D. *Trafalgar and the Spanish Navy.* Annapolis: Naval Institute Press, 1988.

Haythornthwaite, Philip J. *Uniforms of the French Revolutionary Wars, 1789–1802.* Poole: Blandford, 1981; reprinted, London: Weidenfeld and Nicolson, 1997.

Heriot, Angus. *The French in Italy, 1796–1799.* London: Chatto and Windus, 1957.

Herold, J. Christopher. *Napoleon in Egypt.* London: Hamish Hamilton, 1963.

Hollins, D. *Marengo 1800: Napoleon's Greatest Gamble.* Botley: Osprey, 2000.

Howard, Michael. "The Wars of Revolution." Chapter in *War in European History.* Oxford: Oxford University Press, 1976.

Ingram, Edward. *Commitment to Empire: Prophecies of the Great Game in Asia, 1797–1800.* Oxford: Oxford University Press, 1981.

_____. "Where and For What Shall We Fight?" *The International History Review* 7 (May 1985): 271–76.

Kaplan, Lawrence S. *Alexander Hamilton: Ambivalent Anglophile.* Wilmington: Scholarly Resources, 2002.

Keep, John L.H. "Paul I and the Militarization of the Government." In *Paul I: A Reassessment of His Life and Reign.* Edited by H. Ragsdale. Pittsburg: University Center for International Studies, 1979.

_____. "The Russian Army's Response to the French Revolution." *Jahrbücher für Geschichte Osteuropas* 28 (1980): 500–23.

Lefèbvre, Georges. *The French Revolution.* 2 volumes. London: Routledge and Kegan Paul, 1964.

Lojek, Jerzy. "Catherine II's Armed Intervention in Poland: Origins of the Political Decisions at the Russian Court in 1791–1792." *Canadian-American Slavic Studies* 4 (1970): 570–93.

_____. "The International Crisis of 1791: Poland between the Triple Alliance and Russia." *East-Central Europe* 2 (1975): 1–63.

Longworth, Philip. *The Art of Victory: The Life and Achievements of Field-Marshal Suvorov, 1729–1800.* New York: Holt, Rinehart and Winston, 1965.

Lord, Robert H. *The Second Partition of Poland.* Cambridge, Mass.: Harvard University Press, 1915.

_____. "The Third Partition of Poland." *The Slavonic Review* 3 (March 1925): 481–98.

Lukowski, Jerzy. *The Partitions of Poland, 1772, 1793, 1795.* London: Addison, Wesley, Longman, 1999.

Lynn, John A. "En avant!: The Origins of the Revolutionary Attack." In *Tools of War: Instruments, Ideas, and Institutions of Warfare, 1445–1871.* Edited by John A.Lynn. Urbana: University of Illinois Press, 1990.

_____. *The Bayonets of the Republic: Motivation and Tactics in the Army of Revolutionary France, 1791–1794.* Urbana: University of Illinois Press, 1984.

Mackesy, Piers. *British Victory in Egypt, 1801: The End of Napoleon's Conquest.* London: Routledge, 1995.

_____. *Statesmen at War: The Strategy of Overthrow, 1798–1799.* London: Longman, 1974.

_____. *War without Victory: The Downfall of Pitt, 1799–1802.* Oxford: Clarendon Press, 1984.

Madariaga, Isabel de. *Catherine the Great: A Short History.* New Haven: Yale University Press, 1990.

_____. *Russia in the Age of Catherine the Great.* London: Weidenfeld and Nicolson, 1981.

Markham, Felix. *Napoleon.* London: Weidenfeld and Nicolson, 1963.

Mayer, Matthew Z. "Joseph II and the Austro-Ottoman War, 1788–1791." Ph.D. diss., Cambridge University, 2002.

McGrew, Roderick E. "Paul I and the Knights of Malta." In *Paul I: A Reassessment of His Life and Reign.* Edited by H. Ragsdale. Pittsburg: University Center for International Studies, 1979.

_____. *Paul I of Russia, 1754–1801.* Oxford: Clarendon Press, 1992.

Mitchell, H. *The Underground War against Revolutionary France.* Oxford: Oxford University Press, 1965.

Naff, Thomas. "Ottoman Diplomacy and the Great European Powers, 1797–1802." Ph.D. thesis, University of California at Berkeley, 1961.

Palmer, R.R. *The Age of the Democratic Revolution.* 2 volumes. Princeton: Princeton University Press, 1959–64.

Perkins, Bradford. *The First Rapprochement: England and the United States, 1795–1805.* Berkeley: University of California Press, 1967.

Ragsdale, Hugh. "A Continental System in 1801: Paul I and Bonaparte." *The Journal of Modern History* 42 (March 1970): 70–89.

_____, editor. *Paul I: A Reassessment of His Life and Reign.* Pittsburg: University Center for International Studies, 1979.

_____. "Russia, Prussia, and Europe in the Policy of Paul I." *Jahrbücher für Geschichte Osteuropas* 31 (1983): 81–118.

_____. "Russian Influence at Lunéville." *French Historical Studies* 5 (1968): 274–84.

_____. "Was Paul Bonaparte's Fool? The Evidence of Neglected Archives." In *Paul I: A Reassessment of His Life and Reign.* Edited by H. Ragsdale. Pittsburg: University Center for International Studies, 1979.

Reid, Stuart. *King George's Army 1740–1793*. 3 volumes. London: Osprey, 1995–96.

Reinerman, Alan J. "The Papacy, Austria, and the Anti-French Struggle in Italy, 1792–1797." In *Austria in the Age of the French Revolution, 1789–1815*. Edited by K. Brauer and W.E. Wright. Minneapolis: Center for Austrian Studies, University of Minnesota, 1990.

Ritcheson, Charles R. *Aftermath of Revolution: British Policy Toward the United States, 1783–1795*. Dallas: Southern Methodist University Press, 1969.

_____. "Thomas Pinckney's Mission, 1792–1796, and the Impressment Issue." *The International History Review* 2 (October 1980): 523–41.

Rodger, A.B. *The War of the Second Coalition, 1798–1801: A Strategic Commentary*. Oxford: Clarendon Press, 1961.

Roider, Karl A. *Baron Thurgot and Austria's Response to the French Revolution*. Princeton: Princeton University Press, 1987.

Rose, J.H. *The Life of William Pitt*. 2 volumes. Second edition. London: George Bell, 1934.

_____. *William Pitt and the Great War*. London: George Bell and Sons, 1911.

Ross, Steven T. *Quest for Victory: French Military Strategy, 1792–1799*. New York: South Brunswick and New York: A. S. Barnes and Company, 1973.

_____. "The Military Strategy of the Directory: The Campaigns of 1799." *French Historical Studies* 5 (1967): 170–87.

Saxby, R. "The Blockade of Brest in the French Revolutionary Wars." *Mariner's Mirror* 78 (1992): 25–35.

Schroeder, Paul W. "The Collapse of the Second Coalition." *The Journal of Modern History* 59 (June 1987): 244–90.

Scott, Hamish M. "Prussia from Rossbach to Jena." *German History* 12 (1994): 279–85.

Scott, Samuel F. *The Response of the Royal Army to the French Revolution: The Role and Development of the Line Army, 1787–1793.* Oxford: Clarendon Press, 1978.

Sherwig, John M. "Lord Grenville's Plan for a Concert of Europe, 1797–1799." *The Journal of Modern History* 34 (September 1962): 284–93.

Showalter, Dennis E. "Hubertusberg to Auerstädt: The Prussian Army in Decline?" *German History* 12 (1994): 308–33.

Simms, Brendan. *The Impact of Napoleon: Prussian High Politics, Foreign Policy and the Crisis of the Executive, 1797–1806.* Cambridge: Cambridge University Press, 1997.

Stinchcombe, William C. "The Diplomacy of the XYZ Affair." *William and Mary Quarterly* 34 (1977): 590–617.

_____. *The XYZ Affair.* Westport: Greenwood, 1981.

Stine, J.E. "Frederick William II and the Decline of the Prussian Army, 1786–1797." Ph.D. diss., University of South Carolina, 1980.

Sydenham, M.J. *The First French Republic 1792–1804.* London: B.T. Batsford, 1974.

Tucker, Clara J. "The Foreign Policy of Paul I." Ph.D. diss., Syracuse University, 1965.

Warner, Oliver. *The Battle of the Nile.* London: B.T. Batsford, 1960.

Webb, Paul. "Sea Power in the Ochakov Affair of 1791." *The International History Review* 2 (January 1980): 13–33.

Whitaker, Arthur P. *The Spanish-American Frontier, 1783–1795: The Westward Movement and the Spanish Retreat in the Mississippi Valley.* Lincoln: University of Nebraska Press, 1927.

Wright, D.G. *Revolution and Terror in France, 1789–1795.* 2d edition. London: Longman, 1990.

NAPOLEONIC WARS, 1802–1815

Alexander, Don W. *Rod of Iron: French Counterinsurgency Policy in Aragon during the Peninsular War.* Wilmington, Delaware: Scholarly Resources, 1985.

Anderson, Matthew S. "The Continental System and Russo-British Relations during the Napoleonic Wars." In *Studies in International History.* Edited by K. Bourne and D.C. Watt. Hamden: Archon, 1967.

Arnold, J.R. *Crisis on the Danube: Napoleon's Austrian Campaign of 1809.* London: Arms and Armour, 1990.

Bartlett, Christopher J. *Castlereagh.* London: Macmillan, 1966.

Benn, Carl. *The War of 1812.* Botley: Osprey, 2003.

Ben-Atar, Doron S. *The Origins of Jeffersonian Commercial Policy and Diplomacy.* New York: St. Martin's Press, 1993.

Bernard, J.F. *Talleyrand: A Biography.* New York: G.P. Putnam's Sons, 1973.

Bond, Gordon C. *The Grand Expedition: The British Invasion of Holland in 1809.* Athens, Georgia: University of Georgia Press, 1979.

_____. "Louis Bonaparte and the Collapse of the Kingdom of Holland." *Consortium on Revolutionary Europe Proceedings.*Gainsville: University of Florida, 1974.

_____. "The Walcheren Fiasco: A Diversion Turned Failure." *Proceedings of the Annual Meeting of the Western Society for French History* 3 (1976): 206–17.

Buckland, C.S.B. *Metternich and the British Government from 1809–1832.* London: Macmillan, 1932.

Butterfield, Herbert. *The Peace Tactics of Napoleon, 1806–1808.* Cambridge: Cambridge University Press, 1929.

Carr, R. "Gustavus IV and the British Government, 1804–1809." *The English Historical Review* 60 (1945): 36–66.

Castle, Ian. *Aspern and Wagram 1809: Mighty Clash of Empires.* Botley: Osprey, 1998.

_____. *Eggmuhl 1809: Storm over Bavaria.* Botley: Osprey, 1998.

_____. *Wagram 1809: Mighty Clash of Empires.* London: Osprey, 1994.

Cate, Curtis. *The War of the Two Emperors: The Duel between Napoleon and Alexander: Russia, 1812.* New York: Random House, 1985.

Chandler, David G. *Austerlitz 1805: Battle of the Three Emperors.* London: Osprey, 1990.

_____. *Jena 1806: Napoleon Destroys Prussia.* London: Osprey, 1993.

_____. *On the Napoleonic Wars: Collected Essays.* London: Greenhill, 1994.

_____. *The Campaigns of Napoleon.* New York: Macmillan, 1967.

_____. *Waterloo: The Hundred Days.* London: Osprey, 1980.

Chapman, Tim. *The Congress of Vienna: Origins, Processes and Results.* London: Routledge, 1998.

Chappell, Mike. *Wellington's Peninsular Regiments.* 2 volumes. Botley: Osprey, 2003.

Chartrand, Rene. *Fuentes de Onoro: Wellington's Liberation of Portugal.* Botley: Osprey, 2002.

_____. *Portuguese Army of the Napoleonic Wars.* 3 volumes. Botley: Osprey, 2000–1.

_____. *Spanish Army of the Napoleonic Wars.* 3 volumes. Botley: Osprey, 1998–99.

_____. *Vimeiro 1808: Wellesley's First Victory in the Pennisula.* Botley: Osprey, 2001.

Coles, Harry L. *The War of 1812.* Chicago: University of Chicago Press, 1965.

Connelly, Owen. *Blundering to Glory: Napoleon's Military Campaigns.* Wilmington, Delaware: Scholarly Resources, 1987.

_____. *Napoleon's Satellite Kingdoms: Managing Conquered Peoples.* New York: Macmillan, 1965; reprint, Malabar, Florida: Robert E. Krieger, 1990.

Cooper, Randolf G.S. "Wellington and the Marathas in 1803." *The International History Review* 11 (February 1989): 31–38.

Craig, Gordon A. "Problems of Coalition Warfare: The Military Alliance against Napoleon, 1813–1814." In *War, Politics and Diplomacy.* London: Weidenfeld and Nicolson, 1966; reprinted in *The Harman Memorial Lectures in Military History, 1959–1987.* Edited by Lt Col Harry R. Borowski. Washington, D.C.: Office of Air Force History, 1988.

Dakin, Douglas. "The Congress of Vienna, 1814–15, and its Antecedents." In *Europe's Balance of Power, 1815–1848.* Edited by A. Sked. London: Macmillan, 1979.

DeConde, Alexander. *This Affair of Louisiana.* New York: Scribner's, 1976.

Duffy, Christopher. *Austerlitz, 1805.* London: Seeley Service, 1977.

_____. *Borodino and the War of 1812.* New York: Charles Schribner's Sons, 1973.

Dwyer, Philip G. *Talleyrand.* London: Longman, 2002.

_____. "The Politics of Prussian Neutrality, 1795–1805." *German History* 12 (1994): 351–73.

_____. "Two Definitions of Neutrality: Prussia, the European States-System, and the French Invasion of Hanover in 1803." *The International History Review* 19 (August 1997): 522–40.

Egan, Clifford L. *Neither Peace nor War: Franco-American Relations, 1803–1812.* Baton Rouge: Louisiana State University Press, 1983.

Ellis, Geoffrey. *Napoleon.* London: Longman, 1997.

_____. *Napoleon's Continental Blockade: The Case of Alsace*. London: Clarendon Press, 1981.

Elting, John R. *Swords around a Throne: Napoleon's Grande Armée*. New York: Free Press, 1988.

Epstein, Robert M. *Napoleon's Last Victory and the Emergence of Modern War*. Lawrence: University Press of Kansas, 1994.

Esdaile, Charles. *The French Wars, 1792–1815*. London: Routledge, 2001.

_____. *The Spanish Army in the Peninsular War*. Manchester: Manchester University Press, 1988.

_____. *The Peninsular War*. New York: Palgrave, 2003.

_____. *The Wars of Napoleon*. London: Longman, 1995.

_____. "War and Politics in Spain, 1808–1814." *Historical Journal* 31 (1988): 295–317.

_____. "Wellington and the Military Eclipse of Spain, 1808–1814." *The International History Review* 11 (February 1989): 55–67.

Fedorak, Charles John. "In Search of a Necessary Ally: Addington, Hawkesbury, and Russia, 1801–1804." *The International History Review* 13 (May 1991): 221–45.

_____. "Maritime vs. Continental Strategy: Britain and the Defeat of Napoleon." *Consortium on Revolutionary Europe Proceedings*. Tallahassee: University of Florida, 1989.

Ferrero, Guglielmo. *The Reconstruction of Europe: Talleyrand and the Congress of Vienna*. New York: G.P. Putnam's, 1941.

Fisher, H.A.L. *Napoleonic Statesmanship: Germany*. Oxford: Clarendon Press, 1903.

Fisher, Todd. *The Napoleonic Wars: The Empires Fight Back, 1808–1812*. Botley: Osprey, 2001.

_____. *The Napoleonic Wars: The Rise of the Emperor, 1805–1807*. Botley: Osprey, 2001.

Fletcher, Ian. *Badajoz 1812*. Botley: Osprey, 2001.

_____. *Salamanca 1812*. Botley: Osprey, 2001.

_____. *The Lines of Torres Vedras 1809–1810*. Botley: Osprey, 2003.

_____, editor. *The Peninsular War: Aspects of the Struggle for the Iberian Peninsula*. Staplehurst: Spellmount, 1997.

_____. *Vittoria 1813*. Botley: Osprey, 1998.

Fremont-Barnes, Gregory. *The Napoleonic Wars: The Fall of the French Empire, 1813–1815*. Botley: Osprey, 2002.

_____. *The Napoleonic Wars: The Peninsular War, 1807–1814*. Botley: Osprey, 2002.

Gates, David. *The Napoleonic Wars, 1803–1815*. London: Arnold, 1997.

_____. *The Spanish Ulcer: A History of the Peninsular War*. London: Allen and Unwin, 1986.

Gill, John H. *With Eagles to Glory: Napoleon and His German Allies in the 1809 Campaign*. London: Greenhill, 1992.

Glover, Michael. *The Peninsular War, 1807–1814*. London: David and Charles, 1974.

_____. *Wellington as Military Commander*. London: B.T. Batsford, 1968.

_____. *Wellington's Peninsular Victories: Busaco, Salamanca, Vitoria, Nivelle*. New York: Macmillan, 1963.

Glover, Richard. *Britain at Bay: Defence against Bonaparte, 1803–1814*. London: George Allen and Unwin, 1973.

Goldenberg, Joseph A. "The Royal Navy's Blockade in New England Waters, 1812–1815." *The International History Review* 6 (August 1984): 424–39.

Grimsted, Patricia Kennedy. "Czartoryski's System for Russian Foreign Policy, 1803." *California Slavic Studies* 5 (1970): 19–91.

_____. *The Foreign Ministers of Alexander I.* Berkeley: University of California Press, 1969.

Gulick, Edward V. *Europe's Classical Balance of Power: A Case History of the Theory and Practice of One of the Great Concepts of European Statecraft.* Ithaca: Cornell University Press, 1955; reprint, Westport: Greenwood Press, 1982.

_____. "The Final Coalition and the Congress of Vienna, 1813–1815." In *The New Cambridge Modern History*, Volume IX. Edited by C.W. Crawley. Cambridge: Cambridge University Press, 1965.

Hales, E.E.Y. *Napoleon and the Pope: The Story of Napoleon and Pius VII.* London: Eyre and Spottiswoode, 1962.

Hall, Christopher D. *British Strategy in the Napoleonic War, 1803–1815.* Manchester: Manchester University Press,1992; reprint, London: Sandpiper, 1999.

Hall, John A. *A History of the Peninsular War: Volume VIII, The Biographical Dictionary of British Officers Killed and Wounded, 1808–1814.* London: Greenhill, 1998.

Harford, Lee S., Jr. "The Bavarian Army under Napoleon, 1805–1813." Ph.D. diss., Florida State University, 1988.

Hartley, Janet M. *Alexander I.* London: Longman, 1994.

Haythornthwaite, Philip J. *Austrian Army in the Napoleonic Wars.* 2 volumes. London: Osprey, 1986.

_____. *Die Hard!* London: Weidenfeld and Nicolson, 1998.

_____. *Napoleonic Infantry: Weapons and Warfare.* London: Weidenfeld and Nicolson, 2001.

_____. *Napoleon's Military Machine.* Staplehurst: Spellmount, 1995.

_____. *The Armies of Wellington.* London: Arms and Armour Press, 1994; reprint, London: Brockhampton Press, 1998.

_____. *The Russian Army in the Napoleonic Wars.* 2 volumes. London: Osprey, 1987–92.

_____. *Weapons and Equipment of the Napoleonic Wars.* London: Cassell: 1996.

Heckscher, E.F. *The Continental System: An Economic Interpretation.* London: Clarendon Press, 1922.

Helleiner, Karl F. *The Imperial Loans: A Study in Financial and Diplomatic History.* Oxford: Clarendon Press, 1965.

Hickey, Donald R. *The War of 1812: A Forgotten Conflict.* Urbana: University of Illinois Press, 1989.

Hinde, Wendy. *Castlereagh.* London: Collins, 1981.

Hofschröer, Peter. *1815, The Waterloo Campaign: Wellington, His German Allies and the Battles of Ligny and Quatre Bras.* London: Greenhill, 1998.

_____. *1815, The Waterloo Campaign: The German Victory, From Waterloo to the Fall of Napoleon.* London: Greenhill, 1999.

_____. *Leipzig 1813: Battle of the Nations.* London: Osprey, 1993.

_____. *Lutzen and Bautzen 1813.* Botley: Osprey, 2001.

_____. *Prussian Cavalry of the Napoleonic Wars.* London: Osprey, 1985.

Hook, C. *Corunna 1809: Sir John Moore's Fighting Retreat.* Botley: Osprey, 2001.

Horsman, Reginald. *The Causes of the War of 1812.* Philadelphia: University of Pennsylvania Press, 1962.

_____. *The War of 1812.* London: Eyre and Spotiswoode, 1969.

Horward, Donald D. "Wellington and the Defence of Portugal." *The International History Review* 11 (February 1989): 39–54.

Howarth, David. *A Near Run Thing: The Day of Waterloo*. London: Collins, 1968.

Josselson, Michael and Diana. *The Commander: A Life of Barclay de Tolly*. Oxford: Oxford University Press, 1980.

Kaplan, Lawrence S. *Entangling Alliances with None: American Foreign Policy in the Age of Jefferson*. Kent: Kent State University Press, 1987.

_____. *Thomas Jefferson: Westward the Course of Empire*. Wilmington: Scholarly Resources, 1999.

Kissinger, Henry A. *A World Restored: Metternich, Castlereagh and the Problems of Peace 1812–22*. Boston: Houghton Mifflin, 1957.

Kraehe, Enno E. *Metternich's German Policy*. 2 volumes. Princeton: Princeton University Press, 1963–83.

_____. "Wellington and the Reconstruction of the Allied Armies during the Hundred Days." *The International History Review* 11 (February 1989): 84–97.

Lawford, J.P. *Napoleon: The Last Campaigns, 1813–1815*. Maidenhead: Sampson Low, 1977.

Lefèbvre, Georges. *Napoleon*. 2 volumes. Translated by H.F. Stockhold. London: Routledge and Kegan Paul, 1969.

Luvas, Jay, editor. *Napoleon on the Art of War*. New York: Free Press, 1999.

Mackesy, Piers. *The War in the Mediterranean, 1803–1810*. Cambridge, Mass.: Harvard University Press, 1957.

Mansel, Philip. "Wellington and the French Restoration." *The International History Review* 11 (February 1989): 76–83.

Markham, Felix. *Napoleon*. London: Weidenfeld and Nicolson, 1963.

_____. "The Napoleonic Adventure." In *The New Cambridge Modern History*, Volume IX. Edited by C.W. Crawley. Cambridge: Cambridge University Press, 1965.

Marshall-Cornwall, James. *Napoleon as Military Commander*. London: B.T. Batsford, 1967.

Mowat, Robert B. *The Diplomacy of Napoleon*. London: Edward Arnold, 1924; reprint, New York: Russell and Russell, 1971.

Muir, Rory. *Britain and the Defeat of Napoleon, 1807–1815*. New Haven: Yale University Press, 1996.

_____. *Tactics and the Experience of Battle in the Age of Napoleon*. New Haven: Yale University Press, 1998.

Murphy, Orville T. "Napoleon's International Politics: How Much Did He Owe to the Past?." *The Journal of Military History* 54 (April 1990): 163–71.

Nafziger, George. *Napoleon at Leipzig: The Battle of the Nations 1813*. Chicago: Emperor's Press, 1997.

Nicolson, Harold. *The Congress of Vienna: A Study in Allied Unity, 1812–1822*. New York: Harcourt, Brace, and Company, 1946.

Niven, A.C. *Napoleon and Alexander I: A Study in Anglo-Russian Relations, 1807–1812*. Washington, D.C.: University Press of America, 1978.

Oman, Sir Charles. *A History of the Peninsular War*. 7 volumes. Oxford: Oxford University Press, 1902–30; reprint, London: Greenhill, 1995–97.

Padfield, Peter. *Nelson's War*. London: Granada, 1976.

Palmer, Alan. *Alexander I: Tsar of War and Peace*. London: Weidenfeld and Nicolson, 1974.

_____. *Metternich*. London: Weidenfeld and Nicolson, 1972.

_____. *Napoleon in Russia*. New York: Simon and Schuster, 1967.

Paret, Peter. *Yorck and the Era of Prussian Reform, 1807–1815*. Princeton: Princeton University Press, 1966.

Parker, Harold T. *Three Napoleonic Battles*. Durham: Duke University Press, 1944; reprint, 1988.

_____. "Why did Napoleon Invade Russia? A Study in Motivation and the Interrelations of Personality and Social Structure." *The Journal of Military History* 54 (April 1990): 131–46.

Pawley, Ronald. *Wellington's Dutch Allies 1815*. Botley: Osprey, 2002.

Perkins, Bradford. *Castlereagh and Adams: England and the United States, 1812–1823*. Berkeley: University of California Press, 1964.

Petre, F. Loraine. *Napoleon and Archduke Charles: A History of the Franco-Austrian Campaign in the Valley of the Danube in 1809*. London: John Lane, 1909.

_____. *Napoleon at Bay, 1814*. London: John Lane, 1914; reprint, London: Greenhill, 1994.

_____. *Napoleon's Campaign in Poland, 1806–1807*. London: S. Low, Marston and Company, 1901.

_____. *Napoleon's Conquest of Prussia, 1806*. London: John Lane, 1907.

_____. *Napoleon's Last Campaign in Germany, 1813*. London: John Lane, 1912.

Puryear, Vernon. *Napoleon and the Dardanelles*. Cambridge: Cambridge University Press, 1951.

Ragsdale, Hugh. *Détente in the Napoleonic Era*. Lawrence: University of Kansas Press, 1980.

_____. "The Origins of Bonaparte's Russian Policy." *Slavic Review* 27 (1968): 85–90.

Reiner, G. *Great Britain and the Establishment of the Kingdom of the Netherlands, 1813–1815*. The Hague: Martinus Nijhoff, 1930.

Riley, J.P. *Napoleon and the World War of 1813: Lessons in Coalition Warfighting*. London: Frank Cass, 2001.

Roach, Elmo E. "Anglo-Russian Relations from Austerlitz to Tilsit." *The International History Review* 5 (May 1983): 181–200.

Roider, Karl A. "Austria's Road to Austerlitz." In *Austria in the Age of the French Revolution, 1789–1815*. Edited by K. Brauer and W.E. Wright. Minneapolis: Center for Austrian Studies, University of Minnesota, 1990.

_____. "The Habsburg Foreign Ministry and Political Reform, 1801–1805." *Central European History* 22 (June 1989): 160–82.

Ross, Steven T. "Napoleon and Maneuver Warfare." In *The Harman Memorial Lectures in Military History, 1959–1987*. Edited by Lt Col Harry R. Borowski. Washington, D.C.: Office of Air Force History, 1988.

Ryan, Anthony N. "An Ambassador Afloat: Vice-Admiral Sir James Saumarez and the Swedish Court, 1808–1812." In *The British Navy and the Use of Naval Power in the Eighteenth Century*. Edited by J. Black and P. Woodfine. Atlantic Highlands: Humanities Press International, 1989.

_____. "The Causes of the British Attack upon Copenhagen in 1807." *The English Historical Review* 68 (1953): 37–55.

_____. "The Defence of British Trade with the Baltic, 1808–1813." *The English Historical Review* 74 (1959): 443–66.

_____. "Trade with the Enemy in the Scandinavian and Baltic Ports during the Napoleonic Wars." *Transactions of the Royal Historical Society*, Fifth series, 12 (1962): 123–40.

Saul, Norman E. "The Objectives of Paul's Italian Policy," In *Paul I: A Reassessment of His Life and Reign*. Edited by H. Ragsdale. Pittsburg: University Center for International Studies, 1979.

_____. *Russia and the Mediterranean, 1797–1807*. Chicago: University of Chicago Press, 1970.

Schmidt, Oliver. *Prussian Regular Infantrymen 1808–1815*. Botley: Osprey, 2003.

Severn, J.K. *A Wellesley Affair: Richard, Marquess Wellesley, and the Conduct of Anglo-Spanish Diplomacy, 1809–1812*. Tallahassee: University Presses of Florida, 1981.

Schroeder, Paul W. "An Unnatural 'Natural Alliance': Castlereagh, Metternich, and Aberdeen in 1813." *The International History Review* 10 (November 1988): 522–40.

_____. "Napoleon's Foreign Policy: A Criminal Enterprise." *The Journal of Military History* 54 (April 1990): 147–61.

Simms, Brendan. *The Impact of Napoleon: Prussian High Politics, Foreign Policy and the Crisis of the Executive, 1797–1806.* Cambridge: Cambridge University Press, 1997.

_____. "The Road to Jena: Prussian High Politics, 1804–1806." *German History* 12 (1994): 374–94.

Smith, Digby George. *1813, Leipzig: Napoleon and the Battle of the Nations.* London: Greenhill, 2001.

Sondhaus, Lawrence. "Napoleon's Shipbuilding Program at Venice and the Struggle for Naval Mastery in the Adriatic, 1806–1814." *The Journal of Military History* 53 (October 1989): 349–62.

Stagg, J.C.A. *Mr. Madison's War: Politics, Diplomacy, and Warfare in the Early American Republic, 1783–1830.* Princeton: Princeton University Press, 1983.

Stearns, J.B. *The Role of Metternich in Undermining Napoleon.* Urbana: University of Illinois Press, 1948.

Teffeteller, Gordon L. "Wellington and Sir Rowland Hill." *The International History Review* 11 (February 1989): 68–75.

Thomas, R.N.W. "Wellington in the Low Countries, 1794–1795." *The International History Review* 11 (February 1989): 14–30.

Thompson, J.M. *Napoleon Bonaparte: His Rise and Fall,* Oxford: Basil Blackwell, 1951.

Tucker, Robert W. and David C. Hendrickson. *Empire of Liberty: The Statecraft of Thomas Jefferson.* Oxford: Oxford University Press, 1990.

Updyke, Frank A. *The Diplomacy of the War of 1812*. Baltimore: The Johns Hopkins Press, 1915; reprint, Gloucester, Mass.: Peter Smith, 1965.

Vann, J.A. "Habsburg Policy and the Austrian War of 1809." *Central European History* 7 (December 1974): 291–310.

Webster, Charles K. *The Congress of Vienna, 1814–1815*. London: Foreign Office, 1919; reprint, London: G. Bell and Sons, 1945.

_____. *The Foreign Policy of Castlereagh, 1812–1815: Britain and the Reconstruction of Europe*. London: G. Bell and Sons, 1931.

Whitcomb, Edward A. *Napoleon's Diplomatic Service*. Durham: University of North Carolina Press, 1979.

_____. "The Duties and Functions of Napoleon's External Agents." *History* 57 (June 1972): 189–204.

Wooten, Geoffrey. *Waterloo 1815: Birth of Modern Europe*. Botley: Osprey, 1999.

Wright, D.G. *Napoleon and Europe*. London: Longman, 1984.

Zawadzki, W.H. "Russia and the Re-opening of the Polish Question, 1801–1814." *The International History Review* 7 (February 1985): 19–44.

ABOUT THE AUTHOR

Dr. William Young is the Associate Director of International Programs and Lecturer in History at the University of North Dakota. He is a former historian for the United States Air Force History and Museum Program. His graduate work includes study at the University of North Dakota, University of Southern California, and Cambridge University. He holds doctoral and master's degrees in European diplomatic history and a master's degree in international relations. Dr. Young has traveled extensively throughout western and central Europe, living in the United Kingdom, the Netherlands, and Germany for thirteen years. He was awarded the U.S. Air Force Historian of the Year Award in 1985, 1989, and 1991. He is the author of *War and Diplomacy in the Age of Louis XIV: A Historical Study and Annotated Bibliography* (2000), a contributor to *Magill's Guide to Military History* (2001), and a book reviewer for *The Journal of Military History*. He is married to the former Patricia Groves of Shropshire, England, and they have four children.

0-595-29874-5